READINGS FOR THE ASSEMBLY

New Revised Standard Version, Emended

Revised Common Lectionary

Cycle A

Augsburg Fortress
Minneapolis

READINGS FOR THE ASSEMBLY
Study Edition
Editors: Gordon W. Lathrop and Gail Ramshaw

Design: Lecy Design
Typesetting: Peregrine Graphics Services

Manufactured in U.S.A.   ISBN 0-8066-0434-4   AF 3-389
04   03   02   01   00   99   98   97   96   95   1   2   3   4   5   6   7   8   9   10

CONTENTS

Introduction

The word of God

The Scriptures speak of the word of God as light and lamp, imperishable seed, spiritual food and drink, healing balm, cleansing fire. The word sustains life, produces faith, strengthens hope, and inflames love. As the Bible attests, the word of God created the world and all living things. The word of the Lord liberated the Hebrew people from slavery and sustained them on their journey to the promised land. Throughout the history of Israel, this word inspired the judges and spoke to the prophets. In time, the great acts of God's mercy were written down and then proclaimed in the daily and weekly gatherings of the Jewish people. Through an annual cycle of lessons, the Hebrew Scriptures were read, sung, and interpreted in communal worship.

The word among us

"Long ago God spoke to our ancestors in many and various ways by the prophets, but in these last days God has spoken to us by a Son" (Hebrews 1:1-2). In the worship of his people, Jesus read the ancient scriptures and interpreted them anew: "Today this scripture has been fulfilled in your hearing" (Luke 4:21). In his own life, he proclaimed the good news of salvation in word and deed. To his disciples on the road, the risen Lord interpreted in all the scriptures the things concerning himself. In breaking open the word, he gave himself as the bread of life. Indeed, for the early Christian community, Jesus himself was the living Word to be proclaimed and interpreted in new places among new people. "We declare to you what was from the beginning, what we have heard, what we have seen with our eyes, what we have looked at and touched with our hands, concerning the word of life" (1 John 1:1).

The word proclaimed in worship

When the Scriptures are proclaimed in the worshiping assembly today, the living Word continues to speak to his disciples. Through the power of the Holy Spirit, the risen Christ is truly present when the Scriptures are read. Through the ministry of readers, the written word becomes a lively, spoken word addressed to all who listen with faith.

Gathered around the table of God's word, the church follows Christ's pattern of reading and interpreting the Scriptures, so that when the holy book is opened and read, Christ speaks anew this living and active word. In the hearing of this word the church is sustained in faith, drawn to the font and holy supper, and strengthened for witness in the world.

The proclamation of the word

In various ways the word of God is proclaimed in the liturgy by the worshiping assembly and its ministers. In particular, the word is proclaimed in the biblical readings (the

Hebrew Scriptures, the New Testament letters, and the Gospels); in the singing of the psalms, hymns, and acclamations surrounding the readings; and in preaching.

The proclamation of the Gospel in reading and preaching is the high point of the word service. The other readings illuminate this central reading while the psalms, hymns, and acclamations offer musical responses to the readings. Because of the centrality of the Gospel reading, the assembly stands to welcome the Lord who speaks anew in this place and time.

In these varied actions, the dialogue between God and the worshiping assembly takes place. In order to take the word of God to heart and ponder its meaning, intervals of silence are often kept by the assembly and its readers. Just as haste hinders reflection on the word, so a tendency to wordiness on the part of worship leaders can detract from the clear and simple voice of the word proclaimed.

In most instances, baptized members of the worshiping assembly who have been trained in this ministry read the first and second readings. After brief silences, a cantor or choir leads the people in singing the psalm as well as the song or acclamation that greets the Gospel reading. Normally, the preacher reads the Gospel and then preaches the good news for the community and the world. A hymn responds to this word with thanksgiving. A proclamation of faith often continues the assembly's response, leading the community to pray for the church, the world, and those in need.

The medieval custom of two places for the word (lectern and pulpit) has yielded, in many congregations, to a single place (lectern or ambo) from which the readings are proclaimed and the sermon is preached. Here the book of life is opened; here the banquet of scripture is set forth; here the people of God are nourished on the word.

"He interpreted to them the things about himself in all the scriptures. He took bread, blessed and broke it, and gave it to them. Then their eyes were opened, and they recognized him" (Luke 24:27, 30-31). From the table of God's word, the worshiping assembly gathers at the table of the holy supper to receive the bread of life and the cup of blessing. In word and meal, the living Word welcomes, enlightens, and nourishes the people of God for service in the world.

The lectionary

The lectionary sets forth many of the stories, images, and actions through which the living Word sustains the Christian community gathered in public worship during the seasons of the year. It is ordered around the first reading, psalm, second reading, and Gospel reading. Appropriate introductions and conclusions to the readings are provided in this lectionary book. After announcing the reading with the introduction, the reader/minister pauses and then begins the proclamation. At the end of each of the first two readings, it has become customary for the reader to pause and then say, "The word of the Lord." The people respond, "Thanks be to God." At the conclusion of the Gospel reading, the minister says, "The Gospel of the Lord." The people respond with the words, "Praise to you, O Christ" or another appropriate acclamation.

In this lectionary book, the readings and psalms appointed for Lesser Festivals are printed after the Sunday and principal festival readings.

In places where the New Revised Standard Version versification for the psalms differs from that of the translation used in *Lutheran Book of Worship* and *Book of Common Prayer,* LBW/BCP alternate versification is noted in italics.

During the Sundays after Pentecost, an alternate set of semi-continuous first readings and psalms are provided in an appendix. Where it is the practice to read the semi-continuous first reading and psalm response, the lectionary should be opened first to the appropriate page in the appendix. The page in the body of the lectionary where the readings continue will need to be marked clearly.

In a few instances, the Revised Common Lectionary appoints readings and responses from selected books of the Apocrypha. These readings and responses are printed in a second appendix.

The emendations in this edition

One goal of the New Revised Standard Version was to eliminate so-called generic speech, that is, male language which is meant to include also women, as far as could be done without falsely altering the historical androcentrism of biblical cultures. The New Revised Standard Version thus provides contemporary Christians with the most responsible English translation available which addresses the complex issues inherent in linguistic androcentrism. One goal of this present emendation is to continue this search for inclusive speech, while still striving for accurate biblical translation.

Increasingly, the worship books of mainstream Christian churches have provided liturgical materials which not only eliminate generic speech concerning humans but also reduce the masculine designations for God which occur in biblical Hebrew and Greek. A growing conviction is that although most biblical speech describes God in masculine terms, the dominant theological tradition in both Judaism and Christianity has denied that God is actually male, and thus contemporary English ought to avoid continual masculine language for God. A primary goal of this emendation of the New Revised Standard Version of the lectionary is to minimize masculine language for God.

The following are the principles used in this emendation:

Masculine pronouns referring to God have been eliminated. At appropriate places, participial constructions have been used, nouns appropriate to the context supplied, or sentences cast in the passive voice.

The dual rendering of LORD and Lord as translations of the tetragrammaton and of *Kyrios* has been retained. However, see below concerning the liturgical phrase "The word of the Lord."

Masculine pronouns for Jesus have been reduced, but not eliminated. Following the classical christological understanding, no distinction has been made between Jesus of Nazareth and the risen Christ.

In passages from the Hebrew Scriptures which speak of the davidic messiah, originally cast in the masculine and interpreted by Christians as signaling Christ, masculine references have been reduced, but not wholly eliminated.

Father and Son language has been retained as trinitarian titles. When "father" appears in apposition to "God," commas are inserted to distance the word God from the title Father. Jesus' calling of God Father in the gospels has been retained.

Emendations reduce the occurrences in which the biblical text assumes occupational titles or human designations to be masculine. Sometimes, as is common in American English, the sentence has been recast in the plural.

Many biblical passages are inconsistent in grammatical gender, for example alternating between second and third person. Some of these passages have been rendered with a more contemporary consistency, using either the second person or the third person plural throughout, thus reducing the usage of the masculine third person singular.

In narrative and parable, no attempt has been made to generalize the sex of specific persons or to include persons of the opposite sex in a desire for balance.

In sustained conceits, as in the Wisdom or city of Jerusalem poems, the sexual imagery is retained.

Personal names, such as Jacob or Israel, when used as collective nouns, are assumed to be plural.

Supernatural beings, such as angels, demons, and Satan, have been rendered as asexual beings.

In the case of an extremely familiar passage that requires emending, the syntax has been recast so that the emendation does not sound like a mistake.

Sometimes proper names replace pronoun references in narratives to reduce "he" and to assist aural comprehension.

Euphony or specific context have also contributed to the decision in emendation.

It has become customary, at the end of each of the first two readings, for the reader to pause and then say, "The word of the Lord," to which the people respond, "Thanks be to God." Those assemblies wishing to minimize liturgical language that suggests a masculine God may use another acclamation in response to the reading:

reader: The word of life.
people: Thanks be to God.

reader: Holy wisdom, holy word.
people: Thanks be to God.

May this lectionary assist the worshiping assembly in the proclamation of the word and the preaching of the holy gospel.

SEASON OF ADVENT

✝

FIRST SUNDAY IN ADVENT

DECEMBER 3, 1995 NOVEMBER 29, 1998 DECEMBER 2, 2001

FIRST READING: ISAIAH 2:1–5

A reading from Isaiah:

[1]The word that Isaiah son of Amoz saw concerning Judah and Jerusalem.

[2]In days to come
the mountain of the LORD's house
shall be established as the highest of the mountains,
and shall be raised above the hills;
all the nations shall stream to it.

[3]Many peoples shall come and say,
"Come, let us go up to the mountain of the LORD,
to the house of the Jacob's God,
who will teach us the ways of God,
that we may walk in the paths of the LORD."

For out of Zion shall go forth instruction,
and the word of the LORD from Jerusalem.
[4]God shall judge between the nations,
and shall arbitrate for many peoples;
they shall beat their swords into plowshares,
and their spears into pruning hooks;
nation shall not lift up sword against nation,
neither shall they learn war any more.

[5]O house of Jacob,
come, let us walk in the light of the LORD!

PSALMODY: PSALM 122

SECOND READING: ROMANS 13:11–14

A reading from Romans:

[11]Besides this,
you know what time it is,
how it is now the moment for you to wake from sleep.
For salvation is nearer to us now than when we became believers;
[12]the night is far gone, the day is near.

Let us then lay aside the works of darkness
and put on the armor of light;
[13]let us live honorably as in the day,
not in reveling and drunkenness,
not in debauchery and licentiousness,
not in quarreling and jealousy.

[14]Instead, put on the Lord Jesus Christ,
and make no provision for the flesh,
to gratify its desires.

GOSPEL: MATTHEW 24:36–44

The Holy Gospel according to Matthew, the 24th chapter.

Jesus said,
[36]"About that day and hour no one knows,
neither the angels of heaven, nor the Son,
but only the Father.

[37]"For as the days of Noah were,
so will be the coming of the Son-of-Man.
[38]For as in those days before the flood they were eating and drinking,
marrying and giving in marriage,
until the day Noah entered the ark,
[39]and they knew nothing until the flood came and swept them all away,
so too will be the coming of the Son-of-Man.

[40]"Then two men will be in the field;
one will be taken and one will be left.
[41]Two women will be grinding meal together;
one will be taken and one will be left.
[42]Keep awake therefore,
for you do not know on what day your Lord is coming.

[43]"But understand this:
if the owner of the house had known
in what part of the night the thief was coming,
the owner would have stayed awake
and would not have let the house be broken into.

[44]"Therefore you also must be ready,
for the Son-of-Man is coming at an unexpected hour."

The Gospel of the Lord.

SECOND SUNDAY IN ADVENT

DECEMBER 10, 1995   DECEMBER 6, 1998   DECEMBER 9, 2001

FIRST READING: ISAIAH 11:1–10

A reading from Isaiah:

¹A shoot shall come out from the stump of Jesse,
and a branch shall grow out of its roots.
²The spirit of the LORD shall rest on him,
the spirit of wisdom and understanding,
the spirit of counsel and might,
the spirit of knowledge and the fear of the LORD.
³His delight shall be in the fear of the LORD.

He shall not judge by what his eyes see,
or decide by what his ears hear;
⁴but with righteousness shall judge the poor,
and decide with equity for the meek of the earth;
he shall strike the earth with the rod of his mouth,
and with the breath of his lips shall kill the wicked.
⁵Righteousness shall be the belt around his waist,
and faithfulness the belt around his loins.

⁶The wolf shall live with the lamb,
the leopard shall lie down with the kid,
the calf and the lion and the fatling together,
and a little child shall lead them.
⁷The cow and the bear shall graze,
their young shall lie down together;
and the lion shall eat straw like the ox.
⁸The nursing child shall play over the hole of the asp,
and the weaned child shall put its hand on the adder's den.
⁹They will not hurt or destroy on all my holy mountain;
for the earth will be full of the knowledge of the LORD
as the waters cover the sea.

¹⁰On that day there will stand as a signal to the peoples the root of Jesse,
of whom the nations shall inquire,
and whose dwelling shall be glorious.

PSALMODY: PSALM 72:1–7, 18–19

SECOND READING: ROMANS 15:4–13

A reading from Romans:

⁴Whatever was written in former days
was written for our instruction,
so that by steadfastness and by the encouragement of the scriptures
we might have hope.

⁵May the God of steadfastness and encouragement
grant you to live in harmony with one another,
in accordance with Christ Jesus,
⁶so that together you may with one voice
glorify the God and Father of our Lord Jesus Christ.

⁷Welcome one another, therefore,
just as Christ has welcomed you,
for the glory of God.
⁸For I tell you that Christ has become a servant of the Jewish people
on behalf of the truth of God
in order to confirm the promises given to the ancestors,
⁹and in order that the Gentiles might glorify our merciful God.
As it is written,
"Therefore I will confess you among the Gentiles,
and sing praises to your name";
¹⁰and again it is said,
"Rejoice, O Gentiles, with the people of God";
¹¹and again,
"Praise the Lord, all you Gentiles,
and let all the peoples praise the Lord";
¹²and again Isaiah says,
"The root of Jesse shall come,
the one who rises to rule the Gentiles,
in whom the Gentiles shall hope."

¹³May the God of hope
fill you with all joy and peace in believing,
so that you may abound in hope by the power of the Holy Spirit.

The Holy Gospel according to Matthew, the third chapter.

¹In those days John the Baptist appeared in the wilderness of Judea,
proclaiming,
²"Repent, for the dominion of heaven has come near."
³This is the one of whom the prophet Isaiah spoke when he said,
"The voice of one crying out in the wilderness:
'Prepare the way of the Lord,
make straight the paths of the Lord.' "

⁴Now John wore clothing of camel's hair
with a leather belt around his waist,
and his food was locusts and wild honey.
⁵Then the people of Jerusalem and all Judea were going out to him,
and all the region along the Jordan,
⁶and they were baptized by him in the river Jordan,
confessing their sins.

⁷But when John saw many Pharisees and Sadducees coming for baptism,
he said to them,
"You brood of vipers!
Who warned you to flee from the wrath to come?
⁸Bear fruit worthy of repentance.
⁹Do not presume to say to yourselves,
'We have Abraham as our ancestor';
for I tell you,
God is able from these stones to raise up children to Abraham.
¹⁰Even now the ax is lying at the root of the trees;
every tree therefore that does not bear good fruit
is cut down and thrown into the fire.

¹¹"I baptize you with water for repentance,
but one who is more powerful than I is coming after me;
I am not worthy to carry his sandals.
He will baptize you with the Holy Spirit and fire.
¹²With a winnowing fork in hand,
he will clear his threshing floor
and will gather his wheat into the granary;
but the chaff he will burn with unquenchable fire."

The Gospel of the Lord.

✝

Third Sunday in Advent

DECEMBER 17, 1995　　*DECEMBER 13, 1998*　　*DECEMBER 16, 2001*

FIRST READING: Isaiah 35:1–10

A reading from Isaiah:

¹The wilderness and the dry land shall be glad,
the desert shall rejoice and blossom;
like the crocus ²it shall blossom abundantly,
and rejoice with joy and singing.
The glory of Lebanon shall be given to it,
the majesty of Carmel and Sharon.
They shall see the glory of the Lord,
the majesty of our God.

³Strengthen the weak hands,
and make firm the feeble knees.
⁴Say to those who are of a fearful heart,
"Be strong, do not fear!
Behold, your God will come with vengeance,
with terrible recompense.
God will come and save you."

⁵Then the eyes of the blind shall be opened,
and the ears of the deaf unstopped;
⁶then the lame shall leap like a deer,
and the tongue of the speechless sing for joy.
For waters shall break forth in the wilderness,
and streams in the desert;
⁷the burning sand shall become a pool,
and the thirsty ground springs of water;
the haunt of jackals shall become a swamp,
the grass shall become reeds and rushes.

⁸A highway shall be there,
and it shall be called the Holy Way;
the unclean shall not travel on it,
but it shall be for God's people;
no traveler, not even fools, shall go astray.
⁹No lion shall be there,
nor shall any ravenous beast come up on it;
they shall not be found there,
but the redeemed shall walk there.
¹⁰And the ransomed of the LORD shall return,
and come to Zion with singing;
everlasting joy shall be upon their heads;
they shall obtain joy and gladness,
and sorrow and sighing shall flee away.

PSALMODY: PSALM 146:5–10 or LUKE 1:47–55   *Psalm 146:4–9* LBW/BCP

SECOND READING: JAMES 5:7–10

A reading from James:

⁷Be patient, therefore, beloved,
until the coming of the Lord.
The farmer waits for the precious crop from the earth,
being patient with it until it receives the early and the late rains.
⁸You also must be patient.
Strengthen your hearts,
for the coming of the Lord is near.

⁹Beloved, do not grumble against one another,
so that you may not be judged.
See, the Judge is standing at the doors!
¹⁰As an example of suffering and patience, beloved,
take the prophets who spoke in the name of the Lord.

GOSPEL: MATTHEW 11:2–11

The Holy Gospel according to Matthew, the eleventh chapter.

²When John heard in prison what the Messiah was doing,
he sent word by his disciples ³and said to him,
"Are you the one who is to come,
or are we to wait for another?"
⁴Jesus answered them,
"Go and tell John what you hear and see:
⁵those who are blind receive their sight, those who are lame walk,
those with leprosy are cleansed, those who are deaf hear,
the dead are raised, and the poor have good news brought to them.
⁶And blessed is anyone who takes no offense at me."

⁷As they went away,
Jesus began to speak to the crowds about John:
"What did you go out into the wilderness to look at?
A reed shaken by the wind?
⁸What then did you go out to see?
Someone dressed in soft robes?
Look, those who wear soft robes are in royal palaces.
⁹What then did you go out to see?
A prophet?
Yes, I tell you, and more than a prophet.
¹⁰This is the one about whom it is written,
'See, I am sending my messenger ahead of you,
who will prepare your way before you.'
¹¹Truly I tell you, among those born of women
no one has arisen greater than John the Baptist;
yet the least in the dominion of heaven is greater than he."

The Gospel of the Lord.

FOURTH SUNDAY IN ADVENT

DECEMBER 24, 1995   DECEMBER 20, 1998   DECEMBER 23, 2001

FIRST READING: ISAIAH 7:10–16

A reading from Isaiah:

[10]The LORD spoke to Ahaz, saying,
[11]Ask a sign of the LORD your God;
let it be deep as Sheol or high as heaven.
[12]But Ahaz said,
I will not ask, and I will not put the LORD to the test.

[13]Then Isaiah said:
"Hear then, O house of David!
Is it too little for you to weary mortals,
that you weary my God also?
[14]Therefore this very Lord will give you a sign.
Look, the young woman is with child and shall bear a son,
and shall name him Immanuel.
[15]He shall eat curds and honey
by the time he knows how to refuse the evil and choose the good.
[16]For before the child knows how to refuse the evil and choose the good,
the land before whose two kings you are in dread
will be deserted."

PSALMODY: PSALM 80:1–7, 17–19   *Psalm 80:1–7, 16–18*   LBW/BCP

SECOND READING: ROMANS 1:1–7

A reading from Romans:

[1]Paul, a servant of Jesus Christ,
called to be an apostle,
set apart for the gospel of God,
[2]which God promised beforehand
through the prophets in the holy scriptures,
[3]the gospel concerning God's Son,
who was descended from David according to the flesh
[4]and was declared to be Son of God
with power according to the spirit of holiness

by resurrection from the dead,
Jesus Christ our Lord,
⁵through whom we have received grace and apostleship
to bring about the obedience of faith among all the Gentiles
for the sake of his name,
⁶including yourselves who are called to belong to Jesus Christ,

⁷To all God's beloved in Rome,
who are called to be saints:
Grace to you
and peace from God, our Father, and the Lord Jesus Christ.

GOSPEL: MATTHEW 1:18–25

The Holy Gospel according to Matthew, the first chapter.

¹⁸Now the birth of Jesus the Messiah took place in this way.
When his mother Mary had been engaged to Joseph,
but before they lived together,
she was found to be with child from the Holy Spirit.

¹⁹Her husband Joseph, being a righteous man
and unwilling to expose her to public disgrace,
planned to dismiss her quietly.
²⁰But just when he had resolved to do this,
an angel of the Lord appeared to him in a dream and said,
"Joseph, son of David,
do not be afraid to take Mary home as your wife,
for the child conceived in her is from the Holy Spirit.
²¹She will bear a son,
and you are to name him Jesus,
for he will save his people from their sins."
²²All this took place to fulfill
what had been spoken by the Lord through the prophet:
²³"Look, the virgin shall conceive and bear a son,
and they shall name him Emmanuel,"
which means, "God is with us."

²⁴When Joseph awoke from sleep,
he did as the angel of the Lord commanded him;
he took her home as his wife,
²⁵but had no marital relations with her until she had borne a son;
and he named him Jesus.

The Gospel of the Lord.

✝

SEASON OF CHRISTMAS

THE NATIVITY OF OUR LORD
CHRISTMAS EVE (I)

DECEMBER 24

FIRST READING: ISAIAH 9:2–7

A reading from Isaiah:

²The people who walked in darkness have seen a great light;
those who lived in a land of deep darkness—
on them light has shined.
³You have multiplied the nation,
you have increased its joy;
they rejoice before you as with joy at the harvest,
as people exult when dividing plunder.
⁴For the yoke of their burden,
and the bar across their shoulders,
the rod of their oppressor,
you have broken as on the day of Midian.
⁵For all the boots of the tramping warriors
and all the garments rolled in blood
shall be burned as fuel for the fire.

⁶For a child has been born for us,
a son given to us;
authority rests upon his shoulders;
and he is named
Wonderful Counselor, Mighty God,
Everlasting Father, Prince of Peace.
⁷His authority shall grow continually,
and there shall be endless peace
for the throne and dominion of David,
to establish and uphold it
with justice and with righteousness
from this time onward and forevermore.

The zeal of the LORD of hosts will do this.

PSALMODY: PSALM 96

SECOND READING: TITUS 2:11–14

A reading from Titus:

¹¹The grace of God has appeared,
bringing salvation to all,
¹²training us to renounce impiety and worldly passions,
and in the present age
to live lives that are self-controlled, upright, and godly,
¹³while we wait for the blessed hope
and the manifestation of the glory
of our great God and Savior, Jesus Christ.

¹⁴It is Jesus Christ who gave himself for us
to redeem us from all iniquity
and purify for himself a people of his own
who are zealous for good deeds.

GOSPEL: LUKE 2:1–14 [15–20]

The Holy Gospel according to Luke, the second chapter.

¹In those days a decree went out from Emperor Augustus
that all the world should be registered.
²This was the first registration
and was taken while Quirinius was governor of Syria.
³All went to their own towns to be registered.
⁴Joseph also went from the town of Nazareth in Galilee to Judea,
to the city of David called Bethlehem,
because he was descended from the house and family of David.
⁵He went to be registered with Mary,
to whom he was engaged and who was expecting a child.
⁶While they were there, the time came for her to deliver her child.
⁷And she gave birth to her firstborn son
and wrapped him in bands of cloth,
and laid him in a manger,
because there was no place for them in the inn.

[8]In that region there were shepherds living in the fields,
keeping watch over their flock by night.
[9]Then an angel of the Lord stood before them,
and the glory of the Lord shone around them,
and they were terrified.
[10]But the angel said to them,
"Do not be afraid;
for see—
I am bringing you good news of great joy for all the people:
[11]to you is born this day in the city of David
a Savior, who is the Messiah, the Lord.
[12]This will be a sign for you:
you will find a child wrapped in bands of cloth
and lying in a manger."
[13]And suddenly there was with the angel
a multitude of the heavenly host, praising God and saying,
[14]"Glory to God in the highest heaven,
and on earth peace among those whom God favors!"

[[15]When the angels had left them and gone into heaven,
the shepherds said to one another,
"Let us go now to Bethlehem
and see this thing that has taken place,
which the Lord has made known to us."
[16]So they went with haste
and found Mary and Joseph, and the child lying in the manger.
[17]When they saw this,
they made known what had been told them about this child;
[18]and all who heard it were amazed at what the shepherds told them.
[19]But Mary treasured all these words and pondered them in her heart.

[20]The shepherds returned,
glorifying and praising God for all they had heard and seen,
as it had been told them.]

The Gospel of the Lord.

✝

The Nativity of Our Lord
Christmas Dawn (II)

DECEMBER 25

FIRST READING: Isaiah 62:6–12

A reading from Isaiah:

⁶Upon your walls, O Jerusalem,
I have posted sentinels;
all day and all night they shall never be silent.
You who remind the LORD,
take no rest,
⁷and give God no rest
until Jerusalem is established
and made renowned throughout the earth.

⁸The LORD has sworn
by raised right hand and mighty arm:
I will not again give your grain
to be food for your enemies,
and foreigners shall not drink the wine
for which you have labored;
⁹but those who garner it
shall eat it and praise the LORD,
and those who gather it
shall drink it in my holy courts.

¹⁰Go through,
go through the gates,
prepare the way for the people;
build up, build up the highway,
clear it of stones,
lift up an ensign over the peoples.
¹¹The LORD has proclaimed to the end of the earth:
Say to daughter Zion,
"See, your salvation comes;
God comes bearing the reward,
preceded by the recompense."

¹²They shall be called, "The Holy People,
The Redeemed of the LORD";
and you shall be called, "Sought Out,
A City Not Forsaken."

PSALMODY: PSALM 97

SECOND READING: TITUS 3:4–7

A reading from Titus:

⁴When the goodness and loving kindness of God our Savior appeared,
⁵we were saved,
not because of any works of righteousness that we had done,
but according to God's mercy,
through the water of rebirth
and renewal by the Holy Spirit.
⁶This Spirit was poured out on us richly
through Jesus Christ our Savior,
⁷so that, having been justified by God's grace,
we might become heirs
according to the hope of eternal life.

GOSPEL: LUKE 2:[1–7] 8–20

The Holy Gospel according to Luke, the second chapter.

[¹In those days a decree went out from Emperor Augustus
that all the world should be registered.
²This was the first registration
and was taken while Quirinius was governor of Syria.
³All went to their own towns to be registered.
⁴Joseph also went from the town of Nazareth in Galilee to Judea,
to the city of David called Bethlehem,
because he was descended from the house and family of David.
⁵He went to be registered with Mary,
to whom he was engaged and who was expecting a child.
⁶While they were there, the time came for her to deliver her child.
⁷And she gave birth to her firstborn son
and wrapped him in bands of cloth,
and laid him in a manger,
because there was no place for them in the inn.]

[8]In that region there were shepherds living in the fields,
keeping watch over their flock by night.
[9]Then an angel of the Lord stood before them,
and the glory of the Lord shone around them,
and they were terrified.
[10]But the angel said to them,
"Do not be afraid;
for see—
I am bringing you good news of great joy for all the people:
[11]to you is born this day in the city of David
a Savior, who is the Messiah, the Lord.
[12]This will be a sign for you:
you will find a child wrapped in bands of cloth
and lying in a manger."
[13]And suddenly there was with the angel
a multitude of the heavenly host, praising God and saying,
[14]"Glory to God in the highest heaven,
and on earth peace among those whom God favors!"

[15]When the angels had left them and gone into heaven,
the shepherds said to one another,
"Let us go now to Bethlehem
and see this thing that has taken place,
which the Lord has made known to us."
[16]So they went with haste
and found Mary and Joseph, and the child lying in the manger.
[17]When they saw this,
they made known what had been told them about this child;
[18]and all who heard it were amazed at what the shepherds told them.
[19]But Mary treasured all these words and pondered them in her heart.

[20]The shepherds returned,
glorifying and praising God for all they had heard and seen,
as it had been told them.

The Gospel of the Lord.

✝

The Nativity of Our Lord
Christmas Day (III)

DECEMBER 25

FIRST READING: Isaiah 52:7–10

A reading from Isaiah:

⁷How beautiful upon the mountains
are the feet of the messenger who announces peace,
who brings good news,
who announces salvation,
who says to Zion, "Your God reigns."

⁸Listen! Your sentinels lift up their voices,
together they sing for joy;
for in plain sight
they see the return of the LORD to Zion.

⁹Break forth together into singing, you ruins of Jerusalem;
for the LORD has comforted the chosen people,
and has redeemed Jerusalem.
¹⁰The holy arm of the LORD is bared
before the eyes of all the nations;
and all the ends of the earth
shall see the salvation of our God.

PSALMODY: Psalm 98

SECOND READING: HEBREWS 1:1–4 [5–12]

A reading from Hebrews:

1Long ago God spoke to our ancestors
in many and various ways by the prophets,
2but in these last days
God has spoken to us by a Son,
whom God appointed heir of all things,
through whom God also created the worlds.
3He is the reflection of God's glory
and the exact imprint of God's very being,
and sustains all things by his powerful word.
When the Son had made purification for sins,
he sat down at the right hand of the Majesty on high,
4having become as much superior to angels
as the name he has inherited is more excellent than theirs.

[5For to which of the angels did God ever say,
"You are my Son; today I have begotten you"?
Or again,
"I will be a Father to him, and he will be a Son to me"?
6And again, when bringing the firstborn into the world, God says,
"Let all God's angels worship him."
7Of the angels God says,
"God makes the angels winds,
and God's servants flames of fire."

8But of the Son God says,
"Your throne, O God, is forever and ever,
and the righteous scepter is the scepter of your dominion.
9You have loved righteousness and hated wickedness;
therefore God, your God, has anointed you
with the oil of gladness beyond your companions."
10And, "In the beginning, Lord, you founded the earth,
and the heavens are the work of your hands;
11they will perish, but you remain;
they will all wear out like clothing;
12like a cloak you will roll them up,
and like clothing they will be changed.
But you are the same,
and your years will never end."]

The Holy Gospel according to John, the first chapter.

¹In the beginning was the Word,
and the Word was with God,
and the Word was God.
²The Word was in the beginning with God.
³All things came into being through the Word,
without whom not one thing came into being.
What has come into being ⁴in the Word was life,
and the life was the light of all people.
⁵The light shines in the darkness,
and the darkness did not overcome it.

⁶There was a man sent from God, whose name was John.
⁷He came as a witness to testify to the light,
so that all might believe through him.
⁸He himself was not the light,
but he came to testify to the light.
⁹The true light, which enlightens everyone,
was coming into the world.

¹⁰The light was in the world,
and the world came into being through him;
yet the world did not know him.
¹¹He came to what was his own,
and his own people did not accept him.
¹²But to all who received him,
who believed in his name,
he gave power to become children of God,
¹³who were born,
not of blood or of the will of the flesh or of the will of a man,
but of God.

¹⁴And the Word became flesh and lived among us,
and we have seen his glory,
the glory as of a father's only son,
full of grace and truth.

The Gospel of the Lord.

FIRST SUNDAY AFTER CHRISTMAS

DECEMBER 31, 1995   DECEMBER 27, 1998   DECEMBER 30, 2001

FIRST READING: ISAIAH 63:7–9

A reading from Isaiah:

7I will recount the gracious deeds of the LORD,
the praiseworthy acts of the LORD,
because of all that the LORD has done for us,
and the great favor to the house of Israel
that the LORD has shown them out of mercy,
out of abundant steadfast love.

8For the LORD said,
"Surely they are my people,
children who will not deal falsely";
and the LORD became their savior 9in all their distress.

It was no messenger or angel
but the presence of the LORD that saved them;
out of love and pity
the LORD redeemed them,
lifting them up
and carrying them all the days of old.

PSALMODY: PSALM 148

SECOND READING: Hebrews 2:10–18

A reading from Hebrews:

[10]It was fitting that God,
for whom and through whom all things exist,
in bringing many children to glory,
should make the pioneer of their salvation
perfect through sufferings.
[11]For the one who sanctifies
and those who are sanctified
all have one origin.
For this reason
Jesus is not ashamed to call them brothers and sisters, [12]saying,
"I will proclaim your name to my brothers and sisters,
in the midst of the congregation I will praise you."
[13]And again,
"I will put my trust in God."
And again,
"Here am I and the children whom God has given me."

[14]Since, therefore, the children share flesh and blood,
Jesus himself likewise shared the same things,
so that through death
he might destroy the one who has the power of death,
that is, the devil,
[15]and free those who all their lives
were held in slavery by the fear of death.
[16]For it is clear that Jesus did not come to help angels,
but the descendants of Abraham.
[17]Therefore Jesus had to become like his brothers and sisters
in every respect,
so that he might be a merciful and faithful high priest in the service of God,
to make a sacrifice of atonement for the sins of the people.
[18]Because Jesus himself was tested by what he suffered,
he is able to help those who are being tested.

GOSPEL: MATTHEW 2:13–23

The Holy Gospel according to Matthew, the second chapter.

[13]Now after the magi had left,
an angel of the Lord appeared to Joseph in a dream and said,
"Get up, take the child and his mother, and flee to Egypt,
and remain there until I tell you;
for Herod is about to search for the child, to destroy him."

[14]Then Joseph got up,
took the child and his mother by night, and went to Egypt,
[15]and remained there until the death of Herod.
This was to fulfill
what had been spoken by the Lord through the prophet,
"Out of Egypt I have called my son."

[16]When Herod saw that he had been tricked by the magi,
he was infuriated,
and he sent and killed all the children in and around Bethlehem
who were two years old or under,
according to the time that he had learned from the magi.
[17]Then was fulfilled what had been spoken through the prophet Jeremiah:
[18]"A voice was heard in Ramah,
wailing and loud lamentation,
Rachel weeping for her children;
she refused to be consoled, because they are no more."

[19]When Herod died,
an angel of the Lord suddenly appeared in a dream to Joseph in Egypt
        and said,
[20]"Get up, take the child and his mother,
and go to the land of Israel,
for those who were seeking the child's life are dead."
[21]Then Joseph got up, took the child and his mother,
and went to the land of Israel.
[22]But when he heard that Archelaus was ruling over Judea
in place of his father Herod,
he was afraid to go there.
And after being warned in a dream,
he went away to the district of Galilee.
[23]There he made his home in a town called Nazareth,
so that what had been spoken through the prophets might be fulfilled,
"He will be called a Nazorean."

The Gospel of the Lord.

Second Sunday after Christmas

JANUARY 3, 1999

FIRST READING: JEREMIAH 31:7–14   *Alternate Reading: Sirach 24:1–12 (p. 413)*

A reading from Jeremiah:

7Thus says the LORD:
Sing aloud with gladness for Jacob,
and raise shouts for the chief of the nations;
proclaim, give praise, and say,
"Save, O LORD, your people,
the remnant of Israel."

8See, I am going to bring them from the land of the north,
and gather them from the farthest parts of the earth,
among them the blind and the lame,
those with child and those in labor, together;
a great company, they shall return here.
9With weeping they shall come,
and with consolations I will lead them back,
I will let them walk by brooks of water,
in a straight path in which they shall not stumble;
for I am as a father to Israel,
and Ephraim is as my firstborn.

10Hear the word of the LORD, O nations,
and declare it in the coastlands far away;
say, "The one who scattered Israel will gather them,
and will keep them as a shepherd a flock."
11For the LORD has ransomed Jacob,
and has redeemed Jacob's people from hands too strong for them.

¹²They shall come
and sing aloud on the height of Zion,
and they shall be radiant over the goodness of the LORD,
over the grain, the wine, and the oil,
and over the young of the flock and the herd;
their life shall become like a watered garden,
and they shall never languish again.
¹³Then shall the young women rejoice in the dance,
and the young men and the old shall be merry.
I will turn their mourning into joy,
I will comfort them,
and give them gladness for sorrow.
¹⁴I will give the priests their fill of fatness,
and my people shall be satisfied with my bounty, says the LORD.

PSALMODY: PSALM 147:12–20

Psalm 147:13–21 LBW/BCP
Alternate Psalmody: Wisdom of Solomon 10:15–21

SECOND READING: EPHESIANS 1:3–14

A reading from Ephesians:

³Blessed be the God and Father of our Lord Jesus Christ,
who has blessed us in Christ
with every spiritual blessing in the heavenly places,
⁴just as God chose us in Christ before the foundation of the world
that before God we should be holy and blameless in love.
⁵God destined us for adoption as children through Jesus Christ:
this was God's good pleasure and will,
⁶to the praise of God's glorious grace,
freely bestowed on us in the Beloved.

⁷In Christ we have redemption through his blood,
the forgiveness of our trespasses,
according to the riches of God's grace ⁸lavished on us.

With all wisdom and insight
⁹God has made known to us the mystery of the divine will,
according to God's good pleasure set forth in Christ,
¹⁰as a plan for the fullness of time,
to gather up all things in Christ,
things in heaven and things on earth.

¹¹In Christ we have also obtained an inheritance,
having been destined according to the purpose of the one
who accomplishes all things according to divine counsel and will,
¹²so that we, who were the first to set our hope on Christ,
might live for the praise of God's glory.
¹³In Christ you also, when you had heard the word of truth,
the gospel of your salvation, and had believed in him,
were marked with the seal of the promised Holy Spirit;
¹⁴this is the pledge of our inheritance
toward redemption as God's own people,
to the praise of God's glory.

GOSPEL: JOHN 1:[1–9] 10–18

The Holy Gospel according to John, the first chapter.

[¹In the beginning was the Word,
and the Word was with God,
and the Word was God.
²The Word was in the beginning with God.
³All things came into being through the Word,
without whom not one thing came into being.
What has come into being ⁴in the Word was life,
and the life was the light of all people.
⁵The light shines in the darkness,
and the darkness did not overcome it.

⁶There was a man sent from God, whose name was John.
⁷He came as a witness to testify to the light,
so that all might believe through him.
⁸He himself was not the light,
but he came to testify to the light.
⁹The true light, which enlightens everyone,
was coming into the world.]

¹⁰The light was in the world,
and the world came into being through him;
yet the world did not know him.
¹¹He came to what was his own,
and his own people did not accept him.
¹²But to all who received him,
who believed in his name,
he gave power to become children of God,
¹³who were born, not of blood or of the will of the flesh
or of the will of a man,
but of God.

¹⁴And the Word became flesh and lived among us,
and we have seen his glory,
the glory as of a father's only son,
full of grace and truth.

¹⁵(John testified to him and cried out,
"This was the one of whom I said,
'The one who comes after me ranks ahead of me
because he was before me.' ")
¹⁶From his fullness we have all received,
grace upon grace.
¹⁷The law indeed was given through Moses;
grace and truth came through Jesus Christ.

¹⁸No one has ever seen God.
It is God the only Son,
who is close to the Father's heart,
who has made God known.

The Gospel of the Lord.

✚

Season of Epiphany

✝

THE EPIPHANY OF OUR LORD

JANUARY 6

FIRST READING: Isaiah 60:1–6

A reading from Isaiah:

¹Arise, shine; for your light has come,
and the glory of the LORD has risen upon you.
²For darkness shall cover the earth,
and thick darkness the peoples;
but the LORD will arise upon you,
and the glory of the LORD will appear over you.
³Nations shall come to your light,
and rulers to the brightness of your dawn.

⁴Lift up your eyes and look around;
they all gather together, they come to you;
your sons shall come from far away,
and your daughters shall be carried on their nurses' arms.

⁵Then you shall see and be radiant;
your heart shall thrill and rejoice,
because the abundance of the sea shall be brought to you,
the wealth of the nations shall come to you.
⁶A multitude of camels shall cover you,
the young camels of Midian and Ephah;
all those from Sheba shall come.
They shall bring gold and frankincense,
and shall proclaim the praise of the LORD.

PSALMODY: Psalm 72:1–7, 10–14

SECOND READING: EPHESIANS 3:1–12

A reading from Ephesians:

¹This is the reason that I Paul am a prisoner for Christ Jesus
for the sake of you Gentiles—
²for surely you have already heard of the commission of God's grace
that was given me for you,
³and how the mystery was made known to me by revelation,
as I wrote above in a few words,
⁴a reading of which will enable you
to perceive my understanding of the mystery of Christ.

⁵In former generations this mystery was not made known to humankind,
as it has now been revealed to his holy apostles and prophets by the Spirit:
⁶that is, the Gentiles have become heirs with us,
members of the same body,
and sharers in the promise in Christ Jesus through the gospel.

⁷Of this gospel I have become a servant
according to the gift of God's grace
that was given me by the working of God's power.
⁸Although I am the very least of all the saints,
this grace was given to me
to bring to the Gentiles the news of the boundless riches of Christ,
⁹and to make everyone see
what is the plan of the mystery hidden for ages in God
who created all things;
¹⁰so that through the church
the wisdom of God in its rich variety
might now be made known to the rulers and authorities
in the heavenly places.
¹¹This was in accordance with the eternal purpose
that God has carried out in Christ Jesus our Lord,
¹²through faith in whom we have access to God
in boldness and confidence.

The Holy Gospel according to Matthew, the second chapter.

[1]In the time of King Herod,
after Jesus was born in Bethlehem of Judea,
magi from the East came to Jerusalem, [2]asking,
"Where is the child who has been born king of the Jews?
For we observed his star at its rising,
and have come to pay him homage."

[3]When King Herod heard this, he was frightened,
and all Jerusalem with him;
[4]and calling together all the chief priests and scribes of the people,
he inquired of them where the Messiah was to be born.
[5]They told him,
"In Bethlehem of Judea;
for so it has been written by the prophet:

[6]" 'And you, Bethlehem, in the land of Judah,
are by no means least among the rulers of Judah;
for from you shall come a ruler
who is to shepherd my people Israel.' "

[7]Then Herod secretly called for the magi
and learned from them the exact time when the star had appeared.
[8]Then he sent them to Bethlehem, saying,
"Go and search diligently for the child;
and when you have found him,
bring me word so that I may also go and pay him homage."

[9]When they had heard the king, they set out;
and there, ahead of them,
went the star that they had seen at its rising,
until it stopped over the place where the child was.
[10]When they saw that the star had stopped,
they were overwhelmed with joy.

[11]On entering the house, they saw the child with Mary his mother;
and they knelt down and paid him homage.
Then, opening their treasure chests,
they offered him gifts of gold, frankincense, and myrrh.

[12]And having been warned in a dream not to return to Herod,
they left for their own country by another road.

The Gospel of the Lord.

✝

THE BAPTISM OF OUR LORD
(First Sunday after the Epiphany)

JANUARY 7, 1996   *JANUARY 10, 1999*   *JANUARY 13, 2002*

FIRST READING: ISAIAH 42:1–9

A reading from Isaiah:

¹Here is my servant, whom I uphold,
my chosen, in whom my soul delights,
upon whom I have put my spirit,
to bring forth justice to the nations.
²Not crying out, not lifting up his voice,
not making it heard in the street,
³a bruised reed my servant will not break,
nor quench a dimly burning wick,
but will faithfully bring forth justice.
⁴My chosen one will not grow faint or be crushed
until he has established justice in the earth;
and the coastlands wait for his teaching.

⁵Thus says God, the LORD,
who created the heavens and stretched them out,
who spread out the earth and what comes from it,
who gives breath to the people upon it
and spirit to those who walk in it:
⁶I am the LORD,
I have called you in righteousness,
I have taken you by the hand and kept you;
I have given you as a covenant to the people,
a light to the nations,
⁷to open the eyes that are blind,
to bring out the prisoners from the dungeon,
from the prison those who sit in darkness.

⁸I am the LORD, that is my name;
my glory I give to no other,
nor my praise to idols.
⁹See, the former things have come to pass,
and new things I now declare;
before they spring forth, I tell you of them.

PSALMODY: PSALM 29

SECOND READING: ACTS 10:34–43

A reading from Acts:

³⁴Peter began to speak to Cornelius and his household:
"I truly understand that God shows no partiality,
³⁵but in every nation
anyone who is God-fearing and does what is right
is acceptable to God.

³⁶"You know the message God sent to the people of Israel,
preaching peace by Jesus Christ,
who is Lord of all.
³⁷That message spread throughout Judea,
beginning in Galilee after the baptism that John announced:
³⁸how God anointed Jesus of Nazareth with the Holy Spirit and with power;
how Jesus went about doing good
and healing all who were oppressed by the devil,
for God was with him.
³⁹We are witnesses to all that Jesus did both in Judea and in Jerusalem.
They put him to death by hanging him on a tree;
⁴⁰but God raised Jesus on the third day
and allowed him to appear,
⁴¹not to all the people
but to us who were chosen by God as witnesses,
and who ate and drank with him after he rose from the dead.

⁴²"Jesus commanded us to preach to the people
and to testify that he is the one ordained by God
as judge of the living and the dead.
⁴³All the prophets testify about him
that everyone who believes in him
receives forgiveness of sins through his name."

The Holy Gospel according to Matthew, the third chapter.

¹³Jesus came from Galilee to John at the Jordan,
to be baptized by him.
¹⁴John would have prevented him, saying,
"I need to be baptized by you, and do you come to me?"
¹⁵But Jesus answered him,
"Let it be so now;
for it is proper for us in this way to fulfill all righteousness."
Then John consented.

¹⁶And when Jesus had been baptized,
just as he came up from the water,
suddenly the heavens were opened to him
and he saw the Spirit of God descending like a dove
and alighting on him.
¹⁷And a voice from heaven said,
"This is my Son, the Beloved,
with whom I am well pleased."

The Gospel of the Lord.

✛

Second Sunday after the Epiphany

JANUARY 14, 1996   JANUARY 17, 1999   JANUARY 20, 2002

FIRST READING: Isaiah 49:1–7

A reading from Isaiah:

¹Listen to me, O coastlands,
pay attention, you peoples from far away!
The LORD called me before I was born,
and while I was in my mother's womb God named me.
²The LORD made my mouth like a sharp sword;
I was hid in the shadow of God's hand.
The LORD made me a polished arrow;
I was hid away in God's quiver.

³And the LORD said to me, "You are my servant,
Israel, in whom I will be glorified."
⁴But I said, "I have labored in vain,
I have spent my strength for nothing and vanity;
yet surely my cause is with the LORD,
and my reward with my God."

⁵And now the LORD says,
who formed me as a servant from the womb,
to bring Jacob back to God,
and that Israel might be gathered to the LORD,
for I am honored in the sight of the LORD,
and my God has become my strength—
⁶the LORD says,
"It is too light a thing that you should be my servant
to raise up the tribes of Jacob
and to restore the survivors of Israel;
I will give you as a light to the nations,
that my salvation may reach to the end of the earth."

7Thus says the LORD,
the Redeemer of Israel, the Holy One of Israel,
to one deeply despised, abhorred by the nations,
the slave of rulers,
"Monarchs shall see and stand up,
chieftains, and they shall prostrate themselves,
because of the LORD, who is faithful,
the Holy One of Israel, who has chosen you."

PSALMODY: PSALM 40:1–11

SECOND READING: 1 CORINTHIANS 1:1–9

A reading from First Corinthians:

1Paul, called to be an apostle of Christ Jesus by the will of God,
and our brother Sosthenes,
2To the church of God that is in Corinth,
to those who are sanctified in Christ Jesus,
called to be saints,
together with all those who in every place
call on the name of our Lord Jesus Christ,
both their Lord and ours:
3Grace to you and peace
from God, our Father, and the Lord Jesus Christ.

4I give thanks to my God always for you
because of the grace of God that has been given you in Christ Jesus,
5for in every way you have been enriched in Christ,
in speech and knowledge of every kind—
6just as the testimony of Christ has been strengthened among you—
7so that you are not lacking in any spiritual gift
as you wait for the revealing of our Lord Jesus Christ.

8God will also strengthen you to the end,
so that you may be blameless on the day of our Lord Jesus Christ.
9God is faithful,
by whom you were called into the communion of the Son of God,
Jesus Christ our Lord.

GOSPEL: JOHN 1:29–42

The Holy Gospel according to John, the first chapter.

²⁹John the Baptist saw Jesus coming toward him and declared,
"Here is the Lamb of God who takes away the sin of the world!
³⁰This is the one of whom I said,
'After me comes a man who ranks ahead of me
because he was before me.'
³¹I myself did not know him;
but I came baptizing with water for this reason,
that he might be revealed to Israel."

³²And John testified,
"I saw the Spirit descending from heaven like a dove,
and it remained on him.
³³I myself did not know him,
but the one who sent me to baptize with water said to me,
'The one on whom you see the Spirit descend and remain
is the one who baptizes with the Holy Spirit.'
³⁴And I myself have seen and have testified
that this is the Son of God."

³⁵The next day John again was standing with two of his disciples,
³⁶and as he watched Jesus walk by, he exclaimed,
"Look, here is the Lamb of God!"
³⁷The two disciples heard him say this, and they followed Jesus.
³⁸When Jesus turned and saw them following, he said to them,
"What are you looking for?"
They said to him,
"Rabbi" (which translated means Teacher),
"where are you staying?"
³⁹He said to them,
"Come and see."
They came and saw where Jesus was staying,
and they remained with him that day.
It was about four o'clock in the afternoon.

⁴⁰One of the two who heard John speak and followed him
was Andrew, Simon Peter's brother.
⁴¹Andrew first found his brother Simon and said to him,
"We have found the Messiah" (which is translated Anointed).
⁴²He brought Simon to Jesus, who looked at him and said,
"You are Simon son of John.
You are to be called Cephas" (which is translated Peter).

The Gospel of the Lord.

THIRD SUNDAY AFTER THE EPIPHANY

JANUARY 21, 1996   JANUARY 24, 1999   JANUARY 27, 2002

FIRST READING: ISAIAH 9:1–4

A reading from Isaiah:

[1]There will be no gloom for those who were in anguish.
In the former time the LORD brought into contempt
the land of Zebulun and the land of Naphtali,
but in the latter time the LORD will make glorious the way of the sea,
the land beyond the Jordan, Galilee of the nations.

[2]The people who walked in darkness have seen a great light;
those who lived in a land of deep darkness—
on them light has shined.
[3]You have multiplied the nation,
you have increased its joy;
they rejoice before you as with joy at the harvest,
as people exult when dividing plunder.
[4]For the yoke of their burden,
and the bar across their shoulders,
the rod of their oppressor,
you have broken as on the day of Midian.

PSALMODY: PSALM 27:1, 4–9   *Psalm 27:1, 5–10* LBW/BCP

SECOND READING: 1 Corinthians 1:10–18

A reading from First Corinthians:

[10]Now I appeal to you, brothers and sisters,
by the name of our Lord Jesus Christ,
that all of you be in agreement
and that there be no divisions among you,
but that you be united in the same mind and the same purpose.
[11]For it has been reported to me by Chloe's people
that there are quarrels among you, my brothers and sisters.
[12]What I mean is that each of you says,
"I belong to Paul," or "I belong to Apollos,"
or "I belong to Cephas," or "I belong to Christ."
[13]Has Christ been divided?
Was Paul crucified for you?
Or were you baptized in the name of Paul?

[14]I thank God that I baptized none of you except Crispus and Gaius,
[15]so that no one can say that you were baptized in my name.
[16](I did baptize also the household of Stephanas;
beyond that, I do not know whether I baptized anyone else.)
[17]For Christ did not send me to baptize
but to proclaim the gospel,
and not with eloquent wisdom,
so that the cross of Christ might not be emptied of its power.

[18]For the message about the cross
is foolishness to those who are perishing,
but to us who are being saved
it is the power of God.

GOSPEL: MATTHEW 4:12–23

The Holy Gospel according to Matthew, the fourth chapter.

[12]Now when Jesus heard that John had been arrested,
he withdrew to Galilee.
[13]He left Nazareth and made his home in Capernaum by the sea,
in the territory of Zebulun and Naphtali,
[14]so that what had been spoken through the prophet Isaiah
might be fulfilled:

[15]"Land of Zebulun, land of Naphtali,
on the road by the sea, across the Jordan,
Galilee of the Gentiles—
[16]the people who sat in darkness have seen a great light,
and for those who sat in the region and shadow of death
light has dawned."

[17]From that time Jesus began to proclaim,
"Repent, for the dominion of heaven has come near."

[18]As Jesus walked by the Sea of Galilee, he saw two brothers,
Simon, who is called Peter, and Andrew his brother,
casting a net into the sea—for they were fishermen.
[19]And Jesus said to them,
"Follow me, and I will make you fish for human beings."
[20]Immediately they left their nets and followed Jesus.

[21]Going on from there, Jesus saw two other brothers,
James son of Zebedee and his brother John,
in the boat with their father Zebedee, mending their nets,
and he called them.
[22]Immediately they left the boat and their father, and followed him.

[23]Jesus went throughout Galilee, teaching in their synagogues
and proclaiming the good news of the dominion of heaven
and curing every disease and every sickness among the people.

The Gospel of the Lord.

Fourth Sunday after the Epiphany

JANUARY 28, 1996   JANUARY 31, 1999   FEBRUARY 3, 2002

FIRST READING: MICAH 6:1–8

A reading from Micah:

¹Hear what the LORD says:
Rise, plead your case before the mountains,
and let the hills hear your voice.
²Hear, you mountains, the controversy of the LORD,
and you enduring foundations of the earth;
for the LORD has a controversy with the chosen people;
the LORD will contend with Israel.

³"O my people, what have I done to you?
In what have I wearied you?
Answer me!
⁴For I brought you up from the land of Egypt,
and redeemed you from the house of slavery;
and I sent before you Moses, Aaron, and Miriam.
⁵O my people, remember now what King Balak of Moab devised,
what Balaam son of Beor answered him,
and what happened from Shittim to Gilgal,
that you may know the saving acts of the LORD."

⁶"With what shall I come before the LORD,
and bow myself before God on high?
Shall I come before God with burnt offerings, with calves a year old?
⁷Will the LORD be pleased with thousands of rams,
with ten thousands of rivers of oil?
Shall I give my firstborn for my transgression,
the fruit of my body for the sin of my soul?"

⁸The LORD has told you, O mortal, what is good;
and what does the LORD require of you
but to do justice,
and to love kindness,
and to walk humbly with your God?

PSALMODY: Psalm 15

SECOND READING: 1 Corinthians 1:18–31

A reading from First Corinthians:

[18]The message about the cross
is foolishness to those who are perishing,
but to us who are being saved
it is the power of God.

[19]For it is written,
"I will destroy the wisdom of the wise,
and the discernment of the discerning I will thwart."
[20]Where is the one who is wise?
Where is the scribe?
Where is the debater of this age?
Has not God made foolish the wisdom of the world?

[21]For since, in the wisdom of God,
the world did not know God through wisdom,
God decided, through the foolishness of our proclamation,
to save those who believe.
[22]For Jews demand signs and Greeks desire wisdom,
[23]but we proclaim Christ crucified,
a stumbling block to Jews and foolishness to Gentiles,
[24]but to those who are the called, both Jews and Greeks,
Christ the power of God and the wisdom of God.
[25]For God's foolishness is wiser than human wisdom,
and God's weakness is stronger than human strength.

[26]Consider your own call, brothers and sisters:
not many of you were wise by human standards,
not many were powerful,
not many were of noble birth.
[27]But God chose what is foolish in the world to shame the wise;
God chose what is weak in the world to shame the strong;
[28]God chose what is low and despised in the world,
things that are not,
to reduce to nothing things that are,
[29]so that no one might boast in the presence of God.

[30]God is the source of your life in Christ Jesus,
who became for us wisdom from God,
and righteousness and sanctification and redemption,
[31]in order that, as it is written,
"Let the one who boasts, boast in the Lord."

GOSPEL: MATTHEW 5:1–12

The Holy Gospel according to Matthew, the fifth chapter.

[1]When Jesus saw the crowds, he went up the mountain and sat down;
and his disciples came to him.
[2]Then Jesus began to speak, and taught them, saying:

[3]"Blessed are the poor in spirit, for theirs is the dominion of heaven.
[4]Blessed are those who mourn, for they will be comforted.
[5]Blessed are the meek, for they will inherit the earth.
[6]Blessed are those who hunger and thirst for righteousness,
for they will be filled.
[7]Blessed are the merciful, for they will receive mercy.
[8]Blessed are the pure in heart, for they will see God.
[9]Blessed are the peacemakers, for they will be called children of God.

[10]"Blessed are those who are persecuted for righteousness' sake,
for theirs is the dominion of heaven.
[11]Blessed are you when people revile you and persecute you
and utter all kinds of evil against you falsely on my account.
[12]Rejoice and be glad, for your reward is great in heaven,
for in the same way they persecuted the prophets who were before you."

The Gospel of the Lord.

✠

FIFTH SUNDAY AFTER THE EPIPHANY

FEBRUARY 4, 1996   FEBRUARY 7, 1999

FIRST READING: ISAIAH 58:1–9a [9b–12]

A reading from Isaiah:

¹Shout out, do not hold back!
Lift up your voice like a trumpet!
Announce to my people their rebellion,
to the house of Jacob their sins.
²Yet day after day they seek me and delight to know my ways,
as if they were a nation that practiced righteousness
and did not forsake the ordinance of their God;
they ask of me righteous judgments,
they delight to draw near to God.

³"Why do we fast, but you do not see?
Why humble ourselves, but you do not notice?"
Look, you serve your own interest on your fast day,
and oppress all your workers.
⁴Look, you fast only to quarrel and to fight
and to strike with a wicked fist.
Such fasting as you do today
will not make your voice heard on high.

⁵Is such the fast that I choose,
a day to humble oneself?
Is it to bow down the head like a bulrush,
and to lie in sackcloth and ashes?
Will you call this a fast,
a day acceptable to the LORD?

⁶Is not this the fast that I choose:
to loose the bonds of injustice,
to undo the thongs of the yoke,
to let the oppressed go free,
and to break every yoke?
⁷Is it not to share your bread with the hungry,
and bring the homeless poor into your house;

when you see the naked, to cover them,
and not to hide yourself from your own kin?

8Then your light shall break forth like the dawn,
and your healing shall spring up quickly;
your vindicator shall go before you,
the glory of the LORD shall be your rear guard.
9aThen you shall call, and the LORD will answer;
you shall cry for help, and God will say, Here I am.

[9bIf you remove the yoke from among you,
the pointing of the finger, the speaking of evil,
10if you offer your food to the hungry
and satisfy the needs of the afflicted,
then your light shall rise in the darkness
and your gloom be like the noonday.
11The LORD will guide you continually,
and satisfy your needs in parched places,
and make your bones strong;
and you shall be like a watered garden,
like a spring of water, whose waters never fail.
12Your ancient ruins shall be rebuilt;
you shall raise up the foundations of many generations;
you shall be called the repairer of the breach,
the restorer of streets to live in.]

PSALMODY: PSALM 112:1–9 [10]

SECOND READING: 1 CORINTHIANS 2:1–12 [13–16]

A reading from First Corinthians:

1When I came to you, brothers and sisters,
I did not come proclaiming the mystery of God to you
in lofty words or wisdom.
2For I decided to know nothing among you except Jesus Christ,
and him crucified.
3And I came to you in weakness and in fear and in much trembling.
4My speech and my proclamation were not with plausible words of wisdom,
but with a demonstration of the Spirit and of power,
5so that your faith might rest not on human wisdom
but on the power of God.

⁶Yet among the mature we do speak wisdom,
though it is not a wisdom of this age
or of the rulers of this age, who are doomed to perish.
⁷But we speak God's wisdom, secret and hidden,
which God decreed before the ages for our glory.
⁸None of the rulers of this age understood this;
for if they had, they would not have crucified the Lord of glory.

⁹But, as it is written,
"What no eye has seen, nor ear heard,
nor the human heart conceived,
what God has prepared for those who love God"—
¹⁰these things God has revealed to us through the Spirit;
for the Spirit searches everything,
even the depths of God.
¹¹For what human being knows what is truly human
except the human spirit that is within?
So also no one comprehends what is truly God's
except the Spirit of God.

¹²Now we have received not the spirit of the world,
but the Spirit that is from God,
so that we may understand the gifts bestowed on us by God.

[¹³And we speak of these things in words not taught by human wisdom
but taught by the Spirit,
interpreting spiritual things to those who are spiritual.
¹⁴Those who are unspiritual do not receive the gifts of God's Spirit,
for they are foolishness to them,
and they are unable to understand them
because they are spiritually discerned.
¹⁵Those who are spiritual discern all things,
and they are themselves subject to no one else's scrutiny.

¹⁶"For who has known the mind of the Lord
so as to instruct the Lord?"
But we have the mind of Christ.]

GOSPEL: MATTHEW 5:13–20

The Holy Gospel according to Matthew, the fifth chapter.

Jesus said:
[13]"You are the salt of the earth;
but if salt has lost its taste, how can its saltiness be restored?
It is no longer good for anything,
but is thrown out and trampled under foot.

[14]"You are the light of the world.
A city built on a hill cannot be hid.
[15]No one after lighting a lamp puts it under the bushel basket,
but on the lampstand,
and it gives light to all in the house.
[16]In the same way, let your light shine before others,
so that they may see your good works
and give glory to your Father in heaven.

[17]"Do not think that I have come to abolish the law or the prophets;
I have come not to abolish but to fulfill.
[18]For truly I tell you,
until heaven and earth pass away,
not one letter, not one stroke of a letter,
will pass from the law until all is accomplished.
[19]Therefore, whoever breaks one of the least of these commandments,
and teaches others to do the same,
will be called least in the dominion of heaven;
but whoever does them and teaches them
will be called great in the dominion of heaven.

[20]"For I tell you,
unless your righteousness exceeds that of the scribes and Pharisees,
you will never enter the dominion of heaven."

The Gospel of the Lord.

Sixth Sunday after the Epiphany

FEBRUARY 11, 1996

PROPER 1

FIRST READING: Deuteronomy 30:15–20   *Alternate Reading: Sirach 15:15–20 (p.414)*

A reading from Deuteronomy:

Moses said to the people:
¹⁵See, I have set before you today
life and prosperity,
death and adversity.

¹⁶If you obey the commandments of the Lord your God
that I am commanding you today,
by loving the Lord your God,
by walking in the Lord's ways,
and by observing God's commandments, decrees, and ordinances,
then you shall live and become numerous,
and the Lord your God will bless you
in the land that you are entering to possess.

¹⁷But if your heart turns away and you do not hear,
but are led astray to bow down to other deities and serve them,
¹⁸I declare to you today that you shall perish;
you shall not live long in the land
that you are crossing the Jordan to enter and possess.

¹⁹I call heaven and earth to witness against you today
that I have set before you life and death,
blessings and curses.
Choose life so that you and your descendants may live,
²⁰loving the Lord your God,
obeying the Lord,
and holding fast to your God;
for that means life to you and length of days,
so that you may live in the land
that the Lord swore to give to your ancestors,
to Abraham, to Isaac, and to Jacob.

PSALMODY: P<small>SALM</small> 119:1–8

SECOND READING: 1 C<small>ORINTHIANS</small> 3:1–9

A reading from First Corinthians:

¹Brothers and sisters,
I could not speak to you as spiritual people,
but rather as people of the flesh, as infants in Christ.
²I fed you with milk, not solid food,
for you were not ready for solid food.
Even now you are still not ready,
³for you are still of the flesh.

For as long as there is jealousy and quarreling among you,
are you not of the flesh,
and behaving according to human inclinations?
⁴For when one says, "I belong to Paul,"
and another, "I belong to Apollos,"
are you not merely human?
⁵What then is Apollos?
What is Paul?
Servants through whom you came to believe,
as the Lord assigned to each.
⁶I planted, Apollos watered,
but God gave the growth.

⁷So neither the one who plants
nor the one who waters is anything,
but only God who gives the growth.
⁸The one who plants and the one who waters have a common purpose,
and each will receive wages according to the labor of each.
⁹For we are God's servants, working together;
you are God's field, God's building.

GOSPEL: M<small>ATTHEW</small> 5:21–37

The Holy Gospel according to Matthew, the fifth chapter.

Jesus said:
²¹"You have heard that it was said to those of ancient times,
'You shall not murder';
and 'whoever murders shall be liable to judgment.'
²²But I say to you that if you are angry with a brother or sister,
you will be liable to judgment;
and if you insult a brother or sister,
you will be liable to the council;
and if you say, 'You fool,'
you will be liable to the hell of fire.

²³"So when you are offering your gift at the altar,
if you remember that your sister or brother has something against you,
²⁴leave your gift there before the altar and go;
first be reconciled to your sister or brother,
and then come and offer your gift.
²⁵Come to terms quickly with your accuser
while you are going together to court,
or your accuser may hand you over to the judge,
and the judge to the guard,
and you will be thrown into prison.
²⁶Truly I tell you,
you will never get out until you have paid the last penny.

²⁷"You have heard that it was said,
'You shall not commit adultery.'
²⁸But I say to you that every man who looks at a woman with lust
has already committed adultery with her in his heart.
²⁹If your right eye causes you to sin,
tear it out and throw it away;
it is better for you to lose one part of your body
than for your whole body to be thrown into hell.
³⁰And if your right hand causes you to sin,
cut it off and throw it away;
it is better for you to lose one part of your body
than for your whole body to go into hell.

³¹"It was also said,
'Whichever man divorces his wife,
let him give her a certificate of divorce.'
³²But I say to you that any man who divorces his wife,
except on the ground of unchastity,
causes her to commit adultery;
and whichever man marries a divorced woman commits adultery.

³³"Again, you have heard that it was said to those of ancient times,
'You shall not swear falsely,
but carry out the vows you have made to the Lord.'
³⁴But I say to you,
Do not swear at all,
either by heaven, for it is the throne of God,
³⁵or by the earth, for it is God's footstool,
or by Jerusalem, for it is the city of the great Sovereign.
³⁶And do not swear by your head,
for you cannot make one hair white or black.
³⁷Let your word be 'Yes, Yes' or 'No, No';
anything more than this comes from the evil one."

The Gospel of the Lord.

Seventh Sunday after the Epiphany

FIRST READING: Leviticus 19:1–2, 9–18

A reading from Leviticus:

¹The LORD spoke to Moses, saying:
²Speak to all the congregation of the people of Israel and say to them:
You shall be holy,
for I the LORD your God am holy.

⁹When you reap the harvest of your land,
you shall not reap to the very edges of your field,
or gather the gleanings of your harvest.
¹⁰You shall not strip your vineyard bare,
or gather the fallen grapes of your vineyard;
you shall leave them for the poor and the alien:
I am the LORD your God.

¹¹You shall not steal;
you shall not deal falsely;
and you shall not lie to one another.
¹²And you shall not swear falsely by my name,
profaning the name of your God: I am the LORD.

¹³You shall not defraud your neighbor;
you shall not steal;
and you shall not keep for yourself the wages of a laborer until morning.
¹⁴You shall not revile those who are deaf
or put a stumbling block before those who are blind;
you shall fear your God: I am the LORD.

¹⁵You shall not render an unjust judgment;
you shall not be partial to the poor or defer to the great:
with justice you shall judge your neighbor.
¹⁶You shall not go around as a slanderer among your people,
and you shall not profit by the blood of your neighbor:
I am the LORD.

¹⁷You shall not hate in your heart anyone of your kin;
you shall reprove your neighbor,

or you will incur guilt yourself.
18You shall not take vengeance or bear a grudge against any of your people,
but you shall love your neighbor as yourself:
I am the LORD.

PSALMODY: PSALM 119:33–40

SECOND READING: 1 CORINTHIANS 3:10–11, 16–23

A reading from First Corinthians:

10According to the grace of God given to me,
like a skilled master builder I laid a foundation,
and someone else is building on it.
Each builder must choose with care how to build on it.
11For no one can lay any foundation other than the one that has been laid;
that foundation is Jesus Christ.

16Do you not know that you are God's temple
and that God's Spirit dwells in you?
17Anyone who destroys God's temple
will be destroyed by God.
For God's temple is holy,
and you are that temple.

18Do not deceive yourselves.
If you think that you are wise in this age,
you should become fools so that you may become wise.
19For the wisdom of this world is foolishness with God.
For it is written,
"God catches the wise in their craftiness,"
20and again,
"The Lord knows the thoughts of the wise,
that they are futile."
21So let no one boast about human leaders.
For all things are yours,
22whether Paul or Apollos or Cephas
or the world or life or death
or the present or the future—
all belong to you,
23and you belong to Christ,
and Christ belongs to God.

GOSPEL: MATTHEW 5:38–48

The Holy Gospel according to Matthew, the fifth chapter.

Jesus said:
[38]"You have heard that it was said,
'An eye for an eye and a tooth for a tooth.'
[39]But I say to you,
Do not resist an evildoer.
But if anyone strikes you on the right cheek,
turn the other also;
[40]and if anyone wants to sue you and take your coat,
give your cloak as well;
[41]and if anyone forces you to go one mile,
go also the second mile.
[42]Give to everyone who begs from you,
and do not refuse anyone who wants to borrow from you.

[43]"You have heard that it was said,
'You shall love your neighbor and hate your enemy.'
[44]But I say to you,
Love your enemies and pray for those who persecute you,
[45]so that you may be children of your Father in heaven;
for God makes the sun rise on the evil and on the good,
and sends rain on the righteous and on the unrighteous.
[46]For if you love those who love you,
what reward do you have?
Do not even the tax collectors do the same?
[47]And if you greet only your brothers and sisters,
what more are you doing than others?
Do not even the Gentiles do the same?
[48]Be perfect, therefore,
as your heavenly Father is perfect."

The Gospel of the Lord.

Eighth Sunday after the Epiphany

FIRST READING: Isaiah 49:8–16a

A reading from Isaiah:

8Thus says the LORD:
In a time of favor I have answered you,
on a day of salvation I have helped you;
I have kept you and given you
as a covenant to the people,
to establish the land,
to apportion the desolate heritages;
9saying to the prisoners,
"Come out,"
to those who are in darkness,
"Show yourselves."

They shall feed along the ways,
on all the bare heights shall be their pasture;
10they shall not hunger or thirst,
neither scorching wind nor sun shall strike them down,
for the one who has pity on them will lead them,
and by springs of water will guide them.
11And I will turn all my mountains into a road,
and my highways shall be raised up.
12Lo, these shall come from far away,
and lo, these from the north and from the west,
and these from the land of Syene.

13Sing for joy, O heavens, and exult, O earth;
break forth, O mountains, into singing!
For the LORD has comforted the chosen people,
and will have compassion on all the suffering ones.

¹⁴But Zion said, "The LORD has forsaken me,
my LORD has forgotten me."
¹⁵Can a woman forget her nursing child,
or show no compassion for the child of her womb?
Even these may forget,
yet I will not forget you.
¹⁶ªSee, I have inscribed you on the palms of my hands.

PSALMODY: PSALM 131

SECOND READING: 1 CORINTHIANS 4:1–5

A reading from First Corinthians:

¹Think of us in this way,
as servants of Christ and stewards of God's mysteries.
²Moreover, it is required of stewards that they be found trustworthy.
³But with me it is a very small thing
that I should be judged by you or by any human court.
I do not even judge myself.
⁴I am not aware of anything against myself,
but I am not thereby acquitted.
It is the Lord who judges me.

⁵Therefore do not pronounce judgment before the time,
before the Lord comes,
who will bring to light the things now hidden in darkness
and will disclose the purposes of the heart.
Then each one will receive commendation from God.

GOSPEL: MATTHEW 6:24–34

The Holy Gospel according to Matthew, the sixth chapter.

Jesus said:
²⁴"No one can serve two masters;
for a slave will either hate the one and love the other,
or be devoted to the one and despise the other.
You cannot serve God and wealth.

²⁵"Therefore I tell you,
do not worry about your life,
what you will eat or what you will drink,
or about your body, what you will wear.
Is not life more than food, and the body more than clothing?
²⁶Look at the birds of the air;
they neither sow nor reap nor gather into barns,
and yet your heavenly Father feeds them.
Are you not of more value than they?
²⁷And can any of you by worrying
add a single hour to your span of life?
²⁸And why do you worry about clothing?
Consider the lilies of the field, how they grow;
they neither toil nor spin,
²⁹yet I tell you, even Solomon in all his glory
was not clothed like one of these.
³⁰But if God so clothes the grass of the field,
which is alive today and tomorrow is thrown into the oven,
will God not much more clothe you—you of little faith?

³¹"Therefore do not worry, saying,
'What will we eat?' or 'What will we drink?' or 'What will we wear?'
³²For it is the Gentiles who strive for all these things;
and indeed your heavenly Father knows that you need all these things.
³³But strive first for the dominion and the righteousness of God,
and all these things will be given to you as well.

³⁴"So do not worry about tomorrow,
for tomorrow will bring worries of its own.
Today's trouble is enough for today."

The Gospel of the Lord.

✝

The Transfiguration of Our Lord

(Last Sunday after the Epiphany)

FEBRUARY 18, 1996   FEBRUARY 14, 1999   FEBRUARY 10, 2002

FIRST READING: Exodus 24:12–18

A reading from Exodus:

¹²The LORD said to Moses,
"Come up to me on the mountain, and wait there;
and I will give you the tablets of stone,
with the law and the commandment,
which I have written for their instruction."
¹³So Moses set out with his assistant Joshua,
and Moses went up into the mountain of God.
¹⁴To the elders Moses had said,
"Wait here for us, until we come to you again;
for Aaron and Hur are with you;
whoever has a dispute may go to them."

¹⁵Then Moses went up on the mountain, and the cloud covered the mountain.
¹⁶The glory of the LORD settled on Mount Sinai,
and the cloud covered it for six days;
on the seventh day God called to Moses out of the cloud.
¹⁷Now the appearance of the glory of the LORD
was like a devouring fire on the top of the mountain
in the sight of the people of Israel.
¹⁸Moses entered the cloud, and went up on the mountain.
Moses was on the mountain for forty days and forty nights.

PSALMODY: Psalm 2 or Psalm 99

SECOND READING: 2 Peter 1:16–21

A reading from Second Peter:

¹⁶We did not follow cleverly devised myths when we made known to you
the power and coming of our Lord Jesus Christ,
but we had been eyewitnesses of his majesty.
¹⁷For Jesus received honor and glory from God, the Father,

when that voice was conveyed to him by the Majestic Glory, saying,
"This is my Son, my Beloved,
with whom I am well pleased."
[18]We ourselves heard this voice come from heaven,
while we were with Jesus on the holy mountain.

[19]So we have the prophetic message more fully confirmed.
You will do well to be attentive to this
as to a lamp shining in a dark place,
until the day dawns
and the morning star rises in your hearts.
[20]First of all you must understand this,
that no prophecy of scripture is a matter of one's own interpretation,
[21]because no prophecy ever came by human will,
but men and women moved by the Holy Spirit spoke from God.

GOSPEL: MATTHEW 17:1–9

The Holy Gospel according to Matthew, the 17th chapter.

[1]Six days later, Jesus took with him Peter and James and his brother John
and led them up a high mountain, by themselves.
[2]And Jesus was transfigured before them,
and his face shone like the sun, and his clothes became dazzling white.

[3]Suddenly there appeared to them Moses and Elijah, talking with him.
[4]Then Peter said to Jesus,
"Lord, it is good for us to be here;
if you wish, I will make three dwellings here,
one for you, one for Moses, and one for Elijah."

[5]While Peter was still speaking, suddenly a bright cloud overshadowed them,
and from the cloud a voice said,
"This is my Son, the Beloved, with whom I am well pleased;
listen to him!"
[6]When the disciples heard this,
they fell to the ground and were overcome by fear.
[7]But Jesus came and touched them, saying,
"Get up and do not be afraid."
[8]And when they looked up, they saw no one except Jesus alone.

[9]As they were coming down the mountain, Jesus ordered them,
"Tell no one about the vision
until after the Son-of-Man has been raised from the dead."

The Gospel of the Lord.

✜

SEASON OF LENT

✝

ASH WEDNESDAY

FEBRUARY 21, 1996   FEBRUARY 17, 1999   FEBRUARY 13, 2002

FIRST READING: JOEL 2:1–2, 12–17
Or Isaiah 58:1–12, following

A reading from Joel:

¹Blow the trumpet in Zion;
sound the alarm on my holy mountain!
Let all the inhabitants of the land tremble,
for the day of the LORD is coming, it is near—
²a day of darkness and gloom,
a day of clouds and thick darkness!
Like blackness spread upon the mountains
a great and powerful army comes;
their like has never been from of old,
nor will be again after them in ages to come.

¹²Yet even now, says the LORD,
return to me with all your heart,
with fasting, with weeping, and with mourning;
¹³rend your hearts and not your clothing.
Return to the LORD, your God,
for the LORD is gracious and merciful,
slow to anger, and abounding in steadfast love,
and relents from punishing.
¹⁴Who knows whether the LORD will not turn and relent,
and leave behind a blessing,
a grain offering and a drink offering for the LORD, your God?

¹⁵Blow the trumpet in Zion; sanctify a fast;
call a solemn assembly; ¹⁶gather the people.
Sanctify the congregation; assemble the aged;
gather the children, even infants at the breast.
Let the bridegroom leave his room, and the bride her canopy.

¹⁷Between the vestibule and the altar
let the priests, the ministers of the LORD, weep.
Let them say,

"Spare your people, O LORD,
and do not make your heritage a mockery,
a byword among the nations.
Why should it be said among the peoples,
'Where is their God?' "

OR: ISAIAH 58:1–12

A reading from Isaiah:

¹Shout out, do not hold back!
Lift up your voice like a trumpet!
Announce to my people their rebellion,
to the house of Jacob their sins.
²Yet day after day they seek me
and delight to know my ways,
as if they were a nation that practiced righteousness
and did not forsake the ordinance of their God;
they ask of me righteous judgments,
they delight to draw near to God.

³"Why do we fast, but you do not see?
Why humble ourselves, but you do not notice?"
Look, you serve your own interest on your fast day,
and oppress all your workers.
⁴Look, you fast only to quarrel and to fight
and to strike with a wicked fist.
Such fasting as you do today
will not make your voice heard on high.

⁵Is such the fast that I choose,
a day to humble oneself?
Is it to bow down the head like a bulrush,
and to lie in sackcloth and ashes?
Will you call this a fast,
a day acceptable to the LORD?

⁶Is not this the fast that I choose:
to loose the bonds of injustice,
to undo the thongs of the yoke,
to let the oppressed go free,
and to break every yoke?
⁷Is it not to share your bread with the hungry,
and bring the homeless poor into your house;
when you see the naked, to cover them,
and not to hide yourself from your own kin?

⁸Then your light shall break forth like the dawn,
and your healing shall spring up quickly;
your vindicator shall go before you,
the glory of the L<small>ORD</small> shall be your rear guard.
⁹Then you shall call, and the L<small>ORD</small> will answer;
you shall cry for help, and God will say,
Here I am.

If you remove the yoke from among you,
the pointing of the finger, the speaking of evil,
¹⁰if you offer your food to the hungry
and satisfy the needs of the afflicted,
then your light shall rise in the darkness
and your gloom be like the noonday.
¹¹The L<small>ORD</small> will guide you continually,
and satisfy your needs in parched places, and make your bones strong;
and you shall be like a watered garden,
like a spring of water, whose waters never fail.
¹²Your ancient ruins shall be rebuilt;
you shall raise up the foundations of many generations;
you shall be called the repairer of the breach,
the restorer of streets to live in.

PSALMODY: P<small>SALM</small> 51:1–17   *Psalm 51:1–18* LBW/BCP

SECOND READING: 2 CORINTHIANS 5:20b—6:10

A reading from Second Corinthians:

20bWe entreat you on behalf of Christ,
be reconciled to God.
21For our sake God made him to be sin who knew no sin,
so that in him we might become the righteousness of God.

6:1As we work together with God,
we urge you also not to accept the grace of God in vain.
2For God says,
"At an acceptable time I have listened to you,
and on a day of salvation I have helped you."
See, now is the acceptable time;
see, now is the day of salvation!

3We are putting no obstacle in anyone's way,
so that no fault may be found with our ministry,
4but as servants of God we have commended ourselves in every way:
through great endurance,
in afflictions, hardships, calamities,
5beatings, imprisonments, riots,
labors, sleepless nights, hunger;
6by purity, knowledge, patience,
kindness, holiness of spirit, genuine love,
7truthful speech, and the power of God;
with the weapons of righteousness for the right hand and for the left;
8in honor and dishonor,
in ill repute and good repute.
We are treated as impostors, and yet are true;
9as unknown, and yet are well known;
as dying, and see—we are alive;
as punished, and yet not killed;
10as sorrowful, yet always rejoicing;
as poor, yet making many rich;
as having nothing, and yet possessing everything.

GOSPEL: MATTHEW 6:1–6, 16–21

The Holy Gospel according to Matthew, the sixth chapter.

Jesus said:
¹"Beware of practicing your piety before others
in order to be seen by them;
for then you have no reward from your Father in heaven.
²So whenever you give alms, do not sound a trumpet before you,
as the hypocrites do in the synagogues and in the streets,
so that they may be praised by others.
Truly I tell you,
they have received their reward.
³But when you give alms,
do not let your left hand know what your right hand is doing,
⁴so that your alms may be done in secret;
and your Father who sees in secret will reward you.

⁵"And whenever you pray, do not be like the hypocrites;
for they love to stand and pray in the synagogues and at the street corners,
so that they may be seen by others.
Truly I tell you,
they have received their reward.
⁶But whenever you pray,
go into your room and shut the door
and pray to your Father who is in secret;
and your Father who sees in secret will reward you.

¹⁶"And whenever you fast, do not look dismal, like the hypocrites,
for they disfigure their faces so as to show others that they are fasting.
Truly I tell you,
they have received their reward.
¹⁷But when you fast,
put oil on your head and wash your face,
¹⁸so that your fasting may be seen not by others
but by your Father who is in secret;
and your Father who sees in secret will reward you.

¹⁹"Do not store up for yourselves treasures on earth,
where moth and rust consume
and where thieves break in and steal;
²⁰but store up for yourselves treasures in heaven,
where neither moth nor rust consumes
and where thieves do not break in and steal.
²¹For where your treasure is,
there your heart will be also."

The Gospel of the Lord.

FIRST SUNDAY IN LENT

FEBRUARY 25, 1996   FEBRUARY 21, 1999   FEBRUARY 17, 2002

FIRST READING: GENESIS 2:15–17; 3:1–7

A reading from Genesis:

¹⁵The LORD God took the man
and put him in the garden of Eden to till it and keep it.
¹⁶And the LORD God commanded the man,
"You may freely eat of every tree of the garden;
¹⁷but of the tree of the knowledge of good and evil you shall not eat,
for in the day that you eat of it you shall die."

³:¹Now the serpent was more crafty
than any other wild animal that the LORD God had made.
The serpent said to the woman,
"Did God say, 'You shall not eat from any tree in the garden'?"
²The woman said to the serpent,
"We may eat of the fruit of the trees in the garden;
³but God said,
" 'You shall not eat of the fruit of the tree
that is in the middle of the garden,
nor shall you touch it, or you shall die.' "
⁴But the serpent said to the woman,
"You will not die;
⁵for God knows that when you eat of it your eyes will be opened,
and you will be like God, knowing good and evil."

⁶So when the woman saw that the tree was good for food,
and that it was a delight to the eyes,
and that the tree was to be desired to make one wise,
she took of its fruit and ate;
and she also gave some to her husband, who was with her,
and he ate.

⁷Then the eyes of both were opened, and they knew that they were naked;
and they sewed fig leaves together and made loincloths for themselves.

PSALMODY: Psalm 32

SECOND READING: Romans 5:12–19

A reading from Romans:

¹²Just as sin came into the world through one human being,
and death came through sin,
and so death spread to all because all have sinned—
¹³sin was indeed in the world before the law,
but sin is not reckoned when there is no law.
¹⁴Yet death exercised dominion from Adam to Moses,
even over those whose sins were not like the transgression of Adam,
who is a type of the one who was to come.

¹⁵But the free gift is not like the trespass.
For if the many died through the trespass of one human,
much more surely have the grace of God
and the free gift in the grace of the one human, Jesus Christ,
abounded for the many.
¹⁶And the free gift is not like the effect of the sin of one human being.
For the judgment following one trespass brought condemnation,
but the free gift following many trespasses brings justification.
¹⁷If, because of the trespass of one,
death exercised dominion through that one,
much more surely will those who receive the abundance of grace
and the free gift of righteousness
exercise dominion in life through the one, Jesus Christ.

¹⁸Therefore just as the trespass of one person led to condemnation for all,
so the act of righteousness of one person leads to justification and life for all.
¹⁹For just as by the disobedience of one the many were made sinners,
so by the obedience of one the many will be made righteous.

GOSPEL: MATTHEW 4:1–11

The Holy Gospel according to Matthew, the fourth chapter.

[1]Jesus was led up by the Spirit into the wilderness
to be tempted by the devil.
[2]He fasted forty days and forty nights,
and afterwards was famished.

[3]The tempter came and said to him,
"If you are the Son of God,
command these stones to become loaves of bread."
[4]But Jesus answered,
"It is written,
'One does not live by bread alone,
but by every word that comes from the mouth of God.'"

[5]Then the devil took Jesus to the holy city
and placed him on the pinnacle of the temple, [6]saying to him,
"If you are the Son of God, throw yourself down;
for it is written,
'God will give you into the angels' charge,'
and 'On their hands they will bear you up,
so that you will not dash your foot against a stone.'"
[7]Jesus said to the devil,
"Again it is written,
'Do not put the Lord your God to the test.'"

[8]Again, the devil took Jesus to a very high mountain
and showed him all the realms of the world and their splendor;
[9]and said to him,
"All these I will give you,
if you will fall down and worship me."
[10]Jesus said to the devil,
"Away with you, Satan! for it is written,
'Worship the Lord your God;
serve God alone.'"

[11]Then the devil left him,
and suddenly angels came and waited on him.

The Gospel of the Lord.

Second Sunday in Lent

MARCH 3, 1996   *FEBRUARY 28, 1999*   *FEBRUARY 24, 2002*

FIRST READING: Genesis 12:1–4a

A reading from Genesis:

¹The LORD said to Abram,
"Go from your country and your kindred and your father's house
to the land that I will show you.
²I will make of you a great nation,
and I will bless you, and make your name great,
so that you will be a blessing.
³I will bless those who bless you,
and the one who curses you I will curse;
and in you all the families of the earth shall be blessed."

⁴ᵃSo Abram went, as the LORD had told him; and Lot went with him.

PSALMODY: Psalm 121

SECOND READING: Romans 4:1–5, 13–17

A reading from Romans:

¹What are we to say was gained by Abraham,
our ancestor according to the flesh?
²For if Abraham was justified by works,
he has something to boast about, but not before God.
³For what does the scripture say?
"Abraham believed God,
and it was reckoned to him as righteousness."
⁴Now to one who works,
wages are not reckoned as a gift but as something due.
⁵But to one who without works trusts God who justifies the ungodly,
such faith is reckoned as righteousness.

¹³For the promise that he would inherit the world
did not come to Abraham or to his descendants through the law

but through the righteousness of faith.
¹⁴If it is the adherents of the law who are to be the heirs,
faith is null and the promise is void.
¹⁵For the law brings wrath;
but where there is no law,
neither is there violation.

¹⁶For this reason it depends on faith,
in order that the promise may rest on grace
and be guaranteed to all Abraham's descendants,
not only to the adherents of the law
but also to those who share the faith of Abraham
(for he is the father of all of us, ¹⁷as it is written,
"I have made you the father of many nations")—
in the presence of the God in whom Abraham believed,
who gives life to the dead
and calls into existence the things that do not exist.

GOSPEL: JOHN 3:1–17

The Holy Gospel according to John, the third chapter.

¹Now there was a Pharisee named Nicodemus, a leader of the Jewish people.
²He came to Jesus by night and said to him,
"Rabbi, we know that you are a teacher who has come from God;
for no one can do these signs that you do apart from the presence of God."
³Jesus answered him,
"Very truly, I tell you,
no one can see the dominion of God without being born from above."

⁴Nicodemus said to Jesus,
"How can anyone be born after having grown old?
Can one enter a second time into the mother's womb and be born?"
⁵Jesus answered,
"Very truly, I tell you,
no one can enter the dominion of God without being born of water and Spirit.
⁶What is born of the flesh is flesh,
and what is born of the Spirit is spirit.
⁷Do not be astonished that I said to you,
'You must be born from above.'
⁸The wind blows where it chooses, and you hear the sound of it,
but you do not know where it comes from or where it goes.
So it is with everyone who is born of the Spirit."

⁹Nicodemus said to Jesus,
"How can these things be?"

¹⁰Jesus answered him,
"Are you a teacher of Israel,
and yet you do not understand these things?
¹¹Very truly, I tell you,
we speak of what we know and testify to what we have seen;
yet you do not receive our testimony.
¹²If I have told you about earthly things and you do not believe,
how can you believe if I tell you about heavenly things?

¹³"No one has ascended into heaven
except the one who descended from heaven, the Son-of-Man.
¹⁴And just as Moses lifted up the serpent in the wilderness,
so must the Son-of-Man be lifted up,
¹⁵that whoever believes in him may have eternal life.

¹⁶"For God loved the world in this way,
that God gave the Son,
the only begotten one,
so that everyone who believes in him may not perish
but may have eternal life.
¹⁷Indeed, God did not send the Son into the world to condemn the world,
but in order that the world might be saved through him."

The Gospel of the Lord.

✝

Third Sunday in Lent

MARCH 10, 1996   MARCH 7, 1999   MARCH 3, 2002

FIRST READING: Exodus 17:1–7

A reading from Exodus:

¹From the wilderness of Sin the whole congregation of the Israelites
journeyed by stages, as the Lord commanded.
They camped at Rephidim, but there was no water for the people to drink.
²The people quarreled with Moses, and said,
"Give us water to drink."
Moses said to them,
"Why do you quarrel with me?
Why do you test the Lord?"
³But the people thirsted there for water;
and the people complained against Moses and said,
"Why did you bring us out of Egypt,
to kill us and our children and livestock with thirst?"

⁴So Moses cried out to the Lord,
"What shall I do with this people?
They are almost ready to stone me."
⁵The Lord said to Moses,
"Go on ahead of the people,
and take some of the elders of Israel with you;
take in your hand the staff with which you struck the Nile, and go.
⁶I will be standing there in front of you on the rock at Horeb.
Strike the rock, and water will come out of it, so that the people may drink."

Moses did so, in the sight of the elders of Israel.
⁷He called the place Massah and Meribah,
because the Israelites quarreled and tested the Lord, saying,
"Is the Lord among us or not?"

PSALMODY: Psalm 95

SECOND READING: ROMANS 5:1–11

A reading from Romans:

[1]Since we are justified by faith,
we have peace with God through our Lord Jesus Christ,
[2]through whom we have obtained access to this grace in which we stand;
and we boast in our hope of sharing the glory of God.
[3]And not only that,
but we also boast in our sufferings,
knowing that suffering produces endurance,
[4]and endurance produces character,
and character produces hope,
[5]and hope does not disappoint us,
because God's love has been poured into our hearts
through the Holy Spirit that has been given to us.

[6]For while we were still weak,
at the right time Christ died for the ungodly.
[7]Indeed, rarely will anyone die for a righteous person—
though perhaps for a good person someone might actually dare to die.
[8]But it is proof of God's own love for us
in that while we still were sinners Christ died for us.

[9]Much more surely then, now that we have been justified by his blood,
will we be saved through him from the wrath of God.
[10]For if while we were enemies,
we were reconciled to God through the death of the Son of God,
much more surely, having been reconciled,
will we be saved by the life of the Son of God.
[11]But more than that, we even boast in God through our Lord Jesus Christ,
through whom we have now received reconciliation.

GOSPEL: JOHN 4:5–42

The Holy Gospel according to John, the fourth chapter.

[5]Jesus came to a Samaritan city called Sychar,
near the plot of ground that Jacob had given to his son Joseph.
[6]Jacob's well was there,
and Jesus, tired out by his journey, was sitting by the well.
It was about noon.

[7]A Samaritan woman came to draw water,
and Jesus said to her,
"Give me a drink."
[8](His disciples had gone to the city to buy food.)

[9]The Samaritan woman said to him,
"How is it that you, a Jewish man, ask a drink of me, a woman of Samaria?"
(Jewish people do not share things in common with Samaritans.)
[10]Jesus answered her,
"If you knew the gift of God,
and who it is that is saying to you, 'Give me a drink,'
you would have asked him, and he would have given you living water."
[11]The woman said to him,
"Sir, you have no bucket, and the well is deep.
Where do you get that living water?
[12]Are you greater than our ancestor Jacob, who gave us the well,
and with his children and his flocks drank from it?"

[13]Jesus said to her,
"Everyone who drinks of this water will be thirsty again,
[14]but those who drink of the water that I will give them will never be thirsty.
The water that I will give will become in them a spring of water
gushing up to eternal life."
[15]The woman said to Jesus,
"Sir, give me this water, so that I may never be thirsty
or have to keep coming here to draw water."

[16]Jesus said to her,
"Go, call your husband, and come back."
[17]The woman answered him,
"I have no husband."
Jesus said to her,
"You are right in saying, 'I have no husband';
[18]for you have had five husbands,
and the one you have now is not your husband.
What you have said is true!"
[19]The woman said to Jesus,
"Sir, I see that you are a prophet.
[20]Our ancestors worshiped on this mountain,
but you say that the place where people must worship is in Jerusalem."

[21]Jesus said to her,
"Woman, believe me, the hour is coming
when you will worship the Father neither on this mountain nor in Jerusalem.
[22]You worship what you do not know; we worship what we know,
for salvation is from the Jewish people.
[23]But the hour is coming, and is now here,
when the true worshipers will worship the Father in spirit and truth,
for such worshipers the Father seeks.
[24]God is spirit,
and those who worship God must worship in spirit and truth."
[25]The woman said to him,
"I know that Messiah is coming" (who is called Christ).

"When he comes, he will proclaim all things to us."
²⁶Jesus said to her,
"Here I am, the one who is speaking to you."

²⁷Just then his disciples came.
They were astonished that he was speaking with a woman,
but no one said, "What do you want?"
or, "Why are you speaking with her?"

²⁸Then the woman left her water jar and went back to the city.
She said to the people,
²⁹"Come and see someone who told me everything I have ever done!
Can this be the Messiah?"
³⁰They left the city and were on their way to him.

³¹Meanwhile the disciples were urging Jesus,
"Rabbi, eat something."
³²But he said to them,
"I have food to eat that you do not know about."
³³So the disciples said to one another,
"Surely no one has brought him something to eat?"
³⁴Jesus said to them,
"My food is to do the will and accomplish the work of the one who sent me.
³⁵Do you not say, 'Four months more, then comes the harvest'?
But I tell you, look around you,
and see how the fields are ripe for harvesting.
³⁶The reaper is already receiving wages
and is gathering fruit for eternal life,
so that sower and reaper may rejoice together.
³⁷For here the saying holds true,
'One sows and another reaps.'
³⁸I sent you to reap that for which you did not labor.
Others have labored, and you have entered into their labor."

³⁹Many Samaritans from that city believed in Jesus
because of the woman's testimony,
"He told me everything I have ever done."
⁴⁰So when the Samaritans came to him, they asked him to stay with them;
and Jesus stayed there two days.
⁴¹And many more believed because of his word.
⁴²They said to the woman,
"It is no longer because of what you said that we believe,
for we have heard for ourselves,
and we know that this is truly the Savior of the world."

The Gospel of the Lord.

✝

Fourth Sunday in Lent

MARCH 17, 1996   MARCH 14, 1999   MARCH 10, 2002

FIRST READING: 1 Samuel 16:1–13

A reading from First Samuel:

[1]The LORD said to Samuel,
"How long will you grieve over Saul?
I have rejected him from being king over Israel.
Fill your horn with oil and set out;
I will send you to Jesse the Bethlehemite,
for I have provided for myself a king among his sons."
[2]Samuel said, "How can I go?
If Saul hears of it, he will kill me."
And the LORD said,
"Take a heifer with you, and say,
'I have come to sacrifice to the LORD.'
[3]Invite Jesse to the sacrifice, and I will show you what you shall do;
and you shall anoint for me the one whom I name to you."

[4]Samuel did what the LORD commanded, and came to Bethlehem.
The elders of the city came to meet him trembling, and said,
"Do you come peaceably?"
[5]He said,
"Peaceably; I have come to sacrifice to the LORD;
sanctify yourselves and come with me to the sacrifice."
And he sanctified Jesse and his sons and invited them to the sacrifice.

[6]When they came, Samuel looked on Eliab and thought,
"Surely the LORD's anointed is now before the LORD."
[7]But the LORD said to Samuel,
"Do not look on his appearance or on the height of his stature,
because I have rejected him;
for the LORD does not see as mortals see;
they look on the outward appearance,
but the LORD looks on the heart."
[8]Then Jesse called Abinadab, and made him pass before Samuel.
He said, "Neither has the LORD chosen this one."
[9]Then Jesse made Shammah pass by.
And he said,
"Neither has the LORD chosen this one."

^{10}Jesse made seven of his sons pass before Samuel,
and Samuel said to Jesse,
"The LORD has not chosen any of these."

^{11}Samuel said to Jesse,
"Are all your sons here?"
And he said,
"There remains yet the youngest, but he is keeping the sheep."
And Samuel said to Jesse,
"Send and bring him; for we will not sit down until he comes here."
^{12}Jesse sent and brought him in.
Now he was ruddy, and had beautiful eyes, and was handsome.
The LORD said,
"Rise and anoint him; for this is the one."
^{13}Then Samuel took the horn of oil,
and anointed him in the presence of his brothers;
and the spirit of the LORD came mightily upon David from that day forward.
Samuel then set out and went to Ramah.

PSALMODY: PSALM 23

SECOND READING: EPHESIANS 5:8–14

A reading from Ephesians:

^{8}Once you were darkness, but now in the Lord you are light.
Live as children of light—
^{9}for the fruit of the light is found in all that is good and right and true.
^{10}Try to find out what is pleasing to the Lord.
^{11}Take no part in the unfruitful works of darkness, but instead expose them.
^{12}For it is shameful even to mention what such people do secretly;
^{13}but everything exposed by the light becomes visible,
^{14}for everything that becomes visible is light.

Therefore it says,
"Sleeper, awake!
Rise from the dead, and Christ will shine on you."

The Holy Gospel according to John, the ninth chapter.

[1]As Jesus walked along, he saw a man blind from birth.
[2]His disciples asked him,
"Rabbi, who sinned, this man or his parents, that he was born blind?"
[3]Jesus answered,
"Neither this man nor his parents sinned;
he was born blind so that God's works might be revealed in him.
[4]We must work the works of the one who sent me while it is day;
night is coming when no one can work.
[5]As long as I am in the world, I am the light of the world."

[6]When Jesus had said this, he spat on the ground and made mud with the saliva
and spread the mud on the man's eyes, [7]saying to him,
"Go, wash in the pool of Siloam" (which means Sent).
Then he went and washed and came back able to see.

[8]The neighbors and those who had seen him before as a beggar began to ask,
"Is this not the man who used to sit and beg?"
[9]Some were saying, "It is he."
Others were saying, "No, but it is someone like him."
He kept saying, "I am the man."
[10]But they kept asking him, "Then how were your eyes opened?"
[11]He answered,
"The man called Jesus made mud, spread it on my eyes,
and said to me, 'Go to Siloam and wash.'
Then I went and washed and received my sight."
[12]They said to him, "Where is he?"
He said, "I do not know."

[13]They brought to the Pharisees the man who had formerly been blind.
[14]Now it was a sabbath day when Jesus made the mud and opened his eyes.
[15]Then the Pharisees also began to ask him how he had received his sight.
He said to them,
"He put mud on my eyes. Then I washed, and now I see."
[16]Some of the Pharisees said,
"This man is not from God, for he does not observe the sabbath."
But others said,
"How can a man who is a sinner perform such signs?"
And they were divided.
[17]So they said again to the blind man,
"What do you say about him? It was your eyes he opened."
He said, "He is a prophet."

[18]The Judeans did not believe that he had been blind and had received his sight
until they called the parents of the man who had received his sight

¹⁹and asked them,
"Is this your son, who you say was born blind?
How then does he now see?"
²⁰His parents answered,
"We know that this is our son, and that he was born blind;
²¹but we do not know how it is that now he sees,
nor do we know who opened his eyes.
Ask him; he is of age.
He will speak for himself."
²²His parents said this because they were afraid of the Judeans,
who had already agreed
that anyone who confessed Jesus to be the Messiah
would be put out of the synagogue.
²³Therefore his parents said, "He is of age; ask him."

²⁴So for the second time they called the man who had been blind,
and they said to him,
"Give glory to God! We know that this man is a sinner."
²⁵He answered,
"I do not know whether he is a sinner.
One thing I do know, that though I was blind, now I see."
²⁶They said to him,
"What did he do to you? How did he open your eyes?"
²⁷He answered them,
"I have told you already, and you would not listen.
Why do you want to hear it again?
Do you also want to become his disciples?"
²⁸Then they reviled him, saying,
"You are his disciple, but we are disciples of Moses.
²⁹We know that God has spoken to Moses,
but as for this person, we do not know where he comes from."
³⁰The man answered,
"Here is an astonishing thing!
You do not know where he comes from, and yet he opened my eyes.
³¹We know that God does not listen to sinners,
but does listen to anyone who is devout and obeys God's will.
³²Never since the world began
has it been heard that anyone opened the eyes of someone born blind.
³³If this person were not from God, he could do nothing."
³⁴They answered him,
"You were born entirely in sins,
and are you trying to teach us?"
And they drove him out.

³⁵Jesus heard that they had driven him out,
and when he found him, he said,
"Do you believe in the Son-of-Man?"
³⁶He answered, "And who is he, sir?

Tell me, so that I may believe in him."
[37]Jesus said to him, "You have seen him,
and he is the one speaking with you."
[38]He said, "Lord, I believe."
And he worshiped Jesus.
[39]Jesus said,
"I came into this world for judgment
so that those who do not see may see,
and those who do see may become blind."
[40]Some of the Pharisees near Jesus heard this and said to him,
"Surely we are not blind, are we?"
[41]Jesus said to them,
"If you were blind, you would not have sin.
But now that you say, 'We see,' your sin remains."

The Gospel of the Lord.

✝

FIFTH SUNDAY IN LENT

MARCH 24, 1996   MARCH 21, 1999   MARCH 17, 2002

FIRST READING: Ezekiel 37:1–14

A reading from Ezekiel:

¹The hand of the LORD came upon me,
and brought me out by the spirit of the LORD
and set me down in the middle of a valley;
it was full of bones.
²The LORD led me all around them;
there were very many lying in the valley, and they were very dry.
³The LORD said to me,
"Mortal, can these bones live?"
I answered, "O Lord GOD, you know."

⁴Then the LORD said to me,
"Prophesy to these bones, and say to them:
O dry bones, hear the word of the LORD.
⁵Thus says the Lord GOD to these bones:
I will cause breath to enter you, and you shall live.
⁶I will lay sinews on you,
and will cause flesh to come upon you, and cover you with skin,
and put breath in you, and you shall live;
and you shall know that I am the LORD."

⁷So I prophesied as I had been commanded;
and as I prophesied, suddenly there was a noise, a rattling,
and the bones came together, bone to its bone.
⁸I looked, and there were sinews on them,
and flesh had come upon them, and skin had covered them;
but there was no breath in them.
⁹Then the LORD said to me,
"Prophesy to the breath, prophesy, mortal, and say to the breath:
Thus says the Lord GOD:
Come from the four winds, O breath,
and breathe upon these slain, that they may live."
¹⁰I prophesied as the LORD commanded me,
and the breath came into them,
and they lived, and stood on their feet, a vast multitude.

[11]Then the Lord said to me,
"Mortal, these bones are the whole house of Israel.
They say, 'Our bones are dried up, and our hope is lost;
we are cut off completely.'
[12]Therefore prophesy, and say to them,
Thus says the Lord God:
I am going to open your graves,
and bring you up from your graves, O my people;
and I will bring you back to the land of Israel.
[13]And you shall know that I am the Lord, when I open your graves,
and bring you up from your graves, O my people.
[14]I will put my spirit within you, and you shall live,
and I will place you on your own soil;
then you shall know that I, the Lord, have spoken and will act,"
says the Lord.

PSALMODY: Psalm 130

SECOND READING: Romans 8:6–11

A reading from Romans:

[6]To set the mind on the flesh is death,
but to set the mind on the Spirit is life and peace.
[7]For this reason the mind that is set on the flesh is hostile to God;
it does not submit to God's law—indeed it cannot,
[8]and those who are in the flesh cannot please God.

[9]But you are not in the flesh;
you are in the Spirit, since the Spirit of God dwells in you.
Anyone who does not have the Spirit of Christ does not belong to Christ.
[10]But if Christ is in you, though the body is dead because of sin,
the Spirit is life because of righteousness.
[11]If the Spirit of the one who raised Jesus from the dead dwells in you,
the one who raised Christ from the dead
will give life to your mortal bodies also
through this Spirit dwelling in you.

The Holy Gospel according to John, the eleventh chapter.

¹Now a certain man was ill, Lazarus of Bethany,
the village of Mary and her sister Martha.
²Mary was the one who anointed the Lord with perfume
and wiped his feet with her hair;
her brother Lazarus was ill.

³So the sisters sent a message to Jesus,
"Lord, he whom you love is ill."
⁴But when Jesus heard it, he said,
"This illness does not lead to death;
rather it is for God's glory,
so that the Son of God may be glorified through it."
⁵Accordingly, though Jesus loved Martha and her sister and Lazarus,
⁶after having heard that Lazarus was ill,
he stayed two days longer in the place where he was.

⁷Then after this he said to the disciples,
"Let us go to Judea again."
⁸The disciples said to him,
"Rabbi, the Judeans were just now trying to stone you,
and are you going there again?"
⁹Jesus answered, "Are there not twelve hours of daylight?
Those who walk during the day do not stumble,
because they see the light of this world.
¹⁰But those who walk at night stumble,
because the light is not in them."
¹¹After saying this, he told them,
"Our friend Lazarus has fallen asleep,
but I am going there to awaken him."
¹²The disciples said to him,
"Lord, if he has fallen asleep, he will be all right."
¹³Jesus, however, had been speaking about his death,
but they thought that he was referring merely to sleep.
¹⁴Then Jesus told them plainly, "Lazarus is dead.
¹⁵For your sake I am glad I was not there, so that you may believe.
But let us go to him."
¹⁶Thomas, who was called the Twin, said to the other disciples,
"Let us also go, that we may die with him."

¹⁷When Jesus arrived,
he found that Lazarus had already been in the tomb four days.

¹⁸Now Bethany was near Jerusalem, some two miles away,
¹⁹and many of the Judeans had come to Martha and Mary

to console them about their brother.

²⁰When Martha heard that Jesus was coming,
she went and met him, while Mary stayed at home.
²¹Martha said to Jesus,
"Lord, if you had been here, my brother would not have died.
²²But even now I know that whatever you ask from God, God will give you."
²³Jesus said to her, "Your brother will rise again."
²⁴Martha said to him,
"I know that he will rise again in the resurrection on the last day."
²⁵Jesus said to her,
"I am the resurrection and the life.
Those who believe in me, even though they die, will live,
²⁶and everyone who lives and believes in me will never die.
Do you believe this?"
²⁷She said to him,
"Yes, Lord, I believe that you are the Messiah,
the Son of God, the one coming into the world."

²⁸When she had said this,
she went back and called her sister Mary, and told her privately,
"The Teacher is here and is calling for you."
²⁹And when Mary heard it, she got up quickly and went to him.

³⁰Now Jesus had not yet come to the village,
but was still at the place where Martha had met him.
³¹The Judeans who were with her in the house, consoling her,
saw Mary get up quickly and go out.
They followed her
because they thought that she was going to the tomb to weep there.
³²When Mary came where Jesus was and saw him,
she knelt at his feet and said to him,
"Lord, if you had been here, my brother would not have died."
³³When Jesus saw her weeping,
and the Judeans who came with her also weeping,
he was greatly disturbed in spirit and deeply moved.
³⁴He said, "Where have you laid him?"
They said to him, "Lord, come and see."
³⁵Jesus began to weep.
³⁶So the Judeans said, "See how he loved him!"
³⁷But some of them said,
"Could not the one who opened the eyes of the blind man
have kept this man from dying?"

³⁸Then Jesus, again greatly disturbed, came to the tomb.
It was a cave, and a stone was lying against it.
³⁹Jesus said, "Take away the stone."
Martha, the sister of the dead man, said to him,

"Lord, already there is a stench because he has been dead four days."
⁴⁰Jesus said to her,
"Did I not tell you that if you believed, you would see the glory of God?"

⁴¹So they took away the stone.
And Jesus looked upward and said,
"Father, I thank you for having heard me.
⁴²I knew that you always hear me,
but I have said this for the sake of the crowd standing here,
so that they may believe that you sent me."
⁴³When Jesus had said this,
he cried with a loud voice, "Lazarus, come out!"
⁴⁴The dead man came out,
his hands and feet bound with strips of cloth,
and his face wrapped in a cloth.
Jesus said to them, "Unbind him, and let him go."

⁴⁵Many of the Judeans therefore,
who had come with Mary and had seen what Jesus did,
believed in him.

The Gospel of the Lord.

✝

HOLY WEEK

✝

SUNDAY OF THE PASSION/PALM SUNDAY
Liturgy of the Palms

MARCH 31, 1996   MARCH 28, 1999   MARCH 24, 2002

GOSPEL: MATTHEW 21:1–11

The Holy Gospel according to Matthew, the 21st chapter.

[1]When they had come near Jerusalem
and had reached Bethphage, at the Mount of Olives,
Jesus sent two disciples, [2]saying to them,
"Go into the village ahead of you,
and immediately you will find a donkey tied, and a colt with her;
untie them and bring them to me.
[3]If anyone says anything to you, just say this,
'The Lord needs them.'
And they will be sent immediately."
[4]This took place to fulfill what had been spoken through the prophet, saying,
[5]"Tell the daughter of Zion,
Look, your king is coming to you,
humble, and mounted on a donkey,
and on a colt, the foal of a donkey."

[6]The disciples went and did as Jesus had directed them;
[7]they brought the donkey and the colt,
and put their cloaks on them, and he sat on them.
[8]A very large crowd spread their cloaks on the road,
and others cut branches from the trees and spread them on the road.
[9]The crowds that went ahead of him and that followed were shouting,
"Hosanna to the Son of David!
Blessed is the one who comes in the name of the Lord!
Hosanna in the highest heaven!"
[10]When he entered Jerusalem, the whole city was in turmoil, asking,
"Who is this?"
[11]The crowds were saying,
"This is the prophet Jesus from Nazareth in Galilee."

The Gospel of the Lord.

PSALMODY: PSALM 118:1–2, 19–29

✞

Sunday of the Passion/Palm Sunday
Liturgy of the Passion

MARCH 31, 1996   MARCH 28, 1999   MARCH 24, 2002

FIRST READING: Isaiah 50:4–9a

A reading from Isaiah:

⁴The Lord GOD has given me the tongue of a teacher,
that I may know how to sustain the weary with a word.
Morning by morning the Lord GOD wakens—
wakens my ear to listen as those who are taught.
⁵The Lord GOD has opened my ear,
and I was not rebellious,
I did not turn backward.
⁶I gave my back to those who struck me,
and my cheeks to those who pulled out the beard;
I did not hide my face from insult and spitting.

⁷The Lord GOD helps me;
therefore I have not been disgraced;
therefore I have set my face like flint,
and I know that I shall not be put to shame;
⁸the one who vindicates me is near.
Who will contend with me?
Let us stand up together.
Who are my adversaries?
Let them confront me.
⁹ᵃIt is the Lord GOD who helps me;
who will declare me guilty?

PSALMODY: Psalm 31:9–16

SECOND READING: PHILIPPIANS 2:5–11

A reading from Philippians:

⁵Let the same mind be in you that was in Christ Jesus,
⁶who, although being in the form of God,
did not regard equality with God as something to be exploited,
⁷but relinquished it all, taking the form of a slave,
being born in human likeness.
And being found in human form, ⁸he humbled himself
and became obedient to the point of death—
even death on a cross.

⁹Therefore God also highly exalted him
and gave him the name that is above every name,
¹⁰so that at the name of Jesus every knee should bend,
in heaven and on earth and under the earth,
¹¹and every tongue should confess
that Jesus Christ is Lord,
to the glory of God, the Father.

GOSPEL: MATTHEW 26:14—27:66
Or Matthew 27:11-54, following on p. 104

The Passion of our Lord Jesus Christ according to Matthew.

¹⁴One of the twelve, who was called Judas Iscariot,
went to the chief priests ¹⁵and said,
"What will you give me if I betray him to you?"
They paid him thirty pieces of silver.
¹⁶And from that moment Judas began to look for an opportunity to betray him.

¹⁷On the first day of Unleavened Bread the disciples came to Jesus, saying,
"Where do you want us to make the preparations for you to eat the Passover?"
¹⁸Jesus said,
"Go into the city to a certain man, and say to him,
'The Teacher says, My time is near;
I will keep the Passover at your house with my disciples.' "
¹⁹So the disciples did as Jesus had directed them,
and they prepared the Passover meal.

²⁰When it was evening, Jesus took his place with the twelve;
²¹and while they were eating, he said,
"Truly I tell you, one of you will betray me."
²²And they became greatly distressed
and began to say to him one after another,

"Surely not I, Lord?"
23Jesus answered,
"The one who has dipped his hand into the bowl with me will betray me.
24The Son-of-Man goes as it is written of him,
but woe to that one by whom the Son-of-Man is betrayed!
It would have been better for that one not to have been born."
25Judas, who betrayed him, said,
"Surely not I, Rabbi?"
He replied, "You have said so."

26While they were eating, Jesus took a loaf of bread,
and after blessing it he broke it,
gave it to the disciples, and said,
"Take, eat; this is my body."
27Then he took a cup,
and after giving thanks he gave it to them, saying,
"Drink from it, all of you;
28for this is my blood of the covenant,
which is poured out for many for the forgiveness of sins.
29I tell you, I will never again drink of this fruit of the vine
until that day when I drink it new with you in my Father's dominion."

30When they had sung the hymn, they went out to the Mount of Olives.

31Then Jesus said to them,
"You will all become deserters because of me this night; for it is written,
'I will strike the shepherd,
and the sheep of the flock will be scattered.'
32But after I am raised up, I will go ahead of you to Galilee."
33Peter said to him,
"Though all become deserters because of you, I will never desert you."
34Jesus said to him,
"Truly I tell you, this very night, before the cock crows,
you will deny me three times."
35Peter said to him,
"Even though I must die with you, I will not deny you."
And so said all the disciples.

36Then Jesus went with them to a place called Gethsemane;
and he said to his disciples,
"Sit here while I go over there and pray."
37He took with him Peter and the two sons of Zebedee,
and began to be grieved and agitated.
38Then he said to them,
"I am deeply grieved, even to death;
remain here, and stay awake with me."
39And going a little farther, he threw himself on the ground and prayed,
"My Father, if it is possible, let this cup pass from me;

yet not what I want but what you want."

⁴⁰Then he came to the disciples and found them sleeping;
and he said to Peter,
"So, could you not stay awake with me one hour?
⁴¹Stay awake and pray that you may not come into the time of trial;
the spirit indeed is willing, but the flesh is weak."
⁴²Again Jesus went away for the second time and prayed,
"My Father, if this cannot pass unless I drink it, your will be done."
⁴³Again Jesus came and found them sleeping, for their eyes were heavy.
⁴⁴So leaving them again, he went away and prayed for the third time,
saying the same words.
⁴⁵Then he came to the disciples and said to them,
"Are you still sleeping and taking your rest?
See, the hour is at hand,
and the Son-of-Man is betrayed into the hands of sinners.
⁴⁶Get up, let us be going. See, my betrayer is at hand."

⁴⁷While he was still speaking, Judas, one of the twelve, arrived;
with him was a large crowd with swords and clubs,
from the chief priests and the elders of the people.
⁴⁸Now the betrayer had given them a sign, saying,
"The one I will kiss is the man; arrest him."
⁴⁹At once he came up to Jesus and said,
"Greetings, Rabbi!" and kissed him.
⁵⁰Jesus said to him, "Friend, do what you are here to do."
Then they came and laid hands on Jesus and arrested him.
⁵¹Suddenly, one of those with Jesus put his hand on his sword,
drew it, and struck the slave of the high priest, cutting off his ear.
⁵²Then Jesus said to him,
"Put your sword back into its place;
for all who take the sword will perish by the sword.
⁵³Do you think that I cannot appeal to my Father,
who will at once send me more than twelve legions of angels?
⁵⁴But how then would the scriptures be fulfilled,
which say it must happen in this way?"
⁵⁵At that hour Jesus said to the crowds,
"Have you come out with swords and clubs to arrest me
as though I were a bandit?
Day after day I sat in the temple teaching, and you did not arrest me.
⁵⁶But all this has taken place,
so that the scriptures of the prophets may be fulfilled."
Then all the disciples deserted him and fled.

⁵⁷Those who had arrested Jesus took him to Caiaphas the high priest,
in whose house the scribes and the elders had gathered.
⁵⁸But Peter was following him at a distance,
as far as the courtyard of the high priest;
and going inside, he sat with the guards in order to see how this would end.

59Now the chief priests and the whole council
were looking for false testimony against Jesus
so that they might put him to death,
60but they found none, though many false witnesses came forward.
At last two came forward 61and said,
"This fellow said,
'I am able to destroy the temple of God and to build it in three days.' "
62The high priest stood up and said,
"Have you no answer? What is it that they testify against you?"
63But Jesus was silent.
Then the high priest said to him,
"I put you under oath before the living God,
tell us if you are the Messiah, the Son of God."
64Jesus said to him, "You have said so. But I tell you,
from now on you will see the Son-of-Man seated at the right hand of Power
and coming on the clouds of heaven."
65Then the high priest tore his clothes and said,
"He has blasphemed! Why do we still need witnesses?
You have now heard his blasphemy. 66What is your verdict?"
They answered, "He deserves death."
67Then they spat in his face and struck him;
and some slapped him, 68saying,
"Prophesy to us, you Messiah! Who is it that struck you?"

69Now Peter was sitting outside in the courtyard.
A servant-girl came to him and said,
"You also were with Jesus the Galilean."
70But he denied it before all of them, saying,
"I do not know what you are talking about."
71When he went out to the porch, another servant-girl saw him,
and she said to the bystanders, "This man was with Jesus of Nazareth."
72Again he denied it with an oath, "I do not know the man."
73After a little while the bystanders came up and said to Peter,
"Certainly you are also one of them, for your accent betrays you."
74Then he began to curse, and he swore an oath,
"I do not know the man!"
At that moment the cock crowed.
75Then Peter remembered what Jesus had said:
"Before the cock crows, you will deny me three times."
And he went out and wept bitterly.

27:1When morning came, all the chief priests and the elders of the people
conferred together against Jesus in order to bring about his death.
2They bound him, led him away, and handed him over to Pilate the governor.

3When Judas, his betrayer, saw that Jesus was condemned, he repented
and brought back the thirty pieces of silver to the chief priests and the elders.
4He said, "I have sinned by betraying innocent blood."

But they said, "What is that to us? See to it yourself."
[5]Throwing down the pieces of silver in the temple, he departed;
and he went and hanged himself.
[6]But the chief priests, taking the pieces of silver, said,
"It is not lawful to put them into the treasury, since they are blood money."
[7]After conferring together,
they used the silver to buy the potter's field as a place to bury foreigners.
[8]For this reason that field has been called the Field of Blood to this day.
[9]Then was fulfilled what had been spoken through the prophet Jeremiah,
"And they took the thirty pieces of silver,
the price of the one on whom a price had been set,
on whom some of the people of Israel had set a price,
[10]and they gave the silver for the potter's field, as the Lord commanded me."

[11]Now Jesus stood before the governor; and the governor asked him,
"Are you the King of the Jews?"
Jesus said, "You say so."
[12]But when he was accused by the chief priests and elders,
he did not answer.
[13]Then Pilate said to him,
"Do you not hear how many accusations they make against you?"
[14]But Jesus gave Pilate no answer, not even to a single charge,
so that the governor was greatly amazed.

[15]Now at the festival
the governor was accustomed to release a prisoner for the crowd,
anyone whom they wanted.
[16]At that time they had a notorious prisoner, called Jesus Barabbas.
[17]So after they had gathered, Pilate said to them,
"Whom do you want me to release for you,
Jesus Barabbas or Jesus who is called the Messiah?"
[18]For he realized that it was out of jealousy that they had handed him over.
[19]While he was sitting on the judgment seat, his wife sent word to him,
"Have nothing to do with that innocent man,
for today I have suffered a great deal because of a dream about him."
[20]Now the chief priests and the elders persuaded the crowds to ask for
        Barabbas
and to have Jesus killed.
[21]The governor again said to them,
"Which of the two do you want me to release for you?"
And they said, "Barabbas."
[22]Pilate said to them,
"Then what should I do with Jesus who is called the Messiah?"
All of them said, "Let him be crucified!"
[23]Then Pilate asked, "Why, what evil has he done?"
But they shouted all the more, "Let him be crucified!"

[24]So when Pilate saw that he could do nothing,
but rather that a riot was beginning,
he took some water and washed his hands before the crowd, saying,
"I am innocent of this man's blood; see to it yourselves."
[25]Then all the people answered,
"His blood be on us and on our children!"
[26]So Pilate released Barabbas for them;
and after flogging Jesus, he handed him over to be crucified.

[27]Then the soldiers of the governor took Jesus into the governor's
        headquarters,
and they gathered the whole cohort around him.
[28]They stripped him and put a scarlet robe on him,
[29]and after twisting some thorns into a crown, they put it on his head.
They put a reed in his right hand
and knelt before him and mocked him, saying,
"Hail, King of the Jews!"
[30]They spat on him, and took the reed and struck him on the head.
[31]After mocking him,
they stripped him of the robe and put his own clothes on him.
Then they led him away to crucify him.

[32]As they went out, they came upon a man from Cyrene named Simon;
they compelled this man to carry his cross.
[33]And when they came to a place called Golgotha
(which means Place of a Skull),
[34]they offered Jesus wine to drink, mixed with gall;
but when he tasted it, he would not drink it.
[35]And when they had crucified him,
they divided his clothes among themselves by casting lots;
[36]then they sat down there and kept watch over him.
[37]Over his head they put the charge against him, which read,
"This is Jesus, the King of the Jews."

[38]Then two bandits were crucified with him,
one on his right and one on his left.
[39]Those who passed by derided him, shaking their heads [40]and saying,
"You who would destroy the temple and build it in three days, save yourself!
If you are the Son of God, come down from the cross."
[41]In the same way the chief priests also, along with the scribes and elders,
were mocking him, saying,
[42]"He saved others; he cannot save himself.
He is the King of Israel; let him come down from the cross now,
and we will believe in him.
[43]He trusts in God; let God deliver him now, if God wants to;
for he said, 'I am God's Son.' "
[44]The bandits who were crucified with him also taunted him in the same way.

⁴⁵From noon on,
darkness came over the whole land until three in the afternoon.
⁴⁶And about three o'clock Jesus cried with a loud voice,
"Eli, Eli, lema sabachthani?" that is,
"My God, my God, why have you forsaken me?"
⁴⁷When some of the bystanders heard it, they said,
"This man is calling for Elijah."
⁴⁸At once one of them ran and got a sponge,
filled it with sour wine, put it on a stick,
and gave it to him to drink.
⁴⁹But the others said,
"Wait, let us see whether Elijah will come to save him."
⁵⁰Then Jesus cried again with a loud voice and breathed his last.

⁵¹At that moment the curtain of the temple was torn in two, from top to bottom.
The earth shook, and the rocks were split.
⁵²The tombs also were opened,
and many bodies of the saints who had fallen asleep were raised.
⁵³After his resurrection they came out of the tombs
and entered the holy city and appeared to many.

⁵⁴Now when the centurion and those with him,
who were keeping watch over Jesus,
saw the earthquake and what took place, they were terrified and said,
"Truly this man was God's Son!"

⁵⁵Many women were also there, looking on from a distance;
they had followed Jesus from Galilee and had provided for him.
⁵⁶Among them were Mary Magdalene, and Mary the mother of James and
        Joseph,
and the mother of the sons of Zebedee.

⁵⁷When it was evening, there came a rich man from Arimathea, named Joseph,
who was also a disciple of Jesus.
⁵⁸He went to Pilate and asked for the body of Jesus;
then Pilate ordered it to be given to him.
⁵⁹So Joseph took the body and wrapped it in a clean linen cloth
⁶⁰and laid it in his own new tomb, which he had hewn in the rock.
He then rolled a great stone to the door of the tomb and went away.
⁶¹Mary Magdalene and the other Mary were there, sitting opposite the tomb.

⁶²The next day, that is, after the day of Preparation,
the chief priests and the Pharisees gathered before Pilate ⁶³and said,
"Sir, we remember what that impostor said while he was still alive,
'After three days I will rise again.'
⁶⁴Therefore command the tomb to be made secure until the third day;
otherwise his disciples may go and steal him away,
and tell the people, 'He has been raised from the dead,'

and the last deception would be worse than the first."
⁶⁵Pilate said to them,
"You have a guard of soldiers; go, make it as secure as you can."
⁶⁶So they went with the guard and made the tomb secure by sealing the stone.

The Gospel of the Lord.

OR: MATTHEW 27:11–54

The Passion of our Lord Jesus Christ according to Matthew.

¹¹Now Jesus stood before the governor; and the governor asked him,
"Are you the King of the Jews?"
Jesus said, "You say so."
¹²But when he was accused by the chief priests and elders,
he did not answer.
¹³Then Pilate said to him,
"Do you not hear how many accusations they make against you?"
¹⁴But Jesus gave Pilate no answer, not even to a single charge,
so that the governor was greatly amazed.

¹⁵Now at the festival
the governor was accustomed to release a prisoner for the crowd,
anyone whom they wanted.
¹⁶At that time they had a notorious prisoner, called Jesus Barabbas.
¹⁷So after they had gathered, Pilate said to them,
"Whom do you want me to release for you,
Jesus Barabbas or Jesus who is called the Messiah?"
¹⁸For he realized that it was out of jealousy that they had handed him over.
¹⁹While he was sitting on the judgment seat, his wife sent word to him,
"Have nothing to do with that innocent man,
for today I have suffered a great deal because of a dream about him."
²⁰Now the chief priests and the elders persuaded the crowds to ask for
        Barabbas
and to have Jesus killed.
²¹The governor again said to them,
"Which of the two do you want me to release for you?"
And they said, "Barabbas."
²²Pilate said to them,
"Then what should I do with Jesus who is called the Messiah?"
All of them said, "Let him be crucified!"
²³Then Pilate asked, "Why, what evil has he done?"
But they shouted all the more, "Let him be crucified!"

²⁴So when Pilate saw that he could do nothing,
but rather that a riot was beginning,
he took some water and washed his hands before the crowd, saying,
"I am innocent of this man's blood; see to it yourselves."

²⁵Then all the people answered,
"His blood be on us and on our children!"
²⁶So Pilate released Barabbas for them;
and after flogging Jesus, he handed him over to be crucified.

²⁷Then the soldiers of the governor took Jesus into the governor's
    headquarters,
and they gathered the whole cohort around him.
²⁸They stripped him and put a scarlet robe on him,
²⁹and after twisting some thorns into a crown, they put it on his head.
They put a reed in his right hand
and knelt before him and mocked him, saying,
"Hail, King of the Jews!"
³⁰They spat on him, and took the reed and struck him on the head.
³¹After mocking him,
they stripped him of the robe and put his own clothes on him.
Then they led him away to crucify him.

³²As they went out, they came upon a man from Cyrene named Simon;
they compelled this man to carry his cross.
³³And when they came to a place called Golgotha
(which means Place of a Skull),
³⁴they offered Jesus wine to drink, mixed with gall;
but when he tasted it, he would not drink it.
³⁵And when they had crucified him,
they divided his clothes among themselves by casting lots;
³⁶then they sat down there and kept watch over him.
³⁷Over his head they put the charge against him, which read,
"This is Jesus, the King of the Jews."

³⁸Then two bandits were crucified with him,
one on his right and one on his left.
³⁹Those who passed by derided him, shaking their heads ⁴⁰and saying,
"You who would destroy the temple and build it in three days, save yourself!
If you are the Son of God, come down from the cross."
⁴¹In the same way the chief priests also, along with the scribes and elders,
were mocking him, saying,
⁴²"He saved others; he cannot save himself.
He is the King of Israel; let him come down from the cross now,
and we will believe in him.
⁴³He trusts in God; let God deliver him now, if God wants to;
for he said, 'I am God's Son.'"
⁴⁴The bandits who were crucified with him also taunted him in the same way.

⁴⁵From noon on, darkness came over the whole land until three in the
    afternoon.
⁴⁶And about three o'clock Jesus cried with a loud voice,
"Eli, Eli, lema sabachthani?" that is,

"My God, my God, why have you forsaken me?"
47When some of the bystanders heard it, they said,
"This man is calling for Elijah."
48At once one of them ran and got a sponge,
filled it with sour wine, put it on a stick,
and gave it to him to drink.
49But the others said,
"Wait, let us see whether Elijah will come to save him."
50Then Jesus cried again with a loud voice and breathed his last.

51At that moment the curtain of the temple was torn in two, from top to bottom.
The earth shook, and the rocks were split.
52The tombs also were opened,
and many bodies of the saints who had fallen asleep were raised.
53After his resurrection they came out of the tombs
and entered the holy city and appeared to many.

54Now when the centurion and those with him,
who were keeping watch over Jesus,
saw the earthquake and what took place, they were terrified and said,
"Truly this man was God's Son!"

The Gospel of the Lord.

✝

MONDAY IN HOLY WEEK

APRIL 1, 1996   MARCH 29, 1999   MARCH 25, 2002

FIRST READING: ISAIAH 42:1–9

A reading from Isaiah:

¹Here is my servant, whom I uphold,
my chosen, in whom my soul delights,
upon whom I have put my spirit,
to bring forth justice to the nations.
²Not crying out, not lifting up his voice,
not making it heard in the street,
³a bruised reed my servant will not break,
nor quench a dimly burning wick,
but will faithfully bring forth justice.
⁴My chosen one will not grow faint or be crushed
until he has established justice in the earth;
and the coastlands wait for his teaching.

⁵Thus says God, the LORD,
who created the heavens and stretched them out,
who spread out the earth and what comes from it,
who gives breath to the people upon it
and spirit to those who walk in it:
⁶I am the LORD, I have called you in righteousness,
I have taken you by the hand and kept you;
I have given you as a covenant to the people,
a light to the nations,
⁷to open the eyes that are blind,
to bring out the prisoners from the dungeon,
from the prison those who sit in darkness.
⁸I am the LORD, that is my name;
my glory I give to no other,
nor my praise to idols.

⁹See, the former things have come to pass,
and new things I now declare;
before they spring forth, I tell you of them.

PSALMODY: Psalm 36:5–11

SECOND READING: Hebrews 9:11–15

A reading from Hebrews:

¹¹When Christ came as a high priest of the good things that have come,
then through the greater and perfect tent
(not made with hands, that is, not of this creation),
¹²he entered once for all into the Holy Place,
not with the blood of goats and calves,
but with his own blood, thus obtaining eternal redemption.

¹³For if the blood of goats and bulls,
with the sprinkling of the ashes of a heifer,
sanctifies those who have been defiled so that their flesh is purified,
¹⁴how much more will the blood of Christ,
who through the eternal Spirit offered himself without blemish to God,
purify our conscience from dead works to worship the living God!

¹⁵For this reason Christ is the mediator of a new covenant,
so that those who are called may receive the promised eternal inheritance,
because a death has occurred
that redeems them from the transgressions under the first covenant.

GOSPEL: JOHN 12:1–11

The Holy Gospel according to John, the twelfth chapter.

[1]Six days before the Passover Jesus came to Bethany,
the home of Lazarus, whom he had raised from the dead.
[2]There they gave a dinner for Jesus.
Martha served, and Lazarus was one of those at the table with him.
[3]Mary took a pound of costly perfume made of pure nard,
anointed Jesus' feet, and wiped them with her hair.
The house was filled with the fragrance of the perfume.

[4]But Judas Iscariot, one of his disciples
(the one who was about to betray him), said,
[5]"Why was this perfume not sold for three hundred denarii
and the money given to the poor?"
[6](He said this not because he cared about the poor,
but because he was a thief;
he kept the common purse and used to steal what was put into it.)
[7]Jesus said,
"Leave her alone.
She bought it so that she might keep it for the day of my burial.
[8]You always have the poor with you,
but you do not always have me."

[9]When the great crowd of the Judeans learned that he was there,
they came not only because of Jesus
but also to see Lazarus, whom he had raised from the dead.
[10]So the chief priests planned to put Lazarus to death as well,
[11]since it was on account of him that many of the Judeans were deserting
and were believing in Jesus.

The Gospel of the Lord.

✝

TUESDAY IN HOLY WEEK

APRIL 2, 1996   MARCH 30, 1999   MARCH 26, 2002

FIRST READING: Isaiah 49:1–7

A reading from Isaiah:

¹Listen to me, O coastlands,
pay attention, you peoples from far away!
The LORD called me before I was born,
and while I was in my mother's womb God named me.
²The LORD made my mouth like a sharp sword;
I was hid in the shadow of God's hand.
The LORD made me a polished arrow;
I was hid away in God's quiver.

³And the LORD said to me, "You are my servant,
Israel, in whom I will be glorified."
⁴But I said, "I have labored in vain,
I have spent my strength for nothing and vanity;
yet surely my cause is with the LORD,
and my reward with my God."

⁵And now the LORD says,
who formed me as a servant from the womb,
to bring Jacob back to God,
and that Israel might be gathered to the LORD,
for I am honored in the sight of the LORD,
and my God has become my strength—
⁶the LORD says,
"It is too light a thing that you should be my servant
to raise up the tribes of Jacob
and to restore the survivors of Israel;
I will give you as a light to the nations,
that my salvation may reach to the end of the earth."

⁷Thus says the L<small>ORD</small>,
the Redeemer of Israel, the Holy One of Israel,
to one deeply despised, abhorred by the nations,
the slave of rulers,
"Monarchs shall see and stand up,
chieftains, and they shall prostrate themselves,
because of the L<small>ORD</small>, who is faithful,
the Holy One of Israel, who has chosen you."

PSALMODY: P<small>SALM</small> 71:1–14

SECOND READING: 1 C<small>ORINTHIANS</small> 1:18–31

A reading from First Corinthians:

¹⁸The message about the cross is foolishness to those who are perishing,
but to us who are being saved it is the power of God.
¹⁹For it is written,
"I will destroy the wisdom of the wise,
and the discernment of the discerning I will thwart."
²⁰Where is the one who is wise?
Where is the scribe?
Where is the debater of this age?
Has not God made foolish the wisdom of the world?

²¹For since, in the wisdom of God,
the world did not know God through wisdom,
God decided, through the foolishness of our proclamation,
to save those who believe.
²²For Jews demand signs and Greeks desire wisdom,
²³but we proclaim Christ crucified,
a stumbling block to Jews and foolishness to Gentiles,
²⁴but to those who are the called, both Jews and Greeks,
Christ the power of God and the wisdom of God.
²⁵For God's foolishness is wiser than human wisdom,
and God's weakness is stronger than human strength.

²⁶Consider your own call, brothers and sisters:
not many of you were wise by human standards,
not many were powerful,
not many were of noble birth.
²⁷But God chose what is foolish in the world to shame the wise;
God chose what is weak in the world to shame the strong;
²⁸God chose what is low and despised in the world,
things that are not,
to reduce to nothing things that are,
²⁹so that no one might boast in the presence of God.

³⁰God is the source of your life in Christ Jesus,
who became for us wisdom from God,
and righteousness and sanctification and redemption,
³¹in order that, as it is written,
"Let the one who boasts, boast in the Lord."

GOSPEL: JOHN 12:20–36

The Holy Gospel according to John, the twelfth chapter.

²⁰Now among those who went up to worship at the festival were some Greeks.
²¹They came to Philip, who was from Bethsaida in Galilee,
and said to him, "Sir, we wish to see Jesus."
²²Philip went and told Andrew;
then Andrew and Philip went and told Jesus.
²³Jesus answered them,
"The hour has come for the Son-of-Man to be glorified.
²⁴Very truly, I tell you,
unless a grain of wheat falls into the earth and dies,
it remains just a single grain;
but if it dies, it bears much fruit.
²⁵Those who love their life lose it,
and those who hate their life in this world will keep it for eternal life.
²⁶Whoever serves me must follow me,
and where I am, there will my servant be also.
Whoever serves me, the Father will honor.

²⁷"Now my soul is troubled.
And what should I say—'Father, save me from this hour'?
No, it is for this reason that I have come to this hour.
²⁸Father, glorify your name."
Then a voice came from heaven,
"I have glorified it, and I will glorify it again."
²⁹The crowd standing there heard it and said that it was thunder.
Others said, "An angel has spoken to him."
³⁰Jesus answered,
"This voice has come for your sake, not for mine.
³¹Now is the judgment of this world;
now the ruler of this world will be driven out.
³²And I, when I am lifted up from the earth,
will draw all people to myself."
³³He said this to indicate the kind of death he was to die.
³⁴The crowd answered him,
"We have heard from the law that the Messiah remains forever.
How can you say that the Son-of-Man must be lifted up?
Who is this Son-of-Man?"
³⁵Jesus said to them,

"The light is with you for a little longer.
Walk while you have the light,
so that the darkness may not overtake you.
If you walk in the darkness, you do not know where you are going.
[36]While you have the light, believe in the light,
so that you may become children of light."

After Jesus had said this, he departed and hid from them.

The Gospel of the Lord.

Wednesday in Holy Week

FIRST READING: Isaiah 50:4–9a

A reading from Isaiah:

4The Lord GOD has given me the tongue of a teacher,
that I may know how to sustain the weary with a word.
Morning by morning the Lord GOD wakens—
wakens my ear
to listen as those who are taught.
5The Lord GOD has opened my ear,
and I was not rebellious,
I did not turn backward.
6I gave my back to those who struck me,
and my cheeks to those who pulled out the beard;
I did not hide my face from insult and spitting.

7The Lord GOD helps me;
therefore I have not been disgraced;
therefore I have set my face like flint,
and I know that I shall not be put to shame;
8the one who vindicates me is near.
Who will contend with me?
Let us stand up together.
Who are my adversaries?
Let them confront me.
9aIt is the Lord GOD who helps me;
who will declare me guilty?

PSALMODY: Psalm 70

SECOND READING: Hebrews 12:1–3

A reading from Hebrews:

1Since we are surrounded by so great a cloud of witnesses,
let us also lay aside every weight and the sin that clings so closely,
and let us run with perseverance the race that is set before us,
2looking to Jesus the pioneer and perfecter of our faith,

who for the sake of the joy that was set before him
endured the cross, disregarding its shame,
and is seated at the right hand of the throne of God.

³Consider Jesus who endured such hostility against himself from sinners,
so that you may not grow weary or lose heart.

GOSPEL: JOHN 13:21–32

The Holy Gospel according to John, the 13th chapter.

²¹Jesus was troubled in spirit, and declared,
"Very truly, I tell you, one of you will betray me."
²²The disciples looked at one another,
uncertain of whom he was speaking.

²³One of his disciples—the one whom Jesus loved—was reclining next to him;
²⁴Simon Peter therefore motioned to him to ask Jesus of whom he was speaking.
²⁵So while reclining next to Jesus, he asked him,
"Lord, who is it?"
²⁶Jesus answered,
"It is the one to whom I give this piece of bread
when I have dipped it in the dish."
So when he had dipped the piece of bread,
he gave it to Judas son of Simon Iscariot.
²⁷After Judas received the piece of bread, Satan entered into him.
Jesus said to him,
"Do quickly what you are going to do."
²⁸Now no one at the table knew why Jesus said this to Judas.
²⁹Some thought that, because Judas had the common purse,
Jesus was telling him, "Buy what we need for the festival";
or, that he should give something to the poor.
³⁰So, after receiving the piece of bread, he immediately went out.
And it was night.

³¹When Judas had gone out, Jesus said,
"Now the Son-of-Man has been glorified,
and God has been glorified in him.
³²If God has been glorified in him,
God will also glorify him in God's own self and will glorify him at once."

The Gospel of the Lord.

THE THREE DAYS

✠

MAUNDY THURSDAY

APRIL 4, 1996   APRIL 1, 1999   MARCH 28, 2002

FIRST READING: EXODUS 12:1–4 [5–10] 11–14

A reading from Exodus:

¹The LORD said to Moses and Aaron in the land of Egypt:
²This month shall mark for you the beginning of months;
it shall be the first month of the year for you.
³Tell the whole congregation of Israel
that on the tenth of this month they are to take a lamb for each family,
a lamb for each household.
⁴If a household is too small for a whole lamb,
it shall join its closest neighbor in obtaining one;
the lamb shall be divided in proportion to the number of people who eat of it.

[⁵Your lamb shall be without blemish, a year-old male;
you may take it from the sheep or from the goats.
⁶You shall keep it until the fourteenth day of this month;
then the whole assembled congregation of Israel shall slaughter it at twilight.
⁷They shall take some of the blood and put it on the two doorposts
and the lintel of the houses in which they eat it.
⁸They shall eat the lamb that same night;
they shall eat it roasted over the fire
with unleavened bread and bitter herbs.
⁹Do not eat any of it raw or boiled in water,
but roasted over the fire, with its head, legs, and inner organs.
¹⁰You shall let none of it remain until the morning;
anything that remains until the morning you shall burn.]

¹¹This is how you shall eat it:
your loins girded, your sandals on your feet, and your staff in your hand;
and you shall eat it hurriedly.
It is the passover of the LORD.
¹²For I will pass through the land of Egypt that night,
and I will strike down every firstborn in the land of Egypt,
both human beings and animals;
on all the deities of Egypt I will execute judgments:
I am the LORD.
¹³The blood shall be a sign for you on the houses where you live:
when I see the blood, I will pass over you,

and no plague shall destroy you when I strike the land of Egypt.
[14]This day shall be a day of remembrance for you.
You shall celebrate it as a festival to the LORD;
throughout your generations you shall observe it as a perpetual ordinance.

PSALMODY: PSALM 116:1–2, 12–19   *Psalm 116:1, 10–17*   LBW/BCP

SECOND READING: 1 CORINTHIANS 11:23–26

A reading from First Corinthians:

[23]For I received from the Lord what I also handed on to you,
that the Lord Jesus on the night when he was betrayed
took a loaf of bread,
[24]and when he had given thanks, he broke it and said,
"This is my body that is for you.
Do this in remembrance of me."
[25]In the same way he took the cup also, after supper, saying,
"This cup is the new covenant in my blood.
Do this, as often as you drink it, in remembrance of me."

[26]For as often as you eat this bread and drink the cup,
you proclaim the Lord's death until he comes.

GOSPEL: JOHN 13:1–17, 31b–35

The Holy Gospel according to John, the 13th chapter.

[1]Now before the festival of the Passover,
Jesus knew that his hour had come to depart from this world
and go to the Father.
Having loved his own who were in the world,
he loved them to the end.
[2]The devil had already put it into the heart of Judas son of Simon Iscariot
to betray him.

And during supper
[3]Jesus, knowing that the Father had given all things into his hands,
and that he had come from God and was going to God,
[4]got up from the table,
took off his outer robe, and tied a towel around himself.
[5]Then he poured water into a basin
and began to wash the disciples' feet
and to wipe them with the towel that was tied around him.
[6]He came to Simon Peter, who said to him,
"Lord, are you going to wash my feet?"
[7]Jesus answered,

"You do not know now what I am doing,
but later you will understand."
[8]Peter said to him,
"You will never wash my feet."
Jesus answered,
"Unless I wash you, you have no share with me."
[9]Simon Peter said to him,
"Lord, not my feet only but also my hands and my head!"
[10]Jesus said to him,
"One who has bathed does not need to wash, except for the feet,
but is entirely clean.
And you are clean, though not all of you."
[11]For Jesus knew who was to betray him;
for this reason he said, "Not all of you are clean."

[12]After he had washed their feet, had put on his robe,
and had returned to the table, he said to them,
"Do you know what I have done to you?
[13]You call me Teacher and Lord—
and you are right, for that is what I am.
[14]So if I, your Lord and Teacher, have washed your feet,
you also ought to wash one another's feet.
[15]For I have set you an example,
that you also should do as I have done to you.
[16]Very truly, I tell you,
servants are not greater than their master,
nor are messengers greater than the one who sent them.
[17]If you know these things,
you are blessed if you do them.

[31b]"Now the Son-of-Man has been glorified,
and God has been glorified in him.
[32]If God has been glorified in him,
God will also glorify him in God's own self and will glorify him at once.
[33]Little children, I am with you only a little longer.
You will look for me;
and as I said to the Judeans so now I say to you,
'Where I am going, you cannot come.'

[34]"I give you a new commandment,
that you love one another.
Just as I have loved you, you also should love one another.
[35]By this everyone will know that you are my disciples,
if you have love for one another."

The Gospel of the Lord.

✝

GOOD FRIDAY

APRIL 5, 1996   *APRIL 2, 1999*   *MARCH 29, 2002*

FIRST READING: Isaiah 52:13—53:12

A reading from Isaiah:

13See, my servant shall prosper,
shall be exalted and lifted up,
and shall be very high.
14Just as there were many who were astonished at him
—so marred was his appearance, beyond human semblance,
and his form beyond that of mortals—
15so shall my servant startle many nations;
rulers shall shut their mouths because of him;
for that which had not been told them they shall see,
and that which they had not heard they shall contemplate.

53:1Who has believed what we have heard?
And to whom has the arm of the LORD been revealed?
2For the servant grew up before the LORD like a young plant,
and like a root out of dry ground,
having no form or majesty that we should behold,
and nothing in appearance that we should desire.
3He was despised and rejected by others;
a man of suffering and acquainted with infirmity;
and as one from whom others hide their faces
he was despised, and we held him of no account.

4Surely he has borne our infirmities and carried our diseases;
yet we accounted him stricken,
struck down by God, and afflicted.
5But he was wounded for our transgressions,
crushed for our iniquities;
upon him was the punishment that made us whole,
and by his bruises we are healed.
6All we like sheep have gone astray;
we have all turned to our own way,
and the LORD has laid on him the iniquity of us all.

7He was oppressed, and was afflicted,
yet did not open his mouth;

like a lamb that is led to the slaughter,
and like a ewe that is silent before the shearers,
so he did not open his mouth.
8By a perversion of justice he was taken away.
Who could have imagined his future?
For he was cut off from the land of the living,
stricken for the transgression of my people.
9They made his grave with the wicked
and his tomb with the rich,
although he had done no violence,
and there was no deceit in his mouth.

10Yet it was the will of the LORD to crush him with pain.
When you make his life an offering for sin,
he shall see his offspring, and shall prolong his days;
through him the will of the LORD shall prosper.
11Out of his anguish he shall see light;
he shall find satisfaction through his knowledge.
The righteous one, my servant, shall make many righteous,
and shall bear their iniquities.
12Therefore I will allot him a portion with the great,
and he shall divide the spoil with the strong;
because he poured out himself to death,
and was numbered with the transgressors;
yet he bore the sin of many,
and made intercession for the transgressors.

PSALMODY: PSALM 22

SECOND READING: HEBREWS 10:16–25
Or Hebrews 4:14-16; 5:7-9, following

A reading from Hebrews:

16"This is the covenant that I will make with them after those days,
says the Lord:
I will put my laws in their hearts,
and I will write them on their minds,"
17and then is added,
"I will remember their sins and their lawless deeds no more."
18Where there is forgiveness of these,
there is no longer any offering for sin.

19Therefore, my friends,
since we have confidence to enter the sanctuary by the blood of Jesus,
20by the new and living way that Christ opened for us through the curtain
(that is, through his flesh),

²¹and since we have a great priest over the house of God,
²²let us approach with a true heart in full assurance of faith,
with our hearts sprinkled clean from an evil conscience
and our bodies washed with pure water.
²³Let us hold fast to the confession of our hope without wavering,
for the one who has promised is faithful.
²⁴And let us consider how to provoke one another to love and good deeds,
²⁵not neglecting to meet together, as is the habit of some,
but encouraging one another,
and all the more as you see the Day approaching.

OR: HEBREWS 4:14–16; 5:7–9

A reading from Hebrews:

¹⁴Since, then, we have a great high priest who has passed
      through the heavens,
Jesus, the Son of God,
let us hold fast to our confession.
¹⁵For we do not have a high priest who is unable to sympathize with our
      weaknesses,
but we have one who in every respect has been tested as we are,
yet without sin.
¹⁶Let us therefore approach the throne of grace with boldness,
so that we may receive mercy and find grace
to help in time of need.

^{5:7}In the days of his flesh, Jesus offered up prayers and supplications,
with loud cries and tears,
to the one who was able to save him from death,
and he was heard because of his reverent submission.
⁸Although he was a Son,
he learned obedience through what he suffered;
⁹and having been made perfect,
he became the source of eternal salvation for all who obey him.

The Passion of our Lord Jesus Christ according to John.

[1]Jesus went out with his disciples across the Kidron valley
to a place where there was a garden, which he and his disciples entered.
[2]Now Judas, who betrayed him, also knew the place,
because Jesus often met there with his disciples.
[3]So Judas brought a detachment of soldiers together
with police from the chief priests and the Pharisees,
and they came there with lanterns and torches and weapons.
[4]Then Jesus, knowing all that was to happen to him,
came forward and asked them,
"Whom are you looking for?"
[5]They answered, "Jesus of Nazareth."
Jesus replied, "Here I AM."
Judas, who betrayed him, was standing with them.
[6]When Jesus said to them, "Here I AM,"
they stepped back and fell to the ground.
[7]Again he asked them, "Whom are you looking for?"
And they said, "Jesus of Nazareth."
[8]Jesus answered, "I told you that here I AM.
So if you are looking for me, let these others go."
[9]This was to fulfill the word that he had spoken,
"I did not lose a single one of those whom you gave me."
[10]Then Simon Peter, who had a sword, drew it,
struck the high priest's slave, and cut off his right ear.
The slave's name was Malchus.
[11]Jesus said to Peter,
"Put your sword back into its sheath.
Am I not to drink the cup that the Father has given me?"

[12]So the soldiers, their officer, and the Judean police
arrested Jesus and bound him.
[13]First they took him to Annas,
who was the father-in-law of Caiaphas, the high priest that year.
[14]Caiaphas was the one who had advised the Judeans
that it was better to have one person die for the people.

[15]Simon Peter and another disciple followed Jesus.
Since that disciple was known to the high priest,
he went with Jesus into the courtyard of the high priest,
[16]but Peter was standing outside at the gate.
So the other disciple, who was known to the high priest,
went out, spoke to the woman who guarded the gate,
and brought Peter in.

¹⁷The woman said to Peter,
"You are not also one of this man's disciples, are you?"
He said, "I am not."
¹⁸Now the slaves and the police had made a charcoal fire because it was cold,
and they were standing around it and warming themselves.
Peter also was standing with them and warming himself.

¹⁹Then the high priest questioned Jesus about his disciples
          and about his teaching.
²⁰Jesus answered, "I have spoken openly to the world;
I have always taught in synagogues and in the temple,
where all the Judeans come together.
I have said nothing in secret.
²¹Why do you ask me?
Ask those who heard what I said to them; they know what I said."
²²When he had said this,
one of the police standing nearby struck Jesus on the face, saying,
"Is that how you answer the high priest?"
²³Jesus answered, "If I have spoken wrongly, testify to the wrong.
But if I have spoken rightly, why do you strike me?"
²⁴Then Annas sent him bound to Caiaphas the high priest.

²⁵Now Simon Peter was standing and warming himself.
They asked him, "You are not also one of his disciples, are you?"
He denied it and said, "I am not."
²⁶One of the slaves of the high priest,
a relative of the man whose ear Peter had cut off, asked,
"Did I not see you in the garden with him?"
²⁷Again Peter denied it, and at that moment the cock crowed.

²⁸Then they took Jesus from Caiaphas to Pilate's headquarters.
It was early in the morning.
They themselves did not enter the headquarters,
so as to avoid ritual defilement
and to be able to eat the Passover.
²⁹So Pilate went out to them and said,
"What accusation do you bring against this man?"
³⁰They answered, "If this man were not a criminal,
we would not have handed him over to you."
³¹Pilate said to them,
"Take him yourselves and judge him according to your law."
The Judeans replied,
"We are not permitted to put anyone to death."
³²(This was to fulfill what Jesus had said
when he indicated the kind of death he was to die.)

³³Then Pilate entered the headquarters again,
summoned Jesus, and asked him,
"Are you the King of the Jews?"

³⁴Jesus answered,
"Do you ask this on your own, or did others tell you about me?"
³⁵Pilate replied, "I am not Jewish, am I?
Your own nation and the chief priests have handed you over to me.
What have you done?"
³⁶Jesus answered,
"My kingdom is not from this world.
If my kingdom were from this world,
my followers would be fighting to keep me from being handed over
        to the Judeans.
But as it is, my kingdom is not from here."
³⁷Pilate asked him, "So you are a king?"
Jesus answered,
"You say that I am a king. For this I was born,
and for this I came into the world, to testify to the truth.
Everyone who belongs to the truth listens to my voice."
³⁸Pilate asked him, "What is truth?"

After he had said this, he went out to the Judeans again and told them,
"I find no case against him.
³⁹But you have a custom that I release someone for you at the Passover.
Do you want me to release for you the King of the Jews?"
⁴⁰They shouted in reply,
"Not this man, but Barabbas!"
Now Barabbas was a bandit.

^{19:1}Then Pilate took Jesus and had him flogged.
²And the soldiers wove a crown of thorns and put it on his head,
and they dressed him in a purple robe.
³They kept coming up to him, saying,
"Hail, King of the Jews!" and striking him on the face.
⁴Pilate went out again and said to them,
"Look, I am bringing him out to you
to let you know that I find no case against him."
⁵So Jesus came out, wearing the crown of thorns and the purple robe.
Pilate said to them, "Here is the man!"
⁶When the chief priests and the police saw him, they shouted,
"Crucify him! Crucify him!"
Pilate said to them,
"Take him yourselves and crucify him; I find no case against him."
⁷The Judeans answered him,
"We have a law, and according to that law
he ought to die because he has claimed to be the Son of God."

⁸Now when Pilate heard this, he was more afraid than ever.
⁹He entered his headquarters again and asked Jesus,
"Where are you from?"
But Jesus gave him no answer.

¹⁰Pilate therefore said to him,
"Do you refuse to speak to me?
Do you not know that I have power to release you, and power to crucify you?"
¹¹Jesus answered him,
"You would have no power over me unless it had been given you from above;
therefore the one who handed me over to you is guilty of a greater sin."
¹²From then on Pilate tried to release him,
but the Judeans cried out,
"If you release this man, you are no friend of the emperor.
Everyone who claims to be a king sets himself against the emperor."

¹³When Pilate heard these words, he brought Jesus outside
and sat on the judge's bench at a place called The Stone Pavement,
or in Hebrew Gabbatha.
¹⁴Now it was the day of Preparation for the Passover; and it was about noon.
He said to the Judeans, "Here is your king!"
¹⁵They cried out,
"Away with him! Away with him! Crucify him!"
Pilate asked them, "Shall I crucify your king?"
The chief priests answered,
"We have no king but the emperor."
¹⁶Then he handed him over to them to be crucified.

So they took Jesus; ¹⁷and carrying the cross by himself,
he went out to what is called The Place of the Skull,
which in Hebrew is called Golgotha.
¹⁸There they crucified him,
and with him two others, one on either side, with Jesus between them.
¹⁹Pilate also had an inscription written and put on the cross.
It read, "Jesus of Nazareth, the King of the Jews."
²⁰Many of the Judeans read this inscription,
because the place where Jesus was crucified was near the city;
and it was written in Hebrew, in Latin, and in Greek.
²¹Then the chief priests of the Jews said to Pilate,
"Do not write, 'The King of the Jews,' but,
'This man said, I am King of the Jews.' "
²²Pilate answered,
"What I have written I have written."
²³When the soldiers had crucified Jesus,
they took his clothes and divided them into four parts, one for each soldier.
They also took his tunic;
now the tunic was seamless, woven in one piece from the top.
²⁴So they said to one another,
"Let us not tear it, but cast lots for it to see who will get it."
This was to fulfill what the scripture says,
"They divided my clothes among themselves,
and for my clothing they cast lots."
²⁵And that is what the soldiers did.

Meanwhile, standing near the cross of Jesus were his mother,
and his mother's sister, Mary the wife of Clopas, and Mary Magdalene.
[26]When Jesus saw his mother
and the disciple whom he loved standing beside her,
he said to his mother, "Woman, here is your son."
[27]Then he said to the disciple, "Here is your mother."
And from that hour the disciple took her into his own home.

[28]After this, when Jesus knew that all was now finished,
he said (in order to fulfill the scripture),
"I am thirsty."
[29]A jar full of sour wine was standing there.
So they put a sponge full of the wine on a branch of hyssop
and held it to his mouth.
[30]When Jesus had received the wine, he said,
"It is finished."
Then he bowed his head and gave up his spirit.

[31]Since it was the day of Preparation,
the Judeans did not want the bodies left on the cross during the sabbath,
especially because that sabbath was a day of great solemnity.
So they asked Pilate to have the legs of the crucified men broken
and the bodies removed.
[32]Then the soldiers came and broke the legs of the first
and of the other who had been crucified with him.
[33]But when they came to Jesus and saw that he was already dead,
they did not break his legs.
[34]Instead, one of the soldiers pierced his side with a spear,
and at once blood and water came out.
[35](He who saw this has testified so that you also may believe.
His testimony is true, and he knows that he tells the truth.)
[36]These things occurred so that the scripture might be fulfilled,
"None of his bones shall be broken."
[37]And again another passage of scripture says,
"They will look on the one whom they have pierced."

[38]After these things, Joseph of Arimathea, who was a disciple of Jesus,
though a secret one because of his fear of the Judeans,
asked Pilate to let him take away the body of Jesus.
Pilate gave him permission; so he came and removed his body.
[39]Nicodemus, who had at first come to Jesus by night, also came,
bringing a mixture of myrrh and aloes, weighing about a hundred pounds.
[40]They took the body of Jesus and wrapped it with the spices in linen cloths,
according to the Jewish burial custom.
[41]Now there was a garden in the place where he was crucified,
and in the garden there was a new tomb in which no one had ever been laid.
[42]And so, because it was the Jewish day of Preparation,
and the tomb was nearby, they laid Jesus there.

The Gospel of the Lord.

✝

SATURDAY IN HOLY WEEK
(for services other than the Vigil of Easter)

APRIL 6, 1996   APRIL 3, 1999   MARCH 30, 2002

FIRST READING: JOB 14:1–14
Or Lamentations 3:1-9, 19-24, following

A reading from Job:

¹"A mortal, born of woman, few of days and full of trouble,
²comes up like a flower and withers,
flees like a shadow and does not last.
³Do you fix your eyes on such a one?
Do you bring me into judgment with you?
⁴Who can bring a clean thing out of an unclean?
No one can.
⁵Since their days are determined,
and the number of their months is known to you,
and you have appointed the bounds that they cannot pass,
⁶look away from them, and desist,
that they may enjoy, like laborers, their days.

⁷"For there is hope for a tree, if it is cut down,
that it will sprout again,
and that its shoots will not cease.
⁸Though its root grows old in the earth,
and its stump dies in the ground,
⁹yet at the scent of water it will bud
and put forth branches like a young plant.
¹⁰But mortals die, and are laid low;
humans expire, and where are they?
¹¹As waters fail from a lake,
and a river wastes away and dries up,
¹²so mortals lie down and do not rise again;
until the heavens are no more, they will not awake
or be roused out of their sleep.
¹³Oh that you would hide me in Sheol,
that you would conceal me until your wrath is past,
that you would appoint me a set time, and remember me!
¹⁴If mortals die, will they live again?
All the days of my service I would wait
until my release should come."

OR: LAMENTATIONS 3:1–9, 19–24

A reading from Lamentations:

¹I am one who has seen affliction under the rod of God's wrath;
²God has driven and brought me into darkness without any light;
³against me alone God lashes out,
again and again, all day long.

⁴The LORD has made my flesh and my skin waste away,
and broken my bones;
⁵the LORD has besieged and enveloped me with bitterness and tribulation,
⁶and has made me sit in darkness like the dead of long ago.

⁷The LORD has walled me about so that I cannot escape,
and has put heavy chains on me;
⁸though I call and cry for help,
the LORD shuts out my prayer;
⁹God has blocked my ways with hewn stones,
and has made my paths crooked.

¹⁹The thought of my affliction and my homelessness
is wormwood and gall!
²⁰My soul continually thinks of it
and is bowed down within me.
²¹But this I call to mind, and therefore I have hope:

²²The steadfast love of the LORD never ceases,
the mercies of the LORD never come to an end;
²³they are new every morning;
great is your faithfulness.
²⁴"The LORD is my portion," says my soul,
"therefore in the LORD will I hope."

PSALMODY: PSALM 31:1–4, 15–16

A reading from First Peter:

¹Since therefore Christ suffered in the flesh,
arm yourselves also with the same intention
(for whoever has suffered in the flesh has finished with sin),
²so as to live for the rest of your earthly life
no longer by human desires but by the will of God.
³You have already spent enough time in doing what the Gentiles like to do,
living in licentiousness, passions, drunkenness,
revels, carousing, and lawless idolatry.
⁴They are surprised that you no longer join them
in the same excesses of dissipation, and so they blaspheme.

⁵But they will have to give an accounting to the one who stands ready
to judge the living and the dead.
⁶For this is the reason the gospel was proclaimed even to the dead,
so that, though they had been judged in the flesh as everyone is judged,
they might live in the spirit as God does.

⁷The end of all things is near;
therefore be serious and discipline yourselves for the sake of your prayers.
⁸Above all, maintain constant love for one another,
for love covers a multitude of sins.

GOSPEL: MATTHEW 27:57–66

Or John 19:38-42, following

The Holy Gospel according to Matthew, the 27th chapter:

⁵⁷When it was evening, there came a rich man from Arimathea, named Joseph,
who was also a disciple of Jesus.
⁵⁸He went to Pilate and asked for the body of Jesus;
then Pilate ordered it to be given to him.
⁵⁹So Joseph took the body and wrapped it in a clean linen cloth
⁶⁰and laid it in his own new tomb, which he had hewn in the rock.
He then rolled a great stone to the door of the tomb and went away.
⁶¹Mary Magdalene and the other Mary were there, sitting opposite the tomb.

⁶²The next day, that is, after the day of Preparation,
the chief priests and the Pharisees gathered before Pilate ⁶³and said,
"Sir, we remember what that impostor said while he was still alive,
'After three days I will rise again.'
⁶⁴Therefore command the tomb to be made secure until the third day;
otherwise his disciples may go and steal him away,
and tell the people, 'He has been raised from the dead,'
and the last deception would be worse than the first."

⁶⁵Pilate said to them,
"You have a guard of soldiers;
go, make it as secure as you can."
⁶⁶So they went with the guard and made the tomb secure by sealing the stone.

The Gospel of the Lord.

OR: JOHN 19:38–42

The Holy Gospel according to John, the 19th chapter.

³⁸Joseph of Arimathea, who was a disciple of Jesus,
though a secret one because of his fear of the Judeans,
asked Pilate to let him take away the body of Jesus.
Pilate gave him permission; so he came and removed his body.
³⁹Nicodemus, who had at first come to Jesus by night, also came,
bringing a mixture of myrrh and aloes, weighing about a hundred pounds.
⁴⁰They took the body of Jesus
and wrapped it with the spices in linen cloths,
according to the Jewish burial custom.
⁴¹Now there was a garden in the place where he was crucified,
and in the garden there was a new tomb in which no one had ever been laid.
⁴²And so, because it was the Jewish day of Preparation,
and the tomb was nearby, they laid Jesus there.

The Gospel of the Lord.

✝

THE RESURRECTION OF OUR LORD
VIGIL OF EASTER

APRIL 6, 1996   APRIL 3, 1999   MARCH 30, 2002

FIRST READING: GENESIS 1:1—2:4a
Creation

A reading from Genesis:

¹In the beginning when God created the heavens and the earth,
²the earth was a formless void and darkness covered the face of the deep,
while a wind from God swept over the face of the waters.
³Then God said,
"Let there be light"; and there was light.
⁴And God saw that the light was good;
and God separated the light from the darkness.
⁵God called the light Day,
and the darkness God called Night.
And there was evening and there was morning, the first day.

⁶And God said,
"Let there be a dome in the midst of the waters,
and let it separate the waters from the waters."
⁷So God made the dome
and separated the waters that were under the dome
from the waters that were above the dome.
And it was so.
⁸God called the dome Sky.
And there was evening and there was morning, the second day.

⁹And God said,
"Let the waters under the sky be gathered together into one place,
and let the dry land appear."
And it was so.
¹⁰God called the dry land Earth,
and the waters that were gathered together God called Seas.
And God saw that it was good.
¹¹Then God said,
"Let the earth put forth vegetation:
plants yielding seed,
and fruit trees of every kind on earth that bear fruit with the seed in it."
And it was so.
¹²The earth brought forth vegetation:

plants yielding seed of every kind,
and trees of every kind bearing fruit with the seed in it.
And God saw that it was good.
¹³And there was evening and there was morning, the third day.

¹⁴And God said,
"Let there be lights in the dome of the sky
to separate the day from the night;
and let them be for signs and for seasons and for days and years,
¹⁵and let them be lights in the dome of the sky to give light upon the earth."
And it was so.
¹⁶God made the two great lights—
the greater light to rule the day
and the lesser light to rule the night—and the stars.
¹⁷God set them in the dome of the sky to give light upon the earth,
¹⁸to rule over the day and over the night,
and to separate the light from the darkness.
And God saw that it was good.
¹⁹And there was evening and there was morning, the fourth day.

²⁰And God said,
"Let the waters bring forth swarms of living creatures,
and let birds fly above the earth across the dome of the sky."
²¹So God created the great sea monsters
and every living creature that moves,
of every kind, with which the waters swarm,
and every winged bird of every kind.
And God saw that it was good.
²²God blessed them, saying,
"Be fruitful and multiply and fill the waters in the seas,
and let birds multiply on the earth."
²³And there was evening and there was morning, the fifth day.

²⁴And God said,
"Let the earth bring forth living creatures of every kind:
cattle and creeping things and wild animals of the earth of every kind."
And it was so.
²⁵God made the wild animals of the earth of every kind,
and the cattle of every kind,
and everything that creeps upon the ground of every kind.
And God saw that it was good.

²⁶Then God said,
"Let us make humankind in our image, according to our likeness;
and let them have dominion over the fish of the sea,
and over the birds of the air,
and over the cattle, and over all the wild animals of the earth,
and over every creeping thing that creeps upon the earth."

²⁷So God created humankind in the divine image,
in the image of God humankind was created;
male and female God created them.
²⁸God blessed them, and God said to them,
"Be fruitful and multiply,
and fill the earth and subdue it;
and have dominion over the fish of the sea
and over the birds of the air
and over every living thing that moves upon the earth."
²⁹God said,
"See, I have given you every plant yielding seed
that is upon the face of all the earth,
and every tree with seed in its fruit;
you shall have them for food.
³⁰And to every beast of the earth,
and to every bird of the air,
and to everything that creeps on the earth,
everything that has the breath of life,
I have given every green plant for food."
And it was so.
³¹God saw everything that had been made,
and indeed, it was very good.
And there was evening and there was morning, the sixth day.

²:¹Thus the heavens and the earth were finished, and all their multitude.
²And on the seventh day God finished the work that had been done,
and God rested on the seventh day from all the work that had been done.
³So God blessed the seventh day and hallowed it,
because on it God rested from all the work that God had done in creation.
⁴These are the generations of the heavens and the earth
        when they were created.

RESPONSE: PSALM 136:1–9, 23–26

Antiphon: God's mercy endures forever.

SECOND READING: GENESIS 7:1–5, 11–18; 8:6–18; 9:8–13
The Flood

A reading from Genesis:

¹The LORD said to Noah,
"Go into the ark, you and all your household,
for I have seen that you alone are righteous before me in this generation.
²Take with you seven pairs of all clean animals,
the male and its mate;
and a pair of the animals that are not clean,
the male and its mate;
³and seven pairs of the birds of the air also, male and female,
to keep their kind alive on the face of all the earth.
⁴For in seven days I will send rain on the earth
for forty days and forty nights;
and every living thing that I have made
I will blot out from the face of the ground."
⁵And Noah did all that the LORD had commanded him.

¹¹In the six hundredth year of Noah's life,
in the second month, on the seventeenth day of the month,
on that day all the fountains of the great deep burst forth,
and the windows of the heavens were opened.
¹²The rain fell on the earth forty days and forty nights.
¹³On the very same day Noah with his sons,
Shem and Ham and Japheth,
and Noah's wife and the three wives of his sons entered the ark,
¹⁴they and every wild animal of every kind,
and all domestic animals of every kind,
and every creeping thing that creeps on the earth,
and every bird of every kind—every bird, every winged creature.
¹⁵They went into the ark with Noah,
two and two of all flesh in which there was the breath of life.
¹⁶And those that entered, male and female of all flesh,
went in as God had commanded him;
and the LORD shut him in.

¹⁷The flood continued forty days on the earth;
and the waters increased,
and bore up the ark, and it rose high above the earth.
¹⁸The waters swelled and increased greatly on the earth;
and the ark floated on the face of the waters.

⁸:⁶At the end of forty days
Noah opened the window of the ark that he had made
⁷and sent out the raven;
and it went to and fro until the waters were dried up from the earth.
⁸Then he sent out the dove from him,
to see if the waters had subsided from the face of the ground;
⁹but the dove found no place to set its foot,

and it returned to him to the ark,
for the waters were still on the face of the whole earth.
So Noah put out his hand and took the dove
and brought it into the ark with him.
¹⁰He waited another seven days,
and again he sent out the dove from the ark;
¹¹and the dove came back to him in the evening,
and there in its beak was a freshly plucked olive leaf;
so Noah knew that the waters had subsided from the earth.
¹²Then he waited another seven days, and sent out the dove;
and it did not return to him any more.

¹³In the six hundred first year,
in the first month, the first day of the month,
the waters were dried up from the earth;
and Noah removed the covering of the ark,
and looked, and saw that the face of the ground was drying.
¹⁴In the second month, on the twenty-seventh day of the month,
the earth was dry.
¹⁵Then God said to Noah,
¹⁶"Go out of the ark, you and your wife,
and your sons and your sons' wives with you.
¹⁷Bring out with you every living thing that is with you of all flesh—
birds and animals and every creeping thing that creeps on the earth—
so that they may abound on the earth,
and be fruitful and multiply on the earth."
¹⁸So Noah went out with his sons and his wife and his sons' wives.

⁹:⁸Then God said to Noah and to his sons with him,
⁹"As for me,
I am establishing my covenant with you and your descendants after you,
¹⁰and with every living creature that is with you,
the birds, the domestic animals,
and every animal of the earth with you,
as many as came out of the ark.
¹¹I establish my covenant with you,
that never again shall all flesh be cut off by the waters of a flood,
and never again shall there be a flood to destroy the earth."
¹²God said,
"This is the sign of the covenant that I make
between me and you and every living creature that is with you,
for all future generations:
¹³I have set my bow in the clouds,
and it shall be a sign of the covenant between me and the earth."

RESPONSE: PSALM 46

Antiphon: The LORD of hosts is with us; the God of Jacob is our stronghold.

THIRD READING: GENESIS 22:1–18
The Testing of Abraham

A reading from Genesis:

¹God tested Abraham
and said to him, "Abraham!"
And he said, "Here I am."
²God said,
"Take your son, your only son Isaac, whom you love,
and go to the land of Moriah, and offer him there as a burnt offering
on one of the mountains that I shall show you."

³So Abraham rose early in the morning,
saddled his donkey, and took two of his servants with him,
and his son Isaac;
he cut the wood for the burnt offering,
and set out and went to the place in the distance that God had shown him.
⁴On the third day Abraham looked up and saw the place far away.
⁵Then Abraham said to his servants,
"Stay here with the donkey;
the boy and I will go over there;
we will worship, and then we will come back to you."

⁶Abraham took the wood of the burnt offering
and laid it on his son Isaac,
and he himself carried the fire and the knife.
So the two of them walked on together.
⁷Isaac said to his father Abraham, "Father!"
And he said, "Here I am, my son."
Isaac said, "The fire and the wood are here,
but where is the lamb for a burnt offering?"
⁸Abraham said,
"It is God who will provide the lamb for a burnt offering, my son."
So the two of them walked on together.

⁹When they came to the place that God had shown him,
Abraham built an altar there and laid the wood in order.
He bound his son Isaac,
and laid him on the altar, on top of the wood.
¹⁰Then Abraham reached out his hand
and took the knife to kill his son.
¹¹But the angel of the LORD called to him from heaven, and said,
"Abraham, Abraham!"
And he said, "Here I am."
¹²The angel said,
"Do not lay your hand on the boy or do anything to him;
for now I know that you fear God,

since you have not withheld your son, your only son, from me."

¹³And Abraham looked up and saw a ram, caught in a thicket by its horns.
Abraham went and took the ram
and offered it up as a burnt offering instead of his son.
¹⁴So Abraham called that place "The LORD will provide";
as it is said to this day,
"On the mount of the LORD it shall be provided."

¹⁵The angel of the LORD called to Abraham a second time from heaven,
¹⁶and said,
"By myself I have sworn, says the LORD:
Because you have done this,
and have not withheld your son, your only son,
¹⁷I will indeed bless you,
and I will make your offspring as numerous as the stars of heaven
and as the sand that is on the seashore.
And your offspring shall possess the gate of their enemies,
¹⁸and by your offspring shall all the nations of the earth
gain blessing for themselves,
because you have obeyed my voice."

RESPONSE: PSALM 16

Antiphon: You will show me the path of life.

FOURTH READING: Exodus 14:10–31; 15:20–21
Israel's Deliverance at the Red Sea

A reading from Exodus:

[10]As Pharaoh drew near, the Israelites looked back,
and there were the Egyptians advancing on them.
In great fear the Israelites cried out to the LORD.
[11]They said to Moses,
"Was it because there were no graves in Egypt
that you have taken us away to die in the wilderness?
What have you done to us, bringing us out of Egypt?
[12]Is this not the very thing we told you in Egypt,
'Let us alone and let us serve the Egyptians'?
For it would have been better for us to serve the Egyptians
than to die in the wilderness."
[13]But Moses said to the people,
"Do not be afraid, stand firm,
and see the deliverance that the LORD will accomplish for you today;
for the Egyptians whom you see today you shall never see again.
[14]The LORD will fight for you,
 and you have only to keep still."

[15]Then the LORD said to Moses,
"Why do you cry out to me?
Tell the Israelites to go forward.
[16]But you lift up your staff,
and stretch out your hand over the sea and divide it,
that the Israelites may go into the sea on dry ground.
[17]Then I will harden the hearts of the Egyptians
so that they will go in after them;
and so I will gain glory for myself over Pharaoh and all his army,
his chariots, and his chariot drivers.
[18]And the Egyptians shall know that I am the LORD,
when I have gained glory for myself over Pharaoh,
his chariots, and his chariot drivers."

[19]The angel of God who was going before the Israelite army moved
and went behind them;
and the pillar of cloud moved from in front of them
and took its place behind them.
[20]It came between the army of Egypt and the army of Israel.
And so the cloud was there with the darkness,
and it lit up the night;
one did not come near the other all night.

[21]Then Moses stretched out his hand over the sea.
The LORD drove the sea back by a strong east wind all night,
and turned the sea into dry land;

and the waters were divided.
²²The Israelites went into the sea on dry ground,
the waters forming a wall for them on their right and on their left.
²³The Egyptians pursued, and went into the sea after them,
all of Pharaoh's horses, chariots, and chariot drivers.
²⁴At the morning watch
the LORD in the pillar of fire and cloud looked down upon the Egyptian army,
and threw the Egyptian army into panic,
²⁵clogging their chariot wheels so that they turned with difficulty.
The Egyptians said,
"Let us flee from the Israelites,
for the LORD is fighting for them against Egypt."

²⁶Then the LORD said to Moses,
"Stretch out your hand over the sea,
so that the water may come back upon the Egyptians,
upon their chariots and chariot drivers."
²⁷So Moses stretched out his hand over the sea,
and at dawn the sea returned to its normal depth.
As the Egyptians fled before it,
the LORD tossed the Egyptians into the sea.
²⁸The waters returned and covered the chariots and the chariot drivers,
the entire army of Pharaoh that had followed them into the sea;
not one of them remained.
²⁹But the Israelites walked on dry ground through the sea,
the waters forming a wall for them on their right and on their left.

³⁰Thus the LORD saved Israel that day from the Egyptians;
and Israel saw the Egyptians dead on the seashore.
³¹Israel saw the great work that the LORD did against the Egyptians.
So the people feared the LORD
and believed in the LORD and in Moses, the servant of the LORD.

¹⁵:²⁰Then the prophet Miriam, Aaron's sister, took a tambourine in her hand;
and all the women went out after her with tambourines and with dancing.
²¹And Miriam sang to them:
"Sing to the LORD, who has triumphed gloriously;
horse and rider have been thrown into the sea."

RESPONSE: EXODUS 15:1b–13, 17–18

Antiphon: I will sing to the LORD who has triumphed gloriously.

FIFTH READING: Isaiah 55:1–11
Salvation Offered Freely to All

A reading from Isaiah:

¹Ho, everyone who thirsts, come to the waters;
and you that have no money, come, buy and eat!
Come, buy wine and milk
without money and without price.
²Why do you spend your money for that which is not bread,
and your labor for that which does not satisfy?
Listen carefully to me, and eat what is good,
and delight yourselves in rich food.

³Incline your ear, and come to me;
listen, so that you may live.
I will make with you an everlasting covenant,
my steadfast, sure love for David.
⁴See, I made him a witness to the peoples,
a leader and commander for the peoples.
⁵See, you shall call nations that you do not know,
and nations that do not know you shall run to you,
because of the LORD your God, the Holy One of Israel,
for the LORD has glorified you.

⁶Seek the LORD while the LORD may be found,
call upon God while God is near;
⁷let the wicked forsake their way,
and the unrighteous their thoughts;
let them return to the LORD, who will have mercy on them,
and to our God, who will abundantly pardon.
⁸For my thoughts are not your thoughts,
nor are your ways my ways, says the LORD.
⁹For as the heavens are higher than the earth,
so are my ways higher than your ways
and my thoughts than your thoughts.

¹⁰For as the rain and the snow come down from heaven,
and do not return there until they have watered the earth,
making it bring forth and sprout,
giving seed to the sower and bread to the eater,
¹¹so shall my word be that goes out from my mouth;
it shall not return to me empty,
but it shall accomplish that which I purpose,
and succeed in the thing for which I sent it.

RESPONSE: Isaiah 12:2–6

Antiphon: With joy you will draw water from the wells of salvation.

SIXTH READING: PROVERBS 8:1–8, 19–21; 9:4b–6
The Wisdom of God

Alternate Reading: Baruch 3:9–15, 32—4:4 (p. 415)

A reading from Proverbs:

¹Does not Wisdom call,
and does not Understanding raise her voice?
²On the heights, beside the way,
at the crossroads she takes her stand;
³beside the gates in front of the town,
at the entrance of the portals she cries out:
⁴"To you, O people, I call,
and my cry is to all that live.
⁵O simple ones, learn prudence;
acquire intelligence, you who lack it.
⁶Hear, for I will speak noble things,
and from my lips will come what is right;
⁷for my mouth will utter truth;
wickedness is an abomination to my lips.
⁸All the words of my mouth are righteous;
there is nothing twisted or crooked in them.

¹⁹My fruit is better than gold, even fine gold,
and my yield than choice silver.
²⁰I walk in the way of righteousness,
along the paths of justice,
²¹endowing with wealth those who love me,
and filling their treasuries.
⁹:⁴ᵇTo those without sense she says,
⁵"Come, eat of my bread
and drink of the wine I have mixed.
⁶Lay aside immaturity, and live,
and walk in the way of insight."

RESPONSE: PSALM 19
Antiphon: The statutes of the LORD are just and rejoice the heart.

SEVENTH READING: Ezekiel 36:24–28
A New Heart and a New Spirit

A reading from Ezekiel:

Thus says the Lord GOD:
24I will take you from the nations,
and gather you from all the countries,
and bring you into your own land.
25I will sprinkle clean water upon you,
and you shall be clean from all your uncleannesses,
and from all your idols I will cleanse you.
26A new heart I will give you,
and a new spirit I will put within you;
and I will remove from your body the heart of stone
and give you a heart of flesh.
27I will put my spirit within you,
and make you follow my statutes and be careful to observe my ordinances.
28Then you shall live in the land that I gave to your ancestors;
and you shall be my people, and I will be your God.

RESPONSE: Psalm 42 and 43
Antiphon: My soul is athirst for the living God.

EIGHTH READING: Ezekiel 37:1–14
The Valley of the Dry Bones

A reading from Ezekiel:

1The hand of the LORD came upon me,
and brought me out by the spirit of the LORD
and set me down in the middle of a valley;
it was full of bones.
2The LORD led me all around them;
there were very many lying in the valley, and they were very dry.
3The LORD said to me,
"Mortal, can these bones live?"
I answered, "O Lord GOD, you know."

4Then the LORD said to me,
"Prophesy to these bones, and say to them:
O dry bones, hear the word of the LORD.
5Thus says the Lord GOD to these bones:
I will cause breath to enter you, and you shall live.
6I will lay sinews on you,
and will cause flesh to come upon you, and cover you with skin,

and put breath in you, and you shall live;
and you shall know that I am the LORD."

⁷So I prophesied as I had been commanded;
and as I prophesied, suddenly there was a noise, a rattling,
and the bones came together, bone to its bone.
⁸I looked, and there were sinews on them,
and flesh had come upon them, and skin had covered them;
but there was no breath in them.
⁹Then the LORD said to me,
"Prophesy to the breath, prophesy, mortal, and say to the breath:
Thus says the Lord GOD:
Come from the four winds, O breath,
and breathe upon these slain, that they may live."
¹⁰I prophesied as the LORD commanded me,
and the breath came into them,
and they lived, and stood on their feet, a vast multitude.

¹¹Then the LORD said to me,
"Mortal, these bones are the whole house of Israel.
They say, 'Our bones are dried up, and our hope is lost;
we are cut off completely.'
¹²Therefore prophesy, and say to them,
Thus says the Lord GOD:
I am going to open your graves,
and bring you up from your graves, O my people;
and I will bring you back to the land of Israel.
¹³And you shall know that I am the LORD,
when I open your graves,
and bring you up from your graves, O my people.
¹⁴I will put my spirit within you, and you shall live,
and I will place you on your own soil;
then you shall know that I, the LORD, have spoken and will act,"
says the LORD.

RESPONSE: PSALM 143

Antiphon: Revive me, O LORD, for your name's sake.

NINTH READING: Zephaniah 3:14–20
The Gathering of God's People

A reading from Zephaniah:

¹⁴Sing aloud, O daughter Zion;
shout, O Israel!
Rejoice and exult with all your heart, O daughter Jerusalem!
¹⁵The LORD has taken away the judgments against you,
and has turned away your enemies.
The Sovereign of Israel, the LORD, is in your midst;
you shall fear disaster no more.
¹⁶On that day it shall be said to Jerusalem:
Do not fear, O Zion;
do not let your hands grow weak.
¹⁷The LORD, your God, is in your midst,
a warrior who gives victory;
the LORD will rejoice over you with gladness,
and will renew you with love;
the LORD will exult over you with loud singing
¹⁸as on a day of festival.

I will remove disaster from you,
so that you will not bear reproach for it.
¹⁹I will deal with all your oppressors at that time.
And I will save the lame and gather the outcast,
and I will change their shame into praise
and renown in all the earth.
²⁰At that time I will bring you home,
at the time when I gather you;
for I will make you renowned and praised
among all the peoples of the earth,
when I restore your fortunes
before your eyes, says the LORD.

RESPONSE: Psalm 98
Antiphon: Lift up your voice, rejoice and sing.

Three additional readings from the Hebrew Scriptures follow on pp. 148–152.
The New Testament and Gospel readings continue on p. 153.

TENTH READING: JONAH 3:1–10
The Call of Jonah

A reading from Jonah.

The word from the LORD came to Jonah a second time, saying,
²"Get up, go to Nineveh, that great city,
and proclaim to it the message that I tell you."
³So Jonah set out and went to Nineveh, according to the word of the LORD.

Now Nineveh was an exceedingly large city, a three days' walk across.
⁴Jonah began to go into the city, going a day's walk.
And he cried out,
"Forty days more, and Nineveh shall be overthrown!"
⁵And the people of Nineveh believed God;
they proclaimed a fast,
and everyone, great and small, put on sackcloth.

⁶When the news reached the king of Nineveh,
he rose from his throne, removed his robe,
covered himself with sackcloth, and sat in ashes.
⁷Then he had a proclamation made in Nineveh:
"By the decree of the king and his nobles:
No human being or animal, no herd or flock, shall taste anything.
They shall not feed, nor shall they drink water.
⁸Human beings and animals shall be covered with sackcloth,
and they shall cry mightily to God.
All shall turn from their evil ways
and from the violence that is in their hands.
⁹Who knows? God may relent and have second thoughts,
turning away from fierce anger, so that we do not perish."
¹⁰When God saw what they did,
how they turned from their evil ways,
God had second thoughts about the calamity
that God had said would be done to them;
and God did not do it.

RESPONSE: JONAH 2:1–3 [4–6] 7–9
Antiphon: Deliverance belongs to the LORD.

ELEVENTH READING: Deuteronomy 31:19–30
The Song of Moses

A reading from Deuteronomy.

19Now therefore write this song,
and teach it to the Israelites;
put it in their mouths,
in order that this song may be a witness for me against the Israelites.

20For when I have brought them into the land flowing with milk and honey,
which I promised on oath to their ancestors,
and they have eaten their fill and grown fat,
they will turn to other deities and serve them,
despising me and breaking my covenant.
21And when many terrible troubles come upon them,
this song will confront them as a witness,
because it will not be lost from the mouths of their descendants.
For I know what they are inclined to do even now,
before I have brought them into the land that I promised them on oath."
22That very day Moses wrote this song and taught it to the Israelites.

23Then the LORD commissioned Joshua son of Nun and said,
"Be strong and bold,
for you shall bring the Israelites into the land that I promised them;
I will be with you."

24When Moses had finished writing down in a book
the words of this law to the very end,
25Moses commanded the Levites who carried the ark of the covenant of the
        LORD, saying,
26"Take this book of the law
and put it beside the ark of the covenant of the LORD your God;
let it remain there as a witness against you.
27For I knew well how rebellious and stubborn you are.
If you already have been so rebellious toward the LORD
while I am still alive among you,
how much more after my death!
28Assemble to me all the elders of your tribes and your officials,
so that I may recite these words in their hearing
and call heaven and earth to witness against them.
29For I know that after my death you will surely act corruptly,
turning aside from the way that I have commanded you.
In time to come trouble will befall you,
because you will do what is evil in the sight of the LORD,
provoking the LORD to anger through the work of your hands."

³⁰Then Moses recited the words of this song, to the very end,
in the hearing of the whole assembly of Israel.

RESPONSE: Deuteronomy 32:1–4, 36a, 43a

Antiphon: The Lord *will give his people justice.*

TWELFTH READING: Daniel 3:1–29

A reading from Daniel.

King Nebuchadnezzar made a golden statue whose height was sixty cubits
and whose width was six cubits;
he set it up on the plain of Dura in the province of Babylon.
²Then King Nebuchadnezzar sent for the satraps, the prefects,
    and the governors,
the counselors, the treasurers, the justices, the magistrates,
and all the officials of the provinces to assemble
and come to the dedication of the statue
that King Nebuchadnezzar had set up.

³So the satraps, the prefects, and the governors,
the counselors, the treasurers, the justices, the magistrates,
and all the officials of the provinces,
assembled for the dedication of the statue
that King Nebuchadnezzar had set up.
When they were standing before the statue that Nebuchadnezzar had set up,
⁴the herald proclaimed aloud,
"You are commanded, O peoples, nations, and languages,
⁵that when you hear the sound of the horn, pipe, lyre,
trigon, harp, drum, and entire musical ensemble,
you are to fall down and worship the golden statue
that King Nebuchadnezzar has set up.
⁶Whoever does not fall down and worship
shall immediately be thrown into a furnace of blazing fire."
⁷Therefore, as soon as all the peoples heard the sound of the horn, pipe, lyre,
trigon, harp, drum, and entire musical ensemble,
all the peoples, nations, and languages fell down
and worshiped the golden statue that King Nebuchadnezzar had set up.

⁸Accordingly, at this time
certain Chaldeans came forward and denounced the Jews.
⁹They said to King Nebuchadnezzar,
"O king, live forever!
¹⁰You, O king, have made a decree,
that everyone who hears the sound of the horn, pipe, lyre,
trigon, harp, drum, and entire musical ensemble,
shall fall down and worship the golden statue,

¹¹and whoever does not fall down and worship
shall be thrown into a furnace of blazing fire.
¹²There are certain Jews
whom you have appointed over the affairs of the province of Babylon:
Shadrach, Meshach, and Abednego.
These pay no heed to you, O king.
They do not serve your gods
and they do not worship the golden statue that you have set up."

¹³Then Nebuchadnezzar in furious rage
commanded that Shadrach, Meshach, and Abednego be brought in;
so they brought those men before the king.
¹⁴Nebuchadnezzar said to them,
"Is it true, O Shadrach, Meshach, and Abednego,
that you do not serve my gods
and you do not worship the golden statue that I have set up?
¹⁵Now if you are ready when you hear the sound of the horn, pipe, lyre,
trigon, harp, drum, and entire musical ensemble
to fall down and worship the statue that I have made,
well and good.
But if you do not worship,
you shall immediately be thrown into a furnace of blazing fire,
and who is the god that will deliver you out of my hands?"

¹⁶Shadrach, Meshach, and Abednego answered the king,
"O Nebuchadnezzar,
we have no need to present a defense to you in this matter.
¹⁷If our God whom we serve is able to deliver us
from the furnace of blazing fire and out of your hand, O king,
let God deliver us.
¹⁸But if not, be it known to you, O king,
that we will not serve your gods
and we will not worship the golden statue that you have set up."

¹⁹Then Nebuchadnezzar was so filled with rage
against Shadrach, Meshach, and Abednego
that his face was distorted.
He ordered the furnace heated up seven times more than was customary,
²⁰and ordered some of the strongest guards in his army
to bind Shadrach, Meshach, and Abednego
and to throw them into the furnace of blazing fire.
²¹So the men were bound, still wearing their tunics,
their trousers, their hats, and their other garments,
and they were thrown into the furnace of blazing fire.
²²Because the king's command was urgent and the furnace was so overheated,
the raging flames killed the men who lifted Shadrach, Meshach, and
Abednego.

²³But the three men, Shadrach, Meshach, and Abednego, fell down,
bound, into the furnace of blazing fire.

²⁴Then King Nebuchadnezzar was astonished and rose up quickly.
He said to his counselors,
"Was it not three men that we threw bound into the fire?"
They answered the king, "True, O king."
²⁵He replied, "But I see four men unbound,
walking in the middle of the fire,
and they are not hurt;
and the fourth has the appearance of a god."

²⁶Nebuchadnezzar then approached the door of the furnace of blazing fire
        and said,
"Shadrach, Meshach, and Abednego,
servants of the Most High God,
come out! Come here!"
So Shadrach, Meshach, and Abednego came out from the fire.
²⁷And the satraps, the prefects, the governors,
and the king's counselors gathered together
and saw that the fire had not had any power over the bodies of those men;
the hair of their heads was not singed,
their tunics were not harmed,
and not even the smell of fire came from them.

²⁸Nebuchadnezzar said,
"Blessed be the God of Shadrach, Meshach, and Abednego,
who has sent an angel to deliver these servants who trusted in their God.
They disobeyed the king's command and yielded up their bodies
rather than serve and worship any god except their own God.
²⁹Therefore I make a decree:
Any people, nation, or language that utters blasphemy
against the God of Shadrach, Meshach, and Abednego
shall be torn limb from limb,
and their houses laid in ruins;
for there is no other god who is able to deliver in this way."

RESPONSE: SONG OF THE THREE YOUNG MEN 35–65

Antiphon: Sing praise to the LORD *and highly exalt him forever.*

NEW TESTAMENT READING: ROMANS 6:3–11

A reading from Romans:

³Do you not know that all of us who have been baptized into Christ Jesus
were baptized into his death?
⁴Therefore we have been buried with Christ by baptism into death,
so that, just as Christ was raised from the dead by the glory of the Father,
so we too might walk in newness of life.

⁵For if we have been united with Christ in a death like his,
we will certainly be united with him in a resurrection like his.
⁶We know that our old self was crucified with Christ
so that the body of sin might be destroyed,
and we might no longer be enslaved to sin.
⁷For whoever has died is freed from sin.
⁸But if we have died with Christ,
we believe that we will also live with him.
⁹We know that Christ, being raised from the dead, will never die again;
death no longer has dominion over him.
¹⁰The death he died, he died to sin, once for all;
but the life he lives, he lives to God.

¹¹So you also must consider yourselves dead to sin
and alive to God in Christ Jesus.

RESPONSE: PSALM 114
Antiphon: Tremble, O earth, at the presence of the LORD.

The Holy Gospel according to Matthew, the 28th chapter.

[1]After the sabbath, as the first day of the week was dawning,
Mary Magdalene and the other Mary went to see the tomb.
[2]And suddenly there was a great earthquake;
for an angel of the Lord, descending from heaven,
came and rolled back the stone and sat on it.
[3]The appearance of the angel was like lightning, and its clothing white as snow.
[4]For fear of the angel the guards shook and became as if dead.
[5]But the angel said to the women,
"Do not be afraid;
I know that you are looking for Jesus who was crucified.
[6]He is not here; for he has been raised, as he said.
Come, see the place where he lay.
[7]Then go quickly and tell his disciples,
'He has been raised from the dead,
and indeed he is going ahead of you to Galilee; there you will see him.'
This is my message for you."

[8]So the women left the tomb quickly with fear and great joy,
and ran to tell his disciples.
[9]Suddenly Jesus met them and said, "Greetings!"
And they came to him, took hold of his feet, and worshiped him.
[10]Then Jesus said to them,
"Do not be afraid;
go and tell my brothers to go to Galilee; there they will see me."

The Gospel of the Lord.

✚

SEASON OF EASTER

✝

THE RESURRECTION OF OUR LORD
EASTER DAY

APRIL 7, 1996   APRIL 4, 1999   MARCH 31, 2002

FIRST READING: ACTS 10:34–43
Or Jeremiah 31:1-6, following

A reading from Acts:

[34]Peter began to speak to the people:
"I truly understand that God shows no partiality,
[35]but in every nation anyone who is God-fearing and does what is right
is acceptable to God.

[36]"You know the message God sent to the people of Israel,
preaching peace by Jesus Christ—
who is Lord of all.
[37]That message spread throughout Judea,
beginning in Galilee after the baptism that John announced:
[38]how God anointed Jesus of Nazareth with the Holy Spirit and with power;
how Jesus went about doing good and healing all who were oppressed
        by the devil,
for God was with him.
[39]We are witnesses to all that he did both in Judea and in Jerusalem.
They put him to death by hanging him on a tree;
[40]but God raised him on the third day
and allowed him to appear, [41]not to all the people
but to us who were chosen by God as witnesses,
and who ate and drank with him after he rose from the dead.

[42]"Jesus commanded us to preach to the people
and to testify that he is the one ordained by God
as judge of the living and the dead.
[43]All the prophets testify about him that everyone who believes in him
receives forgiveness of sins through his name."

OR: JEREMIAH 31:1–6

A reading from Jeremiah:

¹At that time, says the LORD,
I will be the God of all the families of Israel,
and they shall be my people.
²Thus says the LORD:
The people who survived the sword found grace in the wilderness;
when Israel sought for rest,
³the LORD appeared to them from far away.
I have loved you with an everlasting love;
therefore I have continued my faithfulness to you.

⁴Again I will build you, and you shall be built, O virgin Israel!
Again you shall take your tambourines,
and go forth in the dance of the merrymakers.
⁵Again you shall plant vineyards on the mountains of Samaria;
the planters shall plant, and shall enjoy the fruit.
⁶For there shall be a day
when sentinels will call in the hill country of Ephraim:
"Come, let us go up to Zion, to the LORD our God."

PSALMODY: PSALM 118:1–2, 14–24

SECOND READING: COLOSSIANS 3:1–4
Or Acts 10:34-43, following

A reading from Colossians:

¹If you have been raised with Christ,
seek the things that are above,
where Christ is, seated at the right hand of God.
²Set your minds on things that are above,
not on things that are on earth,
³for you have died, and your life is hidden with Christ in God.
⁴When Christ who is your life is revealed,
then you also will be revealed with him in glory.

A reading from Acts:

[34]Peter began to speak to the people:
"I truly understand that God shows no partiality,
[35]but in every nation anyone who is God-fearing and does what is right
is acceptable to God.

[36]"You know the message God sent to the people of Israel,
preaching peace by Jesus Christ,
who is Lord of all.
[37]That message spread throughout Judea,
beginning in Galilee after the baptism that John announced:
[38]how God anointed Jesus of Nazareth with the Holy Spirit and with power;
how Jesus went about doing good and healing all who were oppressed
          by the devil,
for God was with him.
[39]We are witnesses to all that he did both in Judea and in Jerusalem.
They put him to death by hanging him on a tree;
[40]but God raised him on the third day
and allowed him to appear, [41]not to all the people
but to us who were chosen by God as witnesses,
and who ate and drank with him after he rose from the dead.

[42]"Jesus commanded us to preach to the people
and to testify that he is the one ordained by God
as judge of the living and the dead.
[43]All the prophets testify about him that everyone who believes in him
receives forgiveness of sins through his name."

Or Matthew 28:1-10, following

The Holy Gospel according to John, the 20th chapter.

[1]Early on the first day of the week, while it was still dark,
Mary Magdalene came to the tomb
and saw that the stone had been removed from the tomb.
[2]So she ran and went to Simon Peter and the other disciple,
the one whom Jesus loved, and said to them,
"They have taken the Lord out of the tomb,
and we do not know where they have laid him."

[3]Then Peter and the other disciple set out and went toward the tomb.
[4]The two were running together,
but the other disciple outran Peter and reached the tomb first.
[5]He bent down to look in and saw the linen wrappings lying there,
but he did not go in.
[6]Then Simon Peter came, following him, and went into the tomb.
He saw the linen wrappings lying there,
[7]and the cloth that had been on Jesus' head,
not lying with the linen wrappings but rolled up in a place by itself.
[8]Then the other disciple, who reached the tomb first,
also went in, and he saw and believed;
[9]for as yet they did not understand the scripture,
that Jesus must rise from the dead.
[10]Then the disciples returned to their homes.

[11]But Mary stood weeping outside the tomb.
As she wept, she bent over to look into the tomb;
[12]and she saw two angels in white,
sitting where the body of Jesus had been lying,
one at the head and the other at the feet.
[13]They said to her, "Woman, why are you weeping?"
She said to them,
"They have taken away my Lord,
and I do not know where they have laid him."
[14]When she had said this, she turned around and saw Jesus standing there,
but she did not know that it was Jesus.
[15]Jesus said to her,
"Woman, why are you weeping? Whom are you looking for?"
Supposing him to be the gardener, she said to him,
"Sir, if you have carried him away,
tell me where you have laid him, and I will take him away."
[16]Jesus said to her, "Mary!"
She turned and said to him in Hebrew,
"Rabbouni!" (which means Teacher).
[17]Jesus said to her,

"Do not hold on to me, because I have not yet ascended to the Father.
But go to my brothers and say to them,
'I am ascending to my Father and your Father,
to my God and your God.'"

18Mary Magdalene went and announced to the disciples,
"I have seen the Lord";
and she told them that Jesus had said these things to her.

The Gospel of the Lord.

OR: MATTHEW 28:1–10

The Holy Gospel according to Matthew, the 28th chapter.

1After the sabbath, as the first day of the week was dawning,
Mary Magdalene and the other Mary went to see the tomb.
2And suddenly there was a great earthquake;
for an angel of the Lord, descending from heaven,
came and rolled back the stone and sat on it.
3The appearance of the angel was like lightning, and its clothing white as snow.
4For fear of the angel
the guards shook and became as if dead.
5But the angel said to the women,
"Do not be afraid;
I know that you are looking for Jesus who was crucified.
6He is not here; for he has been raised, as he said.
Come, see the place where he lay.
7Then go quickly and tell his disciples,
'He has been raised from the dead,
and indeed he is going ahead of you to Galilee; there you will see him.'
This is my message for you."

8So the women left the tomb quickly with fear and great joy,
and ran to tell his disciples.
9Suddenly Jesus met them and said, "Greetings!"
And they came to him, took hold of his feet, and worshiped him.
10Then Jesus said to them,
"Do not be afraid;
go and tell my brothers to go to Galilee; there they will see me."

The Gospel of the Lord.

THE RESURRECTION OF OUR LORD
EASTER EVENING

APRIL 7, 1996   APRIL 4, 1999   MARCH 31, 2002

FIRST READING: ISAIAH 25:6–9

A reading from Isaiah:

⁶On this mountain the LORD of hosts will make for all peoples
a feast of rich food, a feast of well-aged wines,
of rich food filled with marrow, of well-aged wines strained clear.
⁷And the LORD will destroy on this mountain
the shroud that is cast over all peoples,
the sheet that is spread over all nations;
the LORD will swallow up death forever.
⁸Then the Lord GOD will wipe away the tears from all faces,
and the disgrace of the chosen people God will take away from all the earth,
for the LORD has spoken.

⁹It will be said on that day,
Lo, this is our God, for whom we have waited, so that God might save us.
This is the LORD for whom we have waited;
let us be glad and rejoice in the salvation of the LORD.

PSALMODY: PSALM 114

SECOND READING: 1 CORINTHIANS 5:6b–8

A reading from First Corinthians:

⁶ᵇDo you not know that a little yeast leavens the whole batch of dough?
⁷Clean out the old yeast so that you may be a new batch,
as you really are unleavened.
For our paschal lamb, Christ, has been sacrificed.
⁸Therefore, let us celebrate the festival,
not with the old yeast, the yeast of malice and evil,
but with the unleavened bread of sincerity and truth.

The Holy Gospel according to Luke, the 24th chapter.

[13]Now on that same day when Jesus had appeared to Mary Magdalene,
two of them were going to a village called Emmaus,
about seven miles from Jerusalem,
[14]and talking with each other about all these things that had happened.
[15]While they were talking and discussing,
Jesus himself came near and went with them,
[16]but their eyes were kept from recognizing him.
[17]And Jesus said to them,
"What are you discussing with each other while you walk along?"
They stood still, looking sad.
[18]Then one of them, whose name was Cleopas, answered him,
"Are you the only stranger in Jerusalem
who does not know the things that have taken place there in these days?"
[19]He asked them, "What things?"
They replied, "The things about Jesus of Nazareth,
who was a prophet mighty in deed and word before God and all the people,
[20]and how our chief priests and leaders
handed him over to be condemned to death and crucified him.
[21]But we had hoped that he was the one to redeem Israel.
Yes, and besides all this,
it is now the third day since these things took place.
[22]Moreover, some women of our group astounded us.
They were at the tomb early this morning,
[23]and when they did not find his body there, they came back
and told us that they had indeed seen a vision of angels
who said that he was alive.
[24]Some of those who were with us went to the tomb
and found it just as the women had said;
but they did not see him."

[25]Then Jesus said to them,
"Oh, how foolish you are,
and how slow of heart to believe all that the prophets have declared!
[26]Was it not necessary that the Messiah should suffer these things
and then enter into his glory?"
[27]Then beginning with Moses and all the prophets,
he interpreted to them the things about himself in all the scriptures.

[28]As they came near the village to which they were going,
he walked ahead as if he were going on.
[29]But they urged him strongly, saying,
"Stay with us,
because it is almost evening and the day is now nearly over."
So he went in to stay with them.

³⁰When Jesus was at the table with them,
he took bread, blessed and broke it, and gave it to them.
³¹Then their eyes were opened, and they recognized him;
and he vanished from their sight.
³²They said to each other,
"Were not our hearts burning within us
while he was talking to us on the road,
while he was opening the scriptures to us?"

³³That same hour they got up and returned to Jerusalem;
and they found the eleven and their companions gathered together.
³⁴They were saying,
"The Lord has risen indeed, and has appeared to Simon!"
³⁵Then they told what had happened on the road,
and how Jesus had been made known to them in the breaking of the bread.

³⁶While they were talking about this,
Jesus himself stood among them and said to them,
"Peace be with you."
³⁷They were startled and terrified,
and thought that they were seeing a ghost.
³⁸He said to them,
"Why are you frightened, and why do doubts arise in your hearts?
³⁹Look at my hands and my feet; see that it is I myself.
Touch me and see;
for a ghost does not have flesh and bones as you see that I have."
⁴⁰And when he had said this, he showed them his hands and his feet.
⁴¹While in their joy they were disbelieving and still wondering,
he said to them,
"Have you anything here to eat?"
⁴²They gave him a piece of broiled fish,
⁴³and he took it and ate in their presence.

⁴⁴Then Jesus said to them,
"These are my words that I spoke to you while I was still with you—
that everything written about me
in the law of Moses, the prophets, and the psalms must be fulfilled."
⁴⁵Then he opened their minds to understand the scriptures,
⁴⁶and said to them,
"Thus it is written,
that the Messiah is to suffer and to rise from the dead on the third day,
⁴⁷and that repentance and forgiveness of sins
is to be proclaimed in his name to all nations, beginning from Jerusalem.
⁴⁸You are witnesses of these things.
⁴⁹And see, I am sending upon you what my Father promised;
so stay here in the city until you have been clothed with power from on high."

The Gospel of the Lord.

Second Sunday of Easter

APRIL 14, 1996   APRIL 11, 1999   APRIL 7, 2002

FIRST READING: ACTS 2:14a, 22–32

A reading from Acts:

¹⁴Peter, standing with the eleven, raised his voice and addressed the people:

²²"You that are Israelites, listen to what I have to say:
Jesus of Nazareth, a man attested to you by God
with deeds of power, wonders, and signs that God did through him among you,
as you yourselves know—
²³this Jesus, handed over to you according to the definite plan and
    foreknowledge of God,
you crucified and killed by the hands of those outside the law.
²⁴But God raised him up, having freed him from death,
because it was impossible for him to be held in its power.

²⁵"For David says concerning him,
'I saw the Lord always before me,
who is at my right hand so that I will not be shaken;
²⁶therefore my heart was glad, and my tongue rejoiced;
moreover my flesh will live in hope.
²⁷For you will not abandon my soul to Hades,
or let your Holy One experience corruption.
²⁸You have made known to me the ways of life;
you will make me full of gladness with your presence.'

²⁹"Fellow Israelites,
I may say to you confidently of our ancestor David
that he both died and was buried, and his tomb is with us to this day.
³⁰Since he was a prophet,
he knew that God had sworn with an oath to him
that God would put one of his descendants on his throne.
³¹Foreseeing this, David spoke of the resurrection of the Messiah, saying,
'He was not abandoned to Hades, nor did his flesh experience corruption.'
³²This Jesus God raised up, and of that all of us are witnesses."

PSALMODY: Psalm 16

SECOND READING: 1 Peter 1:3–9

A reading from First Peter:

³Blessed be the God and Father of our Lord Jesus Christ,
by whose great mercy we have been given a new birth
into a living hope through the resurrection of Jesus Christ from the dead,
⁴and into an inheritance that is imperishable, undefiled, and unfading,
kept in heaven for you,
⁵who are being protected by the power of God
through faith for a salvation ready to be revealed in the last time.
⁶In this you rejoice,
even if now for a little while you have had to suffer various trials,
⁷so that the genuineness of your faith—
being more precious than gold that, though perishable,
is tested by fire—
may be found to result in praise and glory and honor
when Jesus Christ is revealed.

⁸Although you have not seen him, you love him;
and even though you do not see him now,
you believe in him and rejoice with an indescribable and glorious joy,
⁹for you are receiving the outcome of your faith,
the salvation of your souls.

GOSPEL: John 20:19–31

The Holy Gospel according to John, the 20th chapter.

¹⁹When it was evening on that day, the first day of the week,
and the doors of the house where the disciples had met
were locked for fear of the Judeans,
Jesus came and stood among them and said,
"Peace be with you."
²⁰After he said this, he showed them his hands and his side.
Then the disciples rejoiced when they saw the Lord.
²¹Jesus said to them again,
"Peace be with you.
As the Father has sent me, so I send you."
²²When he had said this, he breathed on them and said to them,
"Receive the Holy Spirit.
²³If you forgive the sins of any, they are forgiven them;
if you retain the sins of any, they are retained."

[24]But Thomas (who was called the Twin), one of the twelve,
was not with them when Jesus came.
[25]So the other disciples told him, "We have seen the Lord."
But he said to them,
"Unless I see the mark of the nails in his hands,
and put my finger in the mark of the nails and my hand in his side,
I will not believe."

[26]A week later his disciples were again in the house,
and Thomas was with them.
Although the doors were shut,
Jesus came and stood among them and said,
"Peace be with you."
[27]Then he said to Thomas,
"Put your finger here and see my hands.
Reach out your hand and put it in my side.
Do not doubt but believe."
[28]Thomas said to Jesus,
"My Lord and my God!"
[29]Jesus said to him,
"Have you believed because you have seen me?
Blessed are those who have not seen and yet have come to believe."

[30]Now Jesus did many other signs in the presence of his disciples,
which are not written in this book.
[31]But these are written
so that you may come to believe that Jesus is the Messiah, the Son of God,
and that through believing you may have life in his name.

The Gospel of the Lord.

THIRD SUNDAY OF EASTER

APRIL 21, 1996   APRIL 18, 1999   APRIL 14, 2002

FIRST READING: ACTS 2:14a, 36–41

A reading from Acts:

[14]Peter, standing with the eleven, raised his voice and addressed the people . . .

[36]"Therefore let the entire house of Israel know with certainty
that God has made this Jesus whom you crucified
to be both Lord and Messiah."

[37]Now when they heard this,
they were cut to the heart and said to Peter and to the other apostles,
"Brothers, what should we do?"
[38]Peter said to them,
"Repent, and be baptized every one of you
in the name of Jesus Christ
so that your sins may be forgiven;
and you will receive the gift of the Holy Spirit.
[39]For the promise is for you, for your children,
and for all who are far away,
everyone whom the Lord our God calls."
[40]And Peter testified with many other arguments and exhorted them, saying,
"Save yourselves from this corrupt generation."

[41]So those who welcomed his message were baptized,
and that day about three thousand persons were added.

PSALMODY: PSALM 116:1–4, 12–19   *Psalm:1–3, 10–17*   LBW/BCP

SECOND READING: 1 PETER 1:17–23

A reading from First Peter:

[17]If you invoke as Father
the one who judges all people impartially according to their deeds,
live in reverent fear during the time of your exile.
[18]You know that you were ransomed from the futile ways
inherited from your ancestors,
not with perishable things like silver or gold,
[19]but with the precious blood of Christ,
like that of a lamb without defect or blemish.
[20]Christ was destined before the foundation of the world,
but was revealed at the end of the ages for your sake.
[21]Through Christ you have come to trust in God,
who raised him from the dead and gave him glory,
so that your faith and hope are set on God.

[22]Now that you have purified your souls by your obedience to the truth
so that you have genuine mutual love,
love one another deeply from the heart.
[23]You have been born anew,
not of perishable but of imperishable seed,
through the living and enduring word of God.

GOSPEL: LUKE 24:13–35

The Holy Gospel according to Luke, the 24th chapter.

[13]Now on that same day when Jesus had appeared to Mary Magdalene,
two of them were going to a village called Emmaus,
about seven miles from Jerusalem,
[14]and talking with each other about all these things that had happened.
[15]While they were talking and discussing,
Jesus himself came near and went with them,
[16]but their eyes were kept from recognizing him.
[17]And Jesus said to them,
"What are you discussing with each other while you walk along?"
They stood still, looking sad.
[18]Then one of them, whose name was Cleopas, answered him,
"Are you the only stranger in Jerusalem
who does not know the things that have taken place there in these days?"
[19]He asked them, "What things?"
They replied, "The things about Jesus of Nazareth,
who was a prophet mighty in deed and word before God and all the people,
[20]and how our chief priests and leaders
handed him over to be condemned to death and crucified him.
[21]But we had hoped that he was the one to redeem Israel.

Yes, and besides all this,
it is now the third day since these things took place.
²²Moreover, some women of our group astounded us.
They were at the tomb early this morning,
²³and when they did not find his body there, they came back
and told us that they had indeed seen a vision of angels
who said that he was alive.
²⁴Some of those who were with us went to the tomb
and found it just as the women had said;
but they did not see him."

²⁵Then Jesus said to them,
"Oh, how foolish you are,
and how slow of heart to believe all that the prophets have declared!
²⁶Was it not necessary that the Messiah should suffer these things
and then enter into his glory?"
²⁷Then beginning with Moses and all the prophets,
he interpreted to them the things about himself in all the scriptures.

²⁸As they came near the village to which they were going,
he walked ahead as if he were going on.
²⁹But they urged him strongly, saying,
"Stay with us,
because it is almost evening and the day is now nearly over."
So he went in to stay with them.

³⁰When Jesus was at the table with them,
he took bread, blessed and broke it, and gave it to them.
³¹Then their eyes were opened, and they recognized him;
and he vanished from their sight.
³²They said to each other,
"Were not our hearts burning within us
while he was talking to us on the road,
while he was opening the scriptures to us?"

³³That same hour they got up and returned to Jerusalem;
and they found the eleven and their companions gathered together.
³⁴They were saying,
"The Lord has risen indeed, and has appeared to Simon!"
³⁵Then they told what had happened on the road,
and how Jesus had been made known to them in the breaking of the bread.

The Gospel of the Lord.

✟

FOURTH SUNDAY OF EASTER

APRIL 28, 1996   APRIL 25, 1999   APRIL 21, 2002

FIRST READING: ACTS 2:42–47

A reading from Acts:

[42]The baptized devoted themselves to the apostles' teaching and common life,
to the breaking of bread and the prayers.
[43]Awe came upon everyone,
because many wonders and signs were being done by the apostles.
[44]All who believed were together and had all things in common;
[45]they would sell their possessions and goods
and distribute the proceeds to all, as any had need.
[46]Day by day, as they spent much time together in the temple,
they broke bread at home and ate their food with glad and generous hearts,
[47]praising God and having the goodwill of all the people.
And day by day the Lord added to their number those who were being saved.

PSALMODY: PSALM 23

SECOND READING: 1 PETER 2:19–25

A reading from First Peter:

[19]It is a credit to you if, being aware of God,
you endure pain while suffering unjustly.
[20]If you endure when you are beaten for doing wrong, what credit is that?
But if you endure when you do right and suffer for it,
you have God's approval.
[21]For to this you have been called,
because Christ also suffered for you, leaving you an example,
so that you should follow in his steps.

[22]"He committed no sin,
and no deceit was found in his mouth."
[23]When abused, Christ did not return abuse;
when suffering, he did not threaten;
but he entrusted himself to the one who judges justly.
[24]Christ himself bore our sins in his body on the tree,
so that, free from sins,

we might live for righteousness;
by his wounds you have been healed.
²⁵For you were going astray like sheep,
but now you have returned to the shepherd and guardian of your souls.

GOSPEL: JOHN 10:1–10

The Holy Gospel according to John, the tenth chapter.

Jesus said:
¹"Very truly, I tell you,
anyone who does not enter the sheepfold by the gate
but climbs in by another way is a thief and a bandit.
²The one who enters by the gate is the shepherd of the sheep.
³The gatekeeper opens the gate for the sheperd, and the sheep hear his voice.
He calls his own sheep by name and leads them out.
⁴When he has brought out all his own, he goes ahead of them,
and the sheep follow him because they know his voice.
⁵They will not follow a stranger,
but they will run away
because they do not know the voice of strangers."

⁶Jesus used this figure of speech with them,
but they did not understand what he was saying to them.
⁷So again Jesus said to them,
"Very truly, I tell you, I am the gate for the sheep.
⁸All who came before me are thieves and bandits;
but the sheep did not listen to them.
⁹I am the gate.
Whoever enters by me will be saved,
and will come in and go out and find pasture.
¹⁰The thief comes only to steal and kill and destroy.
I came that they may have life, and have it abundantly."

The Gospel of the Lord.

FIFTH SUNDAY OF EASTER

FIRST READING: Acts 7:55–60

A reading from Acts:

[55]Filled with the Holy Spirit,
Stephen gazed into heaven and saw the glory of God
and Jesus standing at the right hand of God.
[56]"Look," he said,
"I see the heavens opened
and the Son-of-Man standing at the right hand of God!"
[57]But they covered their ears,
and with a loud shout all rushed together against him.
[58]Then they dragged Stephen out of the city and began to stone him;
and the witnesses laid their coats at the feet of a young man named Saul.
[59]While they were stoning Stephen, he prayed,
"Lord Jesus, receive my spirit."
[60]Then he knelt down and cried out in a loud voice,
"Lord, do not hold this sin against them."
When he had said this, he died.

PSALMODY: Psalm 31:1–5, 15–16

SECOND READING: 1 PETER 2:2–10

A reading from First Peter:

[2]Like newborn infants, long for the pure, spiritual milk,
so that by it you may grow into salvation—
[3]if indeed you have tasted that the Lord is good.

[4]Come to the Lord, a living stone,
though rejected by mortals yet chosen and precious in God's sight,
and [5]like living stones, let yourselves be built into a spiritual house,
to be a holy priesthood,
to offer spiritual sacrifices acceptable to God through Jesus Christ.
[6]For it stands in scripture:
"See, I am laying in Zion a stone,
a cornerstone chosen and precious;
and whoever has faith in it will not be put to shame."
[7]To you then who believe, it is precious;
but for those who do not believe,
"The stone that the builders rejected
has become the very head of the corner,"
[8]and "A stone that makes them stumble,
and a rock that makes them fall."
They stumble because they disobey the word, as they were destined to do.

[9]But you are a chosen race, a royal priesthood, a holy nation,
God's own people,
in order that you may proclaim the mighty acts of the one
who called you out of darkness into the marvelous light of God.
[10]Once you were not a people,
but now you are God's people;
once you had not received mercy,
but now you have received mercy.

GOSPEL: JOHN 14:1–14

The Holy Gospel according to John, the 14th chapter.

Jesus said:
[1]"Do not let your hearts be troubled.
Believe in God, believe also in me.
[2]In my Father's house there are many dwelling places.
If it were not so,
would I have told you that I go to prepare a place for you?
[3]And if I go and prepare a place for you,
I will come again and will take you to myself,
so that where I am, there you may be also.
[4]And you know the way to the place where I am going."

[5]Thomas said to Jesus,
"Lord, we do not know where you are going.
How can we know the way?"
[6]Jesus said to him,
"I am the way, and the truth, and the life.
No one comes to the Father except through me.
[7]If you know me, you will know my Father also.
From now on you do know and have seen my Father."

[8]Philip said to him,
"Lord, show us the Father, and we will be satisfied."
[9]Jesus said to him,
"Have I been with you all this time, Philip,
and you still do not know me?
Whoever has seen me has seen the Father.
How can you say, 'Show us the Father'?
[10]Do you not believe that I am in the Father and the Father is in me?
The words that I say to you I do not speak on my own;
but it is the Father who dwells in me who does these works.
[11]Believe me that I am in the Father and the Father is in me;
but if you do not, then believe me because of the works themselves.

[12]Very truly, I tell you,
the one who believes in me will also do the works that I do and,
in fact, will do greater works than these,
because I am going to the Father.
[13]I will do whatever you ask in my name,
so that the Father may be glorified in the Son.
[14]If in my name you ask me for anything, I will do it.

The Gospel of the Lord.

✝

Sixth Sunday of Easter

MAY 12, 1996   MAY 9, 1999   MAY 5, 2002

FIRST READING: Acts 17:22–31

A reading from Acts:

[22]Paul stood in front of the Areopagus and said,
"Athenians, I see how extremely religious you are in every way.
[23]For as I went through the city
and looked carefully at the objects of your worship,
I found among them an altar with the inscription, 'To an unknown god.'
What therefore you worship as unknown, this I proclaim to you.
[24]The God who made the world and everything in it,
the one who is Lord of heaven and earth,
does not live in shrines made by human hands,
[25]nor is God served by human hands, as though needing anything,
since that very God gives to all mortals life and breath and all things.

[26]"From one ancestor God made all nations to inhabit the whole earth,
and allotted the times of their existence
and the boundaries of the places where they would live,
[27]so that they would search for God
and perhaps grope for and find God—
though indeed God is not far from each one of us.
[28]For 'In God we live and move and have our being';
as even some of your own poets have said,
'For we too are the offspring of God.'

[29]"Since we are God's offspring,
we ought not to think that the deity is like gold, or silver, or stone,
an image formed by the art and imagination of mortals.
[30]While God has overlooked the times of human ignorance,
now God commands all people everywhere to repent,
[31]because God has fixed a day
on which to judge the world in righteousness
by a man whom God has appointed,
and of this God has given assurance to all by raising him from the dead."

PSALMODY: PSALM 66:8–20 *Psalm 66:7–18* LBW/BCP

SECOND READING: 1 PETER 3:13–22

A reading from First Peter:

¹³Who will harm you if you are eager to do what is good?
¹⁴But even if you do suffer for doing what is right, you are blessed.
Do not fear what they fear, and do not be intimidated,
¹⁵but in your hearts sanctify Christ as Lord.
Always be ready to make your defense to anyone
who demands from you an accounting for the hope that is in you;
¹⁶yet do it with gentleness and reverence.
Keep your conscience clear, so that, when you are maligned,
those who abuse you for your good conduct in Christ may be put to shame.
¹⁷For it is better to suffer for doing good,
if suffering should be God's will, than to suffer for doing evil.
¹⁸For Christ also suffered for sins once for all,
the righteous for the unrighteous,
in order to bring you to God.
Christ was put to death in the flesh, but made alive in the spirit,
¹⁹in which also he went and made a proclamation to the spirits in prison,
²⁰who in former times did not obey,
when God waited patiently in the days of Noah,
during the building of the ark,
in which a few, that is, eight persons, were saved through water.

²¹And baptism, which this prefigured, now saves you—
not as a removal of dirt from the body,
but as an appeal to God for a good conscience,
through the resurrection of Jesus Christ,
²²who has gone into heaven and is at the right hand of God,
with angels, authorities, and powers made subject to him.

GOSPEL: John 14:15–21

The Holy Gospel according to John, the 14th chapter.

Jesus said:
¹⁵"If you love me, you will keep my commandments.
¹⁶And I will ask the Father,
who will give you another Advocate, to be with you forever.
¹⁷This is the Spirit of truth, whom the world cannot receive,
whom the world neither sees nor knows.
You know the Spirit, because the Spirit abides with you, and will be in you.

¹⁸ "I will not leave you orphaned; I am coming to you.
¹⁹In a little while the world will no longer see me,
but you will see me;
because I live, you also will live.
²⁰On that day you will know that I am in my Father,
and you in me, and I in you.
²¹They who have my commandments and keep them are those who love me;
and those who love me will be loved by my Father,
and I will love them and reveal myself to them."

The Gospel of the Lord.

$$\dagger$$

The Ascension of Our Lord

MAY 16, 1996   MAY 13, 1999   MAY 9, 2002

FIRST READING: ACTS 1:1–11

A reading from Acts:

Luke writes:
[1]In the first book, Theophilus,
I wrote about all that Jesus did and taught from the beginning
[2]until the day when he was taken up to heaven,
after giving instructions through the Holy Spirit
to the apostles whom he had chosen.
[3]After his suffering Jesus presented himself alive to them
by many convincing proofs,
appearing to them during forty days
and speaking about the dominion of God.
[4]While staying with them, Jesus ordered them not to leave Jerusalem,
but to wait there for the promise of the Father.
"This," he said, "is what you have heard from me;
[5]for John baptized with water,
but you will be baptized with the Holy Spirit not many days from now."

[6]So when they had come together, they asked him,
"Lord, is this the time when you will restore dominion to Israel?"
[7]He replied,
"It is not for you to know the times or periods
that the Father has set by divine authority.
[8]But you will receive power when the Holy Spirit has come upon you;
and you will be my witnesses
in Jerusalem, in all Judea and Samaria, and to the ends of the earth."
[9]When Jesus had said this, as they were watching,
he was lifted up, and a cloud took him out of their sight.

[10]While he was going and they were gazing up toward heaven,
suddenly two men in white robes stood by them.
[11]They said, "You Galileans,
why do you stand looking up toward heaven?
This Jesus, who has been taken up from you into heaven,
will come in the same way as you saw him go into heaven."

PSALMODY: Psalm 47 or Psalm 93

SECOND READING: Ephesians 1:15–23

A reading from Ephesians:

[15]I have heard of your faith in the Lord Jesus
and your love toward all the saints,
and for this reason [16]I do not cease to give thanks for you
as I remember you in my prayers.
[17]I pray that the God of our Lord Jesus Christ, the Father of glory,
may give you a spirit of wisdom and revelation, as you come to know God,
[18]so that, with the eyes of your heart enlightened,
you may know what is the hope to which God has called you,
what are the riches of God's glorious inheritance among the saints,
[19]and what is the immeasurable greatness of God's power for us who believe,
according to the working of God's great power.

[20]God put this power to work in Christ when God raised him from the dead
and seated him at the right hand of Power in the heavenly places,
[21]far above all rule and authority and power and dominion,
and above every name that is named,
not only in this age but also in the age to come.
[22]And God has put all things under the feet of Christ
and has made him the head over all things for the church,
[23]which is the body of Christ, the fullness of the one who fills all in all.

GOSPEL: LUKE 24:44–53

The Holy Gospel according to Luke, the 24th chapter.

44Jesus said,
"These are my words that I spoke to you while I was still with you—
that everything written about me
in the law of Moses, the prophets, and the psalms must be fulfilled."
45Then Jesus opened their minds to understand the scriptures,
46and said to them,
"Thus it is written, that the Messiah is to suffer
and to rise from the dead on the third day,
47and that repentance and forgiveness of sins
is to be proclaimed in his name to all nations,
beginning from Jerusalem.
48You are witnesses of these things.
49And see, I am sending upon you what my Father promised;
so stay here in the city until you have been clothed with power from on high."

50Then Jesus led them out as far as Bethany,
and, lifting up his hands, he blessed them.
51While he was blessing them, he withdrew from them
and was carried up into heaven.
52And they worshiped him, and returned to Jerusalem with great joy;
53and they were continually in the temple blessing God.

The Gospel of the Lord.

✝

SEVENTH SUNDAY OF EASTER

MAY 19, 1996   MAY 16, 1999   MAY 12, 2002

FIRST READING: ACTS 1:6–14

A reading from Acts:

⁶When the apostles had come together, they asked Jesus,
"Lord, is this the time when you will restore dominion to Israel?"
⁷He replied,
"It is not for you to know the times or periods
that the Father has set by divine authority.
⁸But you will receive power when the Holy Spirit has come upon you;
and you will be my witnesses
in Jerusalem, in all Judea and Samaria, and to the ends of the earth."

⁹When he had said this, as they were watching,
he was lifted up, and a cloud took him out of their sight.
¹⁰While he was going and they were gazing up toward heaven,
suddenly two men in white robes stood by them.
¹¹They said,
"You Galileans, why do you stand looking up toward heaven?
This Jesus, who has been taken up from you into heaven,
will come in the same way as you saw him go into heaven."

¹²Then they returned to Jerusalem from the mount called Olivet,
which is near Jerusalem, a sabbath day's journey away.
¹³When they had entered the city,
they went to the room upstairs where they were staying,
Peter, and John, and James, and Andrew, Philip and Thomas,
Bartholomew and Matthew, James son of Alphaeus,
and Simon the Zealot, and Judas son of James.
¹⁴All these were constantly devoting themselves to prayer,
together with certain women,
including Mary the mother of Jesus, as well as his brothers.

PSALMODY: PSALM 68:1–10, 32–35   *Psalm 68:1–10, 33–36* LBW/BCP

SECOND READING: 1 Peter 4:12–14; 5:6–11

A reading from First Peter:

^{12}Beloved, do not be surprised at the fiery ordeal
that is taking place among you to test you,
as though something strange were happening to you.
^{13}But rejoice insofar as you are sharing Christ's sufferings,
so that you may also be glad and shout for joy when his glory is revealed.
^{14}If you are reviled for the name of Christ, you are blessed,
because the spirit of glory, which is the Spirit of God,
is resting on you.

$^{5:6}$Humble yourselves therefore under the mighty hand of God,
so that God may exalt you in due time.
^{7}Cast all your anxiety on God, because God cares for you.
^{8}Discipline yourselves, keep alert.
Like a roaring lion your adversary the devil prowls around,
looking for someone to devour.
^{9}Resist the devil, steadfast in your faith,
for you know that your brothers and sisters in all the world
are undergoing the same kinds of suffering.

^{10}And after you have suffered for a little while,
that very God of all grace, who has called you into eternal glory in Christ,
will restore, support, strengthen, and establish you.
^{11}To God be the power forever and ever. Amen.

GOSPEL: JOHN 17:1–11

The Holy Gospel according to John, the 17th chapter.

[1]After Jesus had spoken these words,
he looked up to heaven and said,
"Father, the hour has come;
glorify your Son so that the Son may glorify you,
[2]since you have given him authority over all people,
to give eternal life to all whom you have given him.
[3]And this is eternal life,
that they may know you, the only true God,
and Jesus Christ whom you have sent.
[4]I glorified you on earth
by finishing the work that you gave me to do.
[5]So now, Father, glorify me in your own presence
with the glory that I had in your presence before the world existed.

[6]"I have made your name known to those whom you gave me from the world.
They were yours, and you gave them to me,
and they have kept your word.
[7]Now they know that everything you have given me is from you;
[8]for the words that you gave to me I have given to them,
and they have received them
and know in truth that I came from you;
and they have believed that you sent me.
[9]I am asking on their behalf;
I am not asking on behalf of the world,
but on behalf of those whom you gave me, because they are yours.
[10]All mine are yours, and yours are mine;
and I have been glorified in them.

[11]"And now I am no longer in the world,
but they are in the world,
and I am coming to you.
Holy Father, protect them in your name that you have given me,
so that they may be one, as we are one."

The Gospel of the Lord.

VIGIL OF PENTECOST

MAY 25, 1996   MAY 22, 1999   MAY 18, 2002

FIRST READING: EXODUS 19:1–9
Or Acts 2:1-11, following

A reading from Exodus:

¹On the third new moon after the Israelites had gone out of the land of Egypt,
on that very day, they came into the wilderness of Sinai.
²They had journeyed from Rephidim,
entered the wilderness of Sinai, and camped in the wilderness;
Israel camped there in front of the mountain.

³Then Moses went up to God;
the LORD called to him from the mountain, saying,
"Thus you shall say to the house of Jacob, and tell the Israelites:
⁴You have seen what I did to the Egyptians,
and how I bore you on eagles' wings and brought you to myself.
⁵Now therefore, if you obey my voice and keep my covenant,
you shall be my treasured possession out of all the peoples.
Indeed, the whole earth is mine,
⁶but you shall be for me a realm of priests and a holy nation.
These are the words that you shall speak to the Israelites."

⁷So Moses came, summoned the elders of the people,
and set before them all these words that the LORD had commanded him.
⁸The people all answered as one:
"Everything that the LORD has spoken we will do."
Moses reported the words of the people to the LORD.
⁹Then the LORD said to Moses,
"I am going to come to you in a dense cloud,
in order that the people may hear when I speak with you
and so trust you ever after."

OR: ACTS 2:1–11

A reading from Acts:

¹When the day of Pentecost had come, they were all together in one place.
²And suddenly from heaven there came a sound like the rush of a violent wind,
and it filled the entire house where they were sitting.
³Divided tongues, as of fire, appeared among them,
and a tongue rested on each of them.
⁴All of them were filled with the Holy Spirit
and began to speak in other languages, as the Spirit gave them ability.

⁵Now there were devout Jews from every nation under heaven
        living in Jerusalem.
⁶And at this sound the crowd gathered and was bewildered,
because each one heard them speaking in the native language of each.
⁷Amazed and astonished, they asked,
"Are not all these who are speaking Galileans?
⁸And how is it that we hear, each of us, in our own native language?
⁹Parthians, Medes, Elamites,
and residents of Mesopotamia, Judea and Cappadocia, Pontus and Asia,
¹⁰Phrygia and Pamphylia, Egypt and the parts of Libya belonging to Cyrene,
and visitors from Rome, both Jewish-born and proselytes, ¹¹Cretans and
        Arabs—
in our own languages we hear them speaking about God's deeds of power."

PSALMODY: PSALM 33:12–22 OR PSALM 130

SECOND READING: ROMANS 8:14–17, 22–27

A reading from Romans:

¹⁴All who are led by the Spirit of God are children of God.
¹⁵For you did not receive a spirit of slavery to fall back into fear,
but you have received a spirit of adoption.
When we cry, "Abba! Father!"
¹⁶it is that very Spirit bearing witness with our spirit
that we are children of God,
¹⁷and if children, then heirs,
heirs of God and joint heirs with Christ—
if, in fact, we suffer with Christ
so that we may also be glorified with Christ.

²²We know that the whole creation has been groaning in labor pains until now;
²³and not only the creation,
but we ourselves, who have the first fruits of the Spirit,
groan inwardly while we wait for adoption, the redemption of our bodies.
²⁴For in hope we were saved.
Now hope that is seen is not hope.
For who hopes for what is seen?
²⁵But if we hope for what we do not see, we wait for it with patience.

²⁶Likewise the Spirit helps us in our weakness;
for we do not know how to pray as we ought,
but that very Spirit intercedes with sighs too deep for words.
²⁷And God, who searches the heart,
knows what is the mind of the Spirit,
because the Spirit intercedes for the saints according to the will of God.

GOSPEL: JOHN 7:37–39

The Holy Gospel according to John, the seventh chapter.

³⁷On the last day of the festival of Booths, the great day,
while Jesus was standing in the temple, he cried out,
"Let anyone who is thirsty come to me,
³⁸and let the one who believes in me drink.
As the scripture has said,
'Out of the believer's heart shall flow rivers of living water.' "
³⁹Now he said this about the Spirit,
which believers in him were to receive;
for as yet there was no Spirit,
because Jesus was not yet glorified.

The Gospel of the Lord.

✝

THE DAY OF PENTECOST

MAY 26, 1996   MAY 23, 1999   MAY 19, 2002

FIRST READING: ACTS 2:1–21
Or Numbers 11:24-30, following

A reading from Acts:

¹When the day of Pentecost had come, they were all together in one place.
²And suddenly from heaven there came a sound like the rush of a violent wind,
and it filled the entire house where they were sitting.
³Divided tongues, as of fire, appeared among them,
and a tongue rested on each of them.
⁴All of them were filled with the Holy Spirit
and began to speak in other languages, as the Spirit gave them ability.

⁵Now there were devout Jews from every nation under heaven
        living in Jerusalem.
⁶And at this sound the crowd gathered and was bewildered,
because each one heard them speaking in the native language of each.
⁷Amazed and astonished, they asked,
"Are not all these who are speaking Galileans?
⁸And how is it that we hear, each of us, in our own native language?
⁹Parthians, Medes, Elamites,
and residents of Mesopotamia, Judea and Cappadocia, Pontus and Asia,
¹⁰Phrygia and Pamphylia, Egypt and the parts of Libya belonging to Cyrene,
and visitors from Rome, both Jewish-born and proselytes, ¹¹Cretans and Arabs—
in our own languages we hear them speaking about God's deeds of power."

¹²All were amazed and perplexed, saying to one another,
"What does this mean?"
¹³But others sneered and said, "They are filled with new wine."

¹⁴But Peter, standing with the eleven, raised his voice and addressed them,
"You Judeans and all who live in Jerusalem,
let this be known to you, and listen to what I say.
¹⁵Indeed, these are not drunk, as you suppose,
for it is only nine o'clock in the morning.
¹⁶No, this is what was spoken through the prophet Joel:

¹⁷'In the last days it will be, God declares,
that I will pour out my Spirit upon all flesh,

and your sons and your daughters shall prophesy,
and your youth shall see visions,
and your elders shall dream dreams.
[18]Even upon my slaves, both men and women,
in those days I will pour out my Spirit;
and they shall prophesy.
[19]And I will show portents in the heaven above and signs on the earth below,
blood, and fire, and smoky mist.
[20]The sun shall be turned to darkness and the moon to blood,
before the coming of the Lord's great and glorious day.
[21]Then everyone who calls on the name of the Lord shall be saved.' "

OR: NUMBERS 11:24–30

A reading from Numbers:

[24]Moses went out and told the people the words of the LORD;
and he gathered seventy elders of the people,
and placed them all around the tent.
[25]Then the LORD came down in the cloud and spoke to Moses,
and took some of the spirit that was on him
and put it on the seventy elders;
and when the spirit rested upon them, they prophesied.
But they did not do so again.

[26]Two men remained in the camp,
one named Eldad, and the other named Medad,
and the spirit rested on them;
they were among those registered,
but they had not gone out to the tent,
and so they prophesied in the camp.
[27]And a young man ran and told Moses,
"Eldad and Medad are prophesying in the camp."
[28]And Joshua son of Nun, the assistant of Moses, one of his chosen ones, said,
"My lord Moses, stop them!"
[29]But Moses said to him,
"Are you jealous for my sake?
Would that all the LORD's people were prophets,
and that the LORD's spirit would be given to them all!"
[30]And Moses and the elders of Israel returned to the camp.

PSALMODY: PSALM 104:24–34, 35b

Psalm 104:25–35, 37 LBW/BCP

SECOND READING: 1 Corinthians 12:3b–13

Or Acts 2:1-21, following

A reading from First Corinthians:

3bNo one can say "Jesus is Lord" except by the Holy Spirit.

4Now there are varieties of gifts, but the same Spirit;
5and there are varieties of services, but the same Lord;
6and there are varieties of activities,
but it is the same God who activates all of them in everyone.
7To each is given the manifestation of the Spirit for the common good.
8To one is given through the Spirit the utterance of wisdom,
and to another the utterance of knowledge according to the same Spirit,
9to another faith by the same Spirit,
to another gifts of healing by the one Spirit,
10to another the working of miracles,
to another prophecy,
to another the discernment of spirits,
to another various kinds of tongues,
to another the interpretation of tongues.
11All these are activated by one and the same Spirit,
who allots to each one individually just as the Spirit chooses.

12For just as the body is one and has many members,
and all the members of the body, though many, are one body,
so it is with Christ.
13For in the one Spirit we were all baptized into one body—
Jews or Greeks, slaves or free—
and we were all made to drink of one Spirit.

OR: Acts 2:1–21

A reading from Acts:

1When the day of Pentecost had come, they were all together in one place.
2And suddenly from heaven there came a sound like the rush of a violent wind,
and it filled the entire house where they were sitting.
3Divided tongues, as of fire, appeared among them,
and a tongue rested on each of them.
4All of them were filled with the Holy Spirit
and began to speak in other languages, as the Spirit gave them ability.

5Now there were devout Jews from every nation under heaven
         living in Jerusalem.
6And at this sound the crowd gathered and was bewildered,
because each one heard them speaking in the native language of each.
7Amazed and astonished, they asked,

"Are not all these who are speaking Galileans?
8And how is it that we hear, each of us, in our own native language?
9Parthians, Medes, Elamites,
and residents of Mesopotamia, Judea and Cappadocia, Pontus and Asia,
10Phrygia and Pamphylia, Egypt and the parts of Libya belonging to Cyrene,
and visitors from Rome, both Jewish-born and proselytes, 11Cretans and
            Arabs—
in our own languages we hear them speaking about God's deeds of power."

12All were amazed and perplexed, saying to one another,
"What does this mean?"
13But others sneered and said, "They are filled with new wine."

14But Peter, standing with the eleven, raised his voice and addressed them,
"You Judeans and all who live in Jerusalem,
let this be known to you, and listen to what I say.
15Indeed, these are not drunk, as you suppose,
for it is only nine o'clock in the morning.
16No, this is what was spoken through the prophet Joel:

17'In the last days it will be, God declares,
that I will pour out my Spirit upon all flesh,
and your sons and your daughters shall prophesy,
and your youth shall see visions,
and your elders shall dream dreams.
18Even upon my slaves, both men and women,
in those days I will pour out my Spirit;
and they shall prophesy.
19And I will show portents in the heaven above and signs on the earth below,
blood, and fire, and smoky mist.
20The sun shall be turned to darkness and the moon to blood,
before the coming of the Lord's great and glorious day.
21Then everyone who calls on the name of the Lord shall be saved.' "

GOSPEL: JOHN 20:19–23

Or John 7:37-39, following

The Holy Gospel according to John, the 20th chapter.

[19]When it was evening on that day, the first day of the week,
and the doors of the house where the disciples had met
were locked for fear of the Judeans,
Jesus came and stood among them and said,
"Peace be with you."
[20]After he said this, he showed them his hands and his side.
Then the disciples rejoiced when they saw the Lord.
[21]Jesus said to them again,
"Peace be with you.
As the Father has sent me, so I send you."

[22]When he had said this, he breathed on them and said to them,
"Receive the Holy Spirit.
[23]If you forgive the sins of any, they are forgiven them;
if you retain the sins of any, they are retained."

The Gospel of the Lord.

OR: JOHN 7:37–39

The Holy Gospel according to John, the seventh chapter.

[37]On the last day of the festival of Booths, the great day,
while Jesus was standing in the temple, he cried out,
"Let anyone who is thirsty come to me,
[38]and let the one who believes in me drink.
As the scripture has said,
'Out of the believer's heart shall flow rivers of living water.' "
[39]Now Jesus said this about the Spirit,
which believers in him were to receive;
for as yet there was no Spirit,
because Jesus was not yet glorified.

The Gospel of the Lord.

✝

SEASON AFTER PENTECOST

✠

THE HOLY TRINITY
First Sunday after Pentecost

JUNE 2, 1996   *MAY 30, 1999*   *MAY 26, 2002*

FIRST READING: GENESIS 1:1—2:4a

A reading from Genesis:

[1]In the beginning when God created the heavens and the earth,
[2]the earth was a formless void
and darkness covered the face of the deep,
while a wind from God swept over the face of the waters.
[3]Then God said,
"Let there be light"; and there was light.
[4]And God saw that the light was good;
and God separated the light from the darkness.
[5]God called the light Day,
and the darkness God called Night.
And there was evening and there was morning, the first day.

[6]And God said,
"Let there be a dome in the midst of the waters,
and let it separate the waters from the waters."
[7]So God made the dome and separated the waters that were under the dome
from the waters that were above the dome.
And it was so.
[8]God called the dome Sky.
And there was evening and there was morning, the second day.

[9]And God said,
"Let the waters under the sky be gathered together into one place,
and let the dry land appear."
And it was so.
[10]God called the dry land Earth,
and the waters that were gathered together God called Seas.
And God saw that it was good.
[11]Then God said,
"Let the earth put forth vegetation:
plants yielding seed,
and fruit trees of every kind on earth that bear fruit with the seed in it."
And it was so.
[12]The earth brought forth vegetation:
plants yielding seed of every kind,

and trees of every kind bearing fruit with the seed in it.
And God saw that it was good.
¹³And there was evening and there was morning, the third day.

¹⁴And God said,
"Let there be lights in the dome of the sky
to separate the day from the night;
and let them be for signs and for seasons and for days and years,
¹⁵and let them be lights in the dome of the sky to give light upon the earth."
And it was so.
¹⁶God made the two great lights—
the greater light to rule the day
and the lesser light to rule the night—and the stars.
¹⁷God set them in the dome of the sky to give light upon the earth,
¹⁸to rule over the day and over the night,
and to separate the light from the darkness.
And God saw that it was good.
¹⁹And there was evening and there was morning, the fourth day.

²⁰And God said,
"Let the waters bring forth swarms of living creatures,
and let birds fly above the earth across the dome of the sky."
²¹So God created the great sea monsters
and every living creature that moves, of every kind, with which the waters
        swarm,
and every winged bird of every kind.
And God saw that it was good.
²²God blessed them, saying,
"Be fruitful and multiply and fill the waters in the seas,
and let birds multiply on the earth."
²³And there was evening and there was morning, the fifth day.

²⁴And God said,
"Let the earth bring forth living creatures of every kind:
cattle and creeping things and wild animals of the earth of every kind."
And it was so.
²⁵God made the wild animals of the earth of every kind,
and the cattle of every kind,
and everything that creeps upon the ground of every kind.
And God saw that it was good.

²⁶Then God said,
"Let us make humankind in our image,
according to our likeness;
and let them have dominion over the fish of the sea,
and over the birds of the air,
and over the cattle, and over all the wild animals of the earth,
and over every creeping thing that creeps upon the earth."

²⁷So God created humankind in the divine image,
in the image of God humankind was created;
male and female God created them.
²⁸God blessed them, and God said to them,
"Be fruitful and multiply,
and fill the earth and subdue it;
and have dominion over the fish of the sea
and over the birds of the air
and over every living thing that moves upon the earth."
²⁹God said,
"See, I have given you every plant yielding seed
that is upon the face of all the earth,
and every tree with seed in its fruit;
you shall have them for food.
³⁰And to every beast of the earth,
and to every bird of the air,
and to everything that creeps on the earth,
everything that has the breath of life,
I have given every green plant for food."
And it was so.
³¹God saw everything that had been made,
and indeed, it was very good.
And there was evening and there was morning, the sixth day.

²:¹Thus the heavens and the earth were finished,
and all their multitude.
²And on the seventh day God finished the work that had been done,
and God rested on the seventh day from all the work that had been done.
³So God blessed the seventh day and hallowed it,
because on it God rested from all the work that God had done in creation.

⁴ᵃThese are the generations of the heavens and the earth
        when they were created.

PSALMODY: PSALM 8

SECOND READING: 2 Corinthians 13:11–13

A reading from Second Corinthians:

Paul writes:
[11]Finally, brothers and sisters, farewell.
Put things in order, listen to my appeal,
agree with one another, live in peace;
and the God of love and peace will be with you.
[12]Greet one another with a holy kiss.
All the saints greet you.

[13]The grace of the Lord Jesus Christ, the love of God,
and the communion of the Holy Spirit be with all of you.

GOSPEL: Matthew 28:16–20

The Holy Gospel according to Matthew, the 28th chapter.

[16]Now the eleven disciples went to Galilee,
to the mountain to which Jesus had directed them.
[17]When they saw Jesus, they worshiped him; but some doubted.

[18]And Jesus came and said to them,
"All authority in heaven and on earth has been given to me.
[19]Go therefore and make disciples of all nations,
baptizing them in the name of the Father and of the Son and of the Holy Spirit,
[20]and teaching them to obey everything that I have commanded you.
And remember, I am with you always, to the end of the age."

The Gospel of the Lord.

SUNDAY BETWEEN MAY 24 AND 28 INCLUSIVE

(if after Trinity Sunday)

PROPER 3

FIRST READING: ISAIAH 49:8–16a

A reading from Isaiah:

⁸Thus says the LORD:
In a time of favor I have answered you,
on a day of salvation I have helped you;
I have kept you and given you as a covenant to the people,
to establish the land,
to apportion the desolate heritages;
⁹saying to the prisoners, "Come out,"
to those who are in darkness, "Show yourselves."
They shall feed along the ways,
on all the bare heights shall be their pasture;
¹⁰they shall not hunger or thirst,
neither scorching wind nor sun shall strike them down,
for the one who has pity on them will lead them,
and by springs of water will guide them.
¹¹And I will turn all my mountains into a road,
and my highways shall be raised up.
¹²Lo, these shall come from far away,
and lo, these from the north and from the west,
and these from the land of Syene.

¹³Sing for joy, O heavens, and exult, O earth;
break forth, O mountains, into singing!
For the LORD has comforted the chosen people,
and will have compassion on all the suffering ones.

¹⁴But Zion said, "The LORD has forsaken me,
my LORD has forgotten me."
¹⁵Can a woman forget her nursing child,
or show no compassion for the child of her womb?
Even these may forget,
yet I will not forget you.
¹⁶See, I have inscribed you on the palms of my hands.

PSALMODY: Psalm 131

SECOND READING: 1 Corinthians 4:1–5

A reading from First Corinthians:

[1]Think of us in this way,
as servants of Christ and stewards of God's mysteries.
[2]Moreover, it is required of stewards that they be found trustworthy.
[3]But with me it is a very small thing that I should be judged by you
or by any human court.
I do not even judge myself.
[4]I am not aware of anything against myself,
but I am not thereby acquitted.
It is the Lord who judges me.
[5]Therefore do not pronounce judgment before the time,
before the Lord comes,
who will bring to light the things now hidden in darkness
and will disclose the purposes of the heart.
Then each one will receive commendation from God.

The Holy Gospel according to Matthew, the sixth chapter.

Jesus said:
[24]"No one can serve two masters;
for a slave will either hate the one and love the other,
or be devoted to the one and despise the other.
You cannot serve God and wealth.

[25]"Therefore I tell you,
do not worry about your life,
what you will eat or what you will drink,
or about your body, what you will wear.
Is not life more than food, and the body more than clothing?
[26]Look at the birds of the air;
they neither sow nor reap nor gather into barns,
and yet your heavenly Father feeds them.
Are you not of more value than they?
[27]And can any of you by worrying
add a single hour to your span of life?
[28]And why do you worry about clothing?
Consider the lilies of the field, how they grow;
they neither toil nor spin,
[29]yet I tell you, even Solomon in all his glory
was not clothed like one of these.
[30]But if God so clothes the grass of the field,
which is alive today and tomorrow is thrown into the oven,
will God not much more clothe you—you of little faith?

[31]"Therefore do not worry, saying,
'What will we eat?' or 'What will we drink?' or 'What will we wear?'
[32]For it is the Gentiles who strive for all these things;
and indeed your heavenly Father knows that you need all these things.
[33]But strive first for the dominion and the righteousness of God,
and all these things will be given to you as well.

[34]"So do not worry about tomorrow,
for tomorrow will bring worries of its own.
Today's trouble is enough for today."

The Gospel of the Lord.

✝

SUNDAY BETWEEN
MAY 29 AND JUNE 4 INCLUSIVE
(if after Trinity Sunday)

JUNE 2, 2002

PROPER 4

FIRST READING: DEUTERONOMY 11:18–21, 26–28

A reading from Deuteronomy:

Moses said to all Israel:
[18]You shall put these words of mine in your heart and soul,
and you shall bind them as a sign on your hand,
and fix them as an emblem on your forehead.
[19]Teach them to your children,
talking about them when you are at home and when you are away,
when you lie down and when you rise.
[20]Write them on the doorposts of your house and on your gates,
[21]so that your days and the days of your children may be multiplied
in the land that the LORD swore to your ancestors to give them,
as long as the heavens are above the earth.

[26]See, I am setting before you today a blessing and a curse:
[27]the blessing, if you obey the commandments of the LORD your God
that I am commanding you today;
[28]and the curse, if you do not obey the commandments of the LORD your God,
but turn from the way that I am commanding you today,
to follow other deities that you have not known.

PSALMODY: PSALM 31:1–5, 19–24

A reading from Romans:

[16]I am not ashamed of the gospel;
it is the power of God for salvation to everyone who has faith,
to the Jew first and also to the Greek.
[17]For in it the righteousness of God is revealed through faith for faith;
as it is written,
"The one who is righteous will live by faith."

[3:22b]For there is no distinction,
[23]since all have sinned and fall short of the glory of God;
[24]they are now justified by God's grace as a gift,
through the redemption that is in Christ Jesus,
[25]whom God put forward as a sacrifice of atonement by his blood,
effective through faith.
This was to show God's righteousness,
because in divine forbearance
God had passed over the sins previously committed;
[26]it was to prove at the present time that God is righteous
and that God justifies the one who has faith in Jesus.
[27]Then what becomes of boasting? It is excluded.
By what law? By that of works?
No, but by the law of faith.
[28]For we hold that a person is justified by faith
apart from works prescribed by the law.

[[29]Or is God the God of Jews only?
Is God not the God of Gentiles also?
Yes, of Gentiles also, [30]since God is one;
and God will justify the people who practice circumcision on the ground of faith
and those who do not through that same faith.
[31]Do we then overthrow the law by this faith?
By no means! On the contrary, we uphold the law.]

The Holy Gospel according to Matthew, the seventh chapter.

Jesus said:
21"Not everyone who says to me, 'Lord, Lord,'
will enter the dominion of heaven,
but only the one who does the will of my Father in heaven.
22On that day many will say to me,
'Lord, Lord, did we not prophesy in your name,
and cast out demons in your name,
and do many deeds of power in your name?'
23Then I will declare to them,
'I never knew you; go away from me, you evildoers.'

24"Everyone then who hears these words of mine and acts on them
will be like a wise man who built his house on rock.
25The rain fell, the floods came, and the winds blew and beat on that house,
but it did not fall, because it had been founded on rock.
26And everyone who hears these words of mine and does not act on them
will be like a foolish man who built his house on sand.
27The rain fell, and the floods came,
and the winds blew and beat against that house, and it fell—
and great was its fall!"

28Now when Jesus had finished saying these things,
the crowds were astounded at his teaching,
29for Jesus taught them as one having authority, and not as their scribes.

The Gospel of the Lord.

✝

SUNDAY BETWEEN
JUNE 5 AND 11 INCLUSIVE
(if after Trinity Sunday)

JUNE 9, 1996   *JUNE 6, 1999*   *JUNE 9, 2002*

PROPER 5

FIRST READING: HOSEA 5:15—6:6

A reading from Hosea:

15I will return again to my place
until they acknowledge their guilt and seek my face.
In their distress they will beg my favor:
6:1"Come, let us return to the LORD;
for having torn, the LORD will heal us;
having struck us down, the LORD will bind us up.
2After two days the LORD will revive us,
and on the third day will raise us up,
that we may live before the face of the LORD.
3Let us know, let us press on to know the LORD,
whose appearing is as sure as the dawn;
the LORD will come to us like the showers,
like the spring rains that water the earth."

4What shall I do with you, O Ephraim?
What shall I do with you, O Judah?
Your love is like a morning cloud,
like the dew that goes away early.
5Therefore I have hewn them by the prophets,
I have killed them by the words of my mouth,
and my judgment goes forth as the light.
6For I desire steadfast love and not sacrifice,
the knowledge of God rather than burnt offerings.

PSALMODY: PSALM 50:7–15

SECOND READING: ROMANS 4:13–25

A reading from Romans:

^{13}The promise that Abraham would inherit the world
did not come to him or to his descendants through the law
but through the righteousness of faith.
^{14}If it is the adherents of the law who are to be the heirs,
faith is null and the promise is void.
^{15}For the law brings wrath;
but where there is no law, neither is there violation.

^{16}For this reason it depends on faith,
in order that the promise may rest on grace
and be guaranteed to all Abraham's descendants,
not only to the adherents of the law
but also to those who share the faith of Abraham
(for he is the father of all of us,
^{17}as it is written, "I have made you the father of many nations")—
in the presence of the God in whom Abraham believed,
who gives life to the dead
and calls into existence the things that do not exist.

^{18}Hoping against hope,
Abraham believed that he would become "the father of many nations,"
according to what was said, "So numerous shall your descendants be."
^{19}He did not weaken in faith when he considered his own body,
which was already as good as dead (for he was about a hundred years old),
or when he considered the barrenness of Sarah's womb.
^{20}No distrust made Abraham waver concerning the promise of God,
but he grew strong in his faith as he gave glory to God,
^{21}being fully convinced that God was able to do what God had promised.
^{22}Therefore his faith "was reckoned to him as righteousness."
^{23}Now the words, "it was reckoned to him,"
were written not for his sake alone, ^{24}but for ours also.
It will be reckoned to us who believe in the one
who raised Jesus our Lord from the dead,
^{25}who was handed over to death for our trespasses
and was raised for our justification.

GOSPEL: MATTHEW 9:9–13, 18–26

The Holy Gospel according to Matthew, the ninth chapter.

⁹As Jesus was walking along,
he saw a man called Matthew sitting at the tax booth;
and he said to him, "Follow me."
And he got up and followed him.

¹⁰And as Jesus sat at dinner in the house,
many tax collectors and sinners came
and were sitting with him and his disciples.
¹¹When the Pharisees saw this, they said to his disciples,
"Why does your teacher eat with tax collectors and sinners?"
¹²But when he heard this, he said,
"Those who are well have no need of a physician,
but those who are sick.
¹³Go and learn what this means, 'I desire mercy, not sacrifice.'
For I have come to call not the righteous but sinners."

¹⁸While Jesus was saying these things to them,
suddenly a leader of the synagogue came in and knelt before him, saying,
"My daughter has just died;
but come and lay your hand on her, and she will live."
¹⁹And Jesus got up and followed him, with his disciples.
²⁰Then suddenly a woman who had been suffering from hemorrhages for
            twelve years
came up behind him and touched the fringe of his cloak,
²¹for she said to herself,
"If I only touch his cloak, I will be made well."
²²Jesus turned, and seeing her he said,
"Take heart, daughter; your faith has made you well."
And instantly the woman was made well.

²³When Jesus came to the leader's house
and saw the flute players and the crowd making a commotion,
²⁴he said, "Go away; for the girl is not dead but sleeping."
And they laughed at him.
²⁵But when the crowd had been put outside,
he went in and took her by the hand, and the girl got up.
²⁶And the report of this spread throughout that district.

The Gospel of the Lord.

✝

SUNDAY BETWEEN
JUNE 12 AND 18 INCLUSIVE
(if after Trinity Sunday)

JUNE 16, 1996   JUNE 13, 1999   JUNE 16, 2002

PROPER 6

FIRST READING: EXODUS 19:2–8a

A reading from Exodus:

²The Israelites had journeyed from Rephidim, entered the wilderness of Sinai,
and camped in the wilderness;
Israel camped there in front of the mountain.
³Then Moses went up to God;
the LORD called to him from the mountain, saying,
"Thus you shall say to the house of Jacob, and tell the Israelites:
⁴You have seen what I did to the Egyptians,
and how I bore you on eagles' wings and brought you to myself.
⁵Now therefore, if you obey my voice and keep my covenant,
you shall be my treasured possession out of all the peoples.
Indeed, the whole earth is mine,
⁶but you shall be for me a realm of priests and a holy nation.
These are the words that you shall speak to the Israelites."

⁷So Moses came, summoned the elders of the people,
and set before them all these words that the LORD had commanded him.
⁸ᵃThe people all answered as one:
"Everything that the LORD has spoken we will do."

PSALMODY: PSALM 100

SECOND READING: ROMANS 5:1–8

A reading from Romans:

[1]Since we are justified by faith,
we have peace with God through our Lord Jesus Christ,
[2]through whom we have obtained access to this grace in which we stand;
and we boast in our hope of sharing the glory of God.
[3]And not only that, but we also boast in our sufferings,
knowing that suffering produces endurance,
[4]and endurance produces character,
and character produces hope,
[5]and hope does not disappoint us,
because God's love has been poured into our hearts
through the Holy Spirit that has been given to us.

[6]For while we were still weak,
at the right time Christ died for the ungodly.
[7]Indeed, rarely will anyone die for a righteous person—
though perhaps for a good person someone might actually dare to die.
[8]But it is proof of God's own love for us
in that while we still were sinners Christ died for us.

GOSPEL: MATTHEW 9:35—10:8 [9–23]

The Holy Gospel according to Matthew, the ninth and tenth chapters.

[35]Jesus went about all the cities and villages,
teaching in their synagogues,
and proclaiming the good news of the dominion of heaven,
and curing every disease and every sickness.
[36]When he saw the crowds, he had compassion for them,
because they were harassed and helpless, like sheep without a shepherd.
[37]Then he said to his disciples,
"The harvest is plentiful, but the laborers are few;
[38]therefore ask the Lord of the harvest to send out laborers for the harvesting."
[10:1]Then Jesus summoned his twelve disciples
and gave them authority over unclean spirits,
to cast them out, and to cure every disease and every sickness.

[2]These are the names of the twelve apostles:
first, Simon, also known as Peter, and his brother Andrew;
James son of Zebedee, and his brother John;
[3]Philip and Bartholomew; Thomas and Matthew the tax collector;
James son of Alphaeus, and Thaddaeus;
[4]Simon the Cananaean, and Judas Iscariot, the one who betrayed him.

⁵These twelve Jesus sent out with the following instructions:
"Go nowhere among the Gentiles, and enter no town of the Samaritans,
⁶but go rather to the lost sheep of the house of Israel.
⁷As you go, proclaim the good news,
'The dominion of heaven has come near.'
⁸Cure the sick, raise the dead, cleanse those with leprosy, cast out demons.
You received without payment; give without payment.
[⁹Take no gold, or silver, or copper in your belts,
¹⁰no bag for your journey, or two tunics, or sandals, or a staff;
for laborers deserve their food.
¹¹Whatever town or village you enter, find out who in it is worthy,
and stay there until you leave.
¹²As you enter the house, greet it.
¹³If the house is worthy, let your peace come upon it;
but if it is not worthy, let your peace return to you.
¹⁴If anyone will not welcome you or listen to your words,
shake off the dust from your feet as you leave that house or town.
¹⁵Truly I tell you,
it will be more tolerable for the land of Sodom and Gomorrah
        on the day of judgment
than for that town.

¹⁶"See, I am sending you out like sheep into the midst of wolves;
so be wise as serpents and innocent as doves.
¹⁷Beware of them, for they will hand you over to councils
and flog you in their synagogues;
¹⁸and you will be dragged before governors and rulers because of me,
as a testimony to them and the Gentiles.
¹⁹When they hand you over,
do not worry about how you are to speak or what you are to say;
for what you are to say will be given to you at that time;
²⁰for it is not you who speak,
but the Spirit of your Father speaking through you.

²¹"Brother and sister will betray one another to death, and the parent the child,
and children will rise against parents and have them put to death;
²²and you will be hated by all because of my name.
But the one who endures to the end will be saved.
²³When they persecute you in one town, flee to the next;
for truly I tell you,
you will not have gone through all the towns of Israel
before the Son-of-Man comes."]

The Gospel of the Lord.

✠

SUNDAY BETWEEN
JUNE 19 AND 25 INCLUSIVE
(if after Trinity Sunday)

JUNE 23, 1996   *JUNE 20, 1999*   *JUNE 23, 2002*

PROPER 7

FIRST READING: JEREMIAH 20:7–13

A reading from Jeremiah:

⁷O LORD, you have enticed me, and I was enticed;
you were too powerful for me, and you have prevailed.
I have become a laughingstock all day long;
everyone mocks me.
⁸For whenever I speak, I must cry out,
I must shout, "Violence and destruction!"
For the word of the LORD has become for me
a reproach and derision all day long.
⁹If I say, "I will not mention the LORD, or speak any more in the name of the LORD,"
then within me there is something like a burning fire shut up in my bones;
I am weary with holding it in, and I cannot.
¹⁰For I hear many whispering:
"Terror is all around!
Denounce him! Let us denounce him!"
All my close friends are watching for me to stumble.
"Perhaps Jeremiah can be enticed,
and we can prevail against him, and take our revenge on him."

¹¹But the LORD is with me like a dread warrior;
therefore my persecutors will stumble, and they will not prevail.
They will be greatly shamed, for they will not succeed.
Their eternal dishonor will never be forgotten.
¹²O LORD of hosts, you test the righteous,
you see the heart and the mind;
let me see your retribution upon them,
for to you I have committed my cause.

¹³Sing to the LORD; praise the LORD!
For the LORD has delivered the life of the needy
from the hands of evildoers.

PSALMODY: PSALM 69:7–10 [11–15] 16–18   *Psalm 69:8–11 [12–17] 18–20* LBW/BCP

SECOND READING: ROMANS 6:1b–11

A reading from Romans:

1bShould we continue in sin in order that grace may abound?
2By no means! How can we who died to sin go on living in it?
3Do you not know that all of us who have been baptized into Christ Jesus
were baptized into his death?
4Therefore we have been buried with him by baptism into death,
so that, just as Christ was raised from the dead by the glory of the Father,
so we too might walk in newness of life.

5For if we have been united with Christ in a death like his,
we will certainly be united with him in a resurrection like his.
6We know that our old self was crucified with him
so that the body of sin might be destroyed,
and we might no longer be enslaved to sin.
7For whoever has died is freed from sin.
8But if we have died with Christ,
we believe that we will also live with him.
9We know that Christ, being raised from the dead, will never die again;
death no longer has dominion over him.
10The death he died, he died to sin, once for all;
but the life he lives, he lives to God.
11So you also must consider yourselves dead to sin
and alive to God in Christ Jesus.

GOSPEL: Matthew 10:24–39

The Holy Gospel according to Matthew, the tenth chapter.

Jesus said:
[24]"A disciple is not above the teacher, nor a slave above the master;
[25]it is enough for the disciple to be like the teacher,
and the slave like the master.
If they have called the master of the house Beelzebul,
how much more will they malign those of the master's household!

[26]"So have no fear of them;
for nothing is covered up that will not be uncovered,
and nothing secret that will not become known.
[27]What I say to you in the dark, tell in the light;
and what you hear whispered, proclaim from the housetops.
[28]Do not fear those who kill the body but cannot kill the soul;
rather fear the one who can destroy both soul and body in hell.
[29]Are not two sparrows sold for a penny?
Yet not one of them will fall to the ground apart from your Father.
[30]And even the hairs of your head are all counted.
[31]So do not be afraid; you are of more value than many sparrows.

[32]"Everyone therefore who acknowledges me before others,
I also will acknowledge before my Father in heaven;
[33]but whoever denies me before others,
I also will deny before my Father in heaven.
[34]Do not think that I have come to bring peace to the earth;
I have not come to bring peace, but a sword.
[35]For I have come to set a son against his father,
and a daughter against her mother,
and in-laws against one another;
[36]and one's foes will be members of one's own household.
[37]Whoever loves father or mother more than me is not worthy of me;
and whoever loves son or daughter more than me is not worthy of me;
[38]and whoever does not take up the cross and follow me is not worthy of me.
[39]Those who find their life will lose it,
and those who lose their life for my sake will find it."

The Gospel of the Lord.

✝

Sunday between June 26 and July 2 inclusive

JUNE 30, 1996   JUNE 27, 1999   JUNE 30, 2002

PROPER 8

FIRST READING: JEREMIAH 28:5–9

A reading from Jeremiah:

⁵The prophet Jeremiah spoke to the prophet Hananiah
in the presence of the priests
and all the people who were standing in the house of the LORD;
⁶and the prophet Jeremiah said,
"Amen! May the LORD do so;
may the LORD fulfill the words that you have prophesied,
and bring back to this place from Babylon
the vessels of the house of the LORD, and all the exiles.

⁷"But listen now to this word that I speak in your hearing
and in the hearing of all the people.
⁸The prophets who preceded you and me from ancient times
prophesied war, famine, and pestilence
against many countries and great realms.
⁹As for the prophet who prophesies peace,
when the word of that prophet comes true,
then it will be known that the LORD has truly sent the prophet."

PSALMODY: PSALM 89:1–4, 15–18

SECOND READING: ROMANS 6:12–23

A reading from Romans:

¹²Do not let sin exercise dominion in your mortal bodies,
to make you obey their passions.
¹³No longer present any parts of your bodies to sin as instruments of wickedness,
but present yourselves to God as those who have been brought from death
       to life,
and present your bodies to God as instruments of righteousness.
¹⁴For sin will have no dominion over you,
since you are not under law but under grace.

¹⁵What then? Should we sin because we are not under law but under grace?
By no means!
¹⁶Do you not know that if you present yourselves to anyone as obedient slaves,
you are slaves of the one whom you obey,
either of sin, which leads to death,
or of obedience, which leads to righteousness?
¹⁷But thanks be to God that you, having once been slaves of sin,
have become obedient from the heart
to the form of teaching to which you were entrusted,
¹⁸and that you, having been set free from sin,
have become slaves of righteousness.
¹⁹I am speaking in human terms because of your natural limitations.
For just as you once presented the parts of your bodies as slaves to impurity
and to greater and greater iniquity,
so now present your bodies as slaves to righteousness for sanctification.

²⁰When you were slaves of sin,
you were free in regard to righteousness.
²¹So what advantage did you then get
from the things of which you now are ashamed?
The end of those things is death.
²²But now that you have been freed from sin and enslaved to God,
the advantage you get is sanctification.
The end is eternal life.
²³For the wages of sin is death,
but the free gift of God is eternal life in Christ Jesus our Lord.

The Holy Gospel according to Matthew, the tenth chapter.

Jesus said:
[40]"Whoever welcomes you welcomes me,
and whoever welcomes me welcomes the one who sent me.
[41]Whoever welcomes a prophet in the name of a prophet
will receive a prophet's reward;
and whoever welcomes a righteous person in the name of a righteous person
will receive the reward of the righteous;
[42]and whoever gives even a cup of cold water to one of these little ones
in the name of a disciple—
truly I tell you, none of these will lose their reward."

The Gospel of the Lord.

SUNDAY BETWEEN
JULY 3 AND 9 INCLUSIVE

JULY 7, 1996   JULY 4, 1999   JULY 7, 2002

PROPER 9

FIRST READING: ZECHARIAH 9:9–12

A reading from Zechariah:

[9]Rejoice greatly, O daughter Zion!
Shout aloud, O daughter Jerusalem!
Lo, your king comes to you;
triumphant and victorious is he,
humble and riding on a donkey,
on a colt, the foal of a donkey.
[10]The king will cut off the chariot from Ephraim
and the war horse from Jerusalem;
and the battle bow shall be cut off,
and he shall command peace to the nations;
his dominion shall be from sea to sea,
and from the River to the ends of the earth.

[11]As for you also, because of the blood of my covenant with you,
I will set your prisoners free from the waterless pit.
[12]Return to your stronghold, O prisoners of hope;
today I declare that I will restore to you double.

PSALMODY: PSALM 145:8–14

Psalm 145:8–15 LBW/BCP

SECOND READING: Romans 7:15–25a

A reading from Romans:

15I do not understand my own actions.
For I do not do what I want,
but I do the very thing I hate.
16Now if I do what I do not want, I agree that the law is good.
17But in fact it is no longer I that do it,
but sin that dwells within me.
18For I know that nothing good dwells within me, that is, in my flesh.
I can will what is right, but I cannot do it.
19For I do not do the good I want,
but the evil I do not want is what I do.
20Now if I do what I do not want, it is no longer I that do it,
but sin that dwells within me.
21So I find it to be a law that when I want to do what is good,
evil lies close at hand.
22For I delight in the law of God in my inmost self,
23but I see in my physical body another law at war with the law of my mind,
making me captive to the law of sin that dwells in my body.

24Wretched man that I am!
Who will rescue me from this body of death?
25aThanks be to God through Jesus Christ our Lord!

GOSPEL: MATTHEW 11:16–19, 25–30

The Holy Gospel according to Matthew, the eleventh chapter.

Jesus said:
16"To what will I compare this generation?
It is like children sitting in the marketplaces and calling to one another,
17'We played the flute for you, and you did not dance;
we wailed, and you did not mourn.'
18For John came neither eating nor drinking,
and they say, 'He has a demon';
19the Son-of-Man came eating and drinking, and they say,
'Look, a glutton and a drunkard, a friend of tax collectors and sinners!'
Yet wisdom is vindicated by wise deeds."

25At that time Jesus said,
"I thank you, Father, Lord of heaven and earth,
because you have hidden these things from the wise and the intelligent
and have revealed them to infants;
26yes, Father, for such was your gracious will.
27All things have been handed over to me by my Father;
and no one knows the Son except the Father,
and no one knows the Father except the Son
and anyone to whom the Son chooses to reveal the Father.

28"Come to me, all you that are weary and are carrying heavy burdens,
and I will give you rest.
29Take my yoke upon you, and learn from me;
for I am gentle and humble in heart,
and you will find rest for your souls.
30For my yoke is easy, and my burden is light."

The Gospel of the Lord.

✝

SUNDAY BETWEEN
JULY 10 AND 16 INCLUSIVE

JULY 14, 1996   *JULY 11, 1999*   *JULY 14, 2002*

PROPER 10

FIRST READING: ISAIAH 55:10–13

A reading from Isaiah:

¹⁰For as the rain and the snow come down from heaven,
and do not return there until they have watered the earth,
making it bring forth and sprout,
giving seed to the sower and bread to the eater,
¹¹so shall my word be that goes out from my mouth;
it shall not return to me empty,
but it shall accomplish that which I purpose,
and succeed in the thing for which I sent it.

¹²For you shall go out in joy,
and be led back in peace;
the mountains and the hills before you shall burst into song,
and all the trees of the field shall clap their hands.
¹³Instead of the thorn shall come up the cypress;
instead of the brier shall come up the myrtle;
and it shall be to the LORD for a memorial,
for an everlasting sign that shall not be cut off.

PSALMODY: PSALM 65:[1–8] 9–13   *Psalm 65:[1–8] 9–14*   LBW/BCP

SECOND READING: ROMANS 8:1–11

A reading from Romans:

¹There is therefore now no condemnation for those who are in Christ Jesus.
²For the law of the Spirit of life in Christ Jesus
has set you free from the law of sin and of death.
³For God has done what the law, weakened by the flesh, could not do:
sending God's own Son in the likeness of sinful flesh,
and to deal with sin, God condemned sin in the flesh,
⁴so that the just requirement of the law might be fulfilled in us,
who walk not according to the flesh but according to the Spirit.
⁵For those who live according to the flesh
set their minds on the things of the flesh,
but those who live according to the Spirit
set their minds on the things of the Spirit.
⁶To set the mind on the flesh is death,
but to set the mind on the Spirit is life and peace.
⁷For this reason the mind that is set on the flesh is hostile to God;
it does not submit to God's law—indeed it cannot,
⁸and those who are in the flesh cannot please God.

⁹But you are not in the flesh; you are in the Spirit,
since the Spirit of God dwells in you.
Anyone who does not have the Spirit of Christ does not belong to him.
¹⁰But if Christ is in you, though the body is dead because of sin,
the Spirit is life because of righteousness.
¹¹If the Spirit of the one who raised Jesus from the dead dwells in you,
the one who raised Christ from the dead will give life to your mortal bodies also
through this Spirit dwelling in you.

The Holy Gospel according to Matthew, the thirteenth chapter.

[1]That same day Jesus went out of the house and sat beside the sea.
[2]Such great crowds gathered around him that he got into a boat and sat there,
while the whole crowd stood on the beach.
[3]And he told them many things in parables, saying:
"Listen! A sower went out to sow.
[4]And in the sowing, some seeds fell on the path,
and the birds came and ate them up.
[5]Other seeds fell on rocky ground, where they did not have much soil,
and they sprang up quickly, since they had no depth of soil.
[6]But when the sun rose, they were scorched;
and since they had no root, they withered away.
[7]Other seeds fell among thorns, and the thorns grew up and choked them.
[8]Other seeds fell on good soil and brought forth grain,
some a hundredfold, some sixty, some thirty.
[9]Let anyone with ears listen!"

[18]"Hear then the parable of the sower.
[19]When anyone hears the word of the dominion of heaven
and does not understand it,
the evil one comes and snatches away what is sown in the heart;
this is what was sown on the path.
[20]As for what was sown on rocky ground,
this is the one who hears the word and immediately receives it with joy;
[21]yet such a person has no root, but endures only for a while,
and when trouble or persecution arises on account of the word,
that person immediately falls away.
[22]As for what was sown among thorns,
this is the one who hears the word,
but the cares of the world and the lure of wealth choke the word,
and it yields nothing.
[23]But as for what was sown on good soil,
this is the one who hears the word and understands it,
who indeed bears fruit and yields,
in one case a hundredfold, in another sixty, and in another thirty."

The Gospel of the Lord.

SUNDAY BETWEEN JULY 17 AND 23 INCLUSIVE

JULY 21, 1996   *JULY 18, 1999*   *JULY 21, 2002*

PROPER 11

FIRST READING: ISAIAH 44:6–8   *Alternate Reading: Wisdom of Solomon 12:13, 16-19 (p. 417)*

A reading from Isaiah:

⁶Thus says the LORD, the Sovereign of Israel,
and Israel's Redeemer, the LORD of hosts:
I am the first and I am the last;
besides me there is no god.
⁷Who is like me?
Let them proclaim it,
let them declare and set it forth before me.
Who has announced from of old the things to come?
Let them tell us what is yet to be.
⁸Do not fear, or be afraid;
have I not told you from of old and declared it?
You are my witnesses!
Is there besides me any other deity?
There is no other rock; I know not one.

PSALMODY: PSALM 86:11–17

SECOND READING: ROMANS 8:12–25

A reading from Romans:

^{12}So then, brothers and sisters, we are debtors, not to the flesh,
to live according to the flesh—
^{13}for if you live according to the flesh, you will die;
but if by the Spirit you put to death the deeds of the body, you will live.
^{14}For all who are led by the Spirit of God are children of God.

^{15}For you did not receive a spirit of slavery to fall back into fear,
but you have received a spirit of adoption.
When we cry, "Abba! Father!"
^{16}it is that very Spirit bearing witness with our spirit
that we are children of God,
^{17}and if children, then heirs,
heirs of God and joint heirs with Christ—
if, in fact, we suffer with Christ so that we may also be glorified with Christ.

^{18}I consider that the sufferings of this present time
are not worth comparing with the glory about to be revealed to us.
^{19}For the creation waits with eager longing
for the revealing of the children of God;
^{20}for the creation was subjected to futility,
not of its own will but by the will of the one who subjected it,
in hope ^{21}that the creation itself will be set free from its bondage to decay
and will obtain the freedom of the glory of the children of God.
^{22}We know that the whole creation has been groaning in labor pains until now;
^{23}and not only the creation, but we ourselves,
who have the first fruits of the Spirit,
groan inwardly while we wait for adoption, the redemption of our bodies.

^{24}For in hope we were saved.
Now hope that is seen is not hope.
For who hopes for what is seen?
^{25}But if we hope for what we do not see, we wait for it with patience.

GOSPEL: MATTHEW 13:24–30, 36–43

The Holy Gospel according to Matthew, the thirteenth chapter.

24Jesus put before the crowds another parable:
"The dominion of heaven may be compared a man who sowed good seed in his
      field;
25but while everybody was asleep,
an enemy came and sowed weeds among the wheat, and then went away.
26So when the plants came up and bore grain,
then the weeds appeared as well.
27And the slaves of the householder came and said to him,
'Master, did you not sow good seed in your field?
Where, then, did these weeds come from?'
28He answered, 'An enemy has done this.'
The slaves said to him, 'Then do you want us to go and gather them?'
29But he replied,
'No; for in gathering the weeds you would uproot the wheat along with them.
30Let both of them grow together until the harvest;
and at harvest time I will tell the reapers,
Collect the weeds first and bind them in bundles to be burned,
but gather the wheat into my barn.' "

36Then Jesus left the crowds and went into the house.
And his disciples approached him, saying,
"Explain to us the parable of the weeds of the field."
37Jesus answered,
"The one who sows the good seed is the Son-of-Man;
38the field is the world,
and the good seed are the children of God's dominion;
the weeds are the children of the evil one,
39and the enemy who sowed them is the devil;
the harvest is the end of the age, and the reapers are angels.
40Just as the weeds are collected and burned up with fire,
so will it be at the end of the age.

41"The Son-of-Man will send his angels,
and they will collect out of his dominion all causes of sin and all evildoers,
42and they will throw them into the furnace of fire,
where there will be weeping and gnashing of teeth.
43Then the righteous will shine like the sun in the dominion of their Father.
Let anyone with ears listen!"

The Gospel of the Lord.

✝

FIRST READING: 1 KINGS 3:5–12

A reading from First Kings:

[5]At Gibeon the LORD appeared to Solomon in a dream by night;
and God said, "Ask what I should give you."
[6]And Solomon said,
"You have shown great and steadfast love to your servant my father David,
because he walked before you in faithfulness, in righteousness,
and in uprightness of heart toward you;
and you have kept for him this great and steadfast love,
and have given him a son to sit on his throne today.
[7]And now, O LORD my God,
you have made your servant king in place of my father David,
although I am only a little child;
I do not know how to go out or come in.
[8]And your servant is in the midst of the people whom you have chosen,
a great people, so numerous they cannot be numbered or counted.
[9]Give your servant therefore an understanding mind to govern your people,
able to discern between good and evil;
for who can govern this your great people?"

[10]It pleased the LORD that Solomon had asked this.
[11]God said to him,
"Because you have asked this,
and have not asked for yourself long life or riches,
or for the life of your enemies,
but have asked for yourself understanding to discern what is right,
[12]I now do according to your word.
Indeed I give you a wise and discerning mind;
no one like you has been before you
and no one like you shall arise after you."

PSALMODY: PSALM 119:129–136

SECOND READING: ROMANS 8:26–39

A reading from Romans:

²⁶The Spirit helps us in our weakness;
for we do not know how to pray as we ought,
but that very Spirit intercedes with sighs too deep for words.
²⁷And God, who searches the heart, knows what is the mind of the Spirit,
because the Spirit intercedes for the saints according to the will of God.

²⁸We know that all things work together for good for those who love God,
who are called according to God's purpose.
²⁹For those whom God foreknew God also predestined
to be conformed to the image of the Son of God,
in order that the Son might be the firstborn within a large family.
³⁰And those whom God predestined God also called;
and those whom God called God also justified;
and those whom God justified God also glorified.

³¹What then are we to say about these things?
If God is for us, who is against us?
³²The very Son of God was not withheld,
but was given up for all of us;
will God not along with the Son also give us everything else?
³³Who will bring any charge against God's elect?
It is God who justifies. ³⁴Who is to condemn?
It is Christ Jesus, who died, yes, who was raised,
who is at the right hand of God,
who indeed intercedes for us.
³⁵Who will separate us from the love of Christ?
Will hardship, or distress, or persecution,
or famine, or nakedness, or peril, or sword?
³⁶As it is written,
"For your sake we are being killed all day long;
we are accounted as sheep to be slaughtered."

³⁷No, in all these things we are more than conquerors
through the one who loved us.
³⁸For I am convinced that neither death, nor life,
nor angels, nor rulers, nor things present, nor things to come,
nor powers, ³⁹nor height, nor depth, nor anything else in all creation,
will be able to separate us from the love of God in Christ Jesus our Lord.

GOSPEL: MATTHEW 13:31–33, 44–52

The Gospel according to Matthew, the thirteenth chapter.

31Jesus put before the crowds another parable:
"The dominion of heaven is like a mustard seed
that someone took and sowed in a field;
32it is the smallest of all the seeds,
but when it has grown it is the greatest of shrubs and becomes a tree,
so that the birds of the air come and make nests in its branches."

33Jesus told them another parable:
"The dominion of heaven is like yeast
that a woman took and mixed in with three measures of flour
until all of it was leavened."

44"The dominion of heaven is like treasure hidden in a field,
which a man found and hid;
then in his joy he goes and sells all that he has and buys that field.

45"Again, the dominion of heaven is like a merchant in search of fine pearls;
46on finding one pearl of great value,
he went and sold all that he had and bought it.

47"Again, the dominion of heaven is like a net that was thrown into the sea
and caught fish of every kind;
48when it was full, they drew it ashore,
sat down, and put the good into baskets but threw out the bad.
49So it will be at the end of the age.
The angels will come out and separate the evil from the righteous
50and throw them into the furnace of fire,
where there will be weeping and gnashing of teeth.

51"Have you understood all this?"
They answered, "Yes."
52And Jesus said to them,
"Therefore every scribe who has been trained for the dominion of heaven
is like a householder
who brings out of the household treasure what is new and what is old."

The Gospel of the Lord.

✝

SUNDAY BETWEEN
JULY 31 AND AUGUST 6 INCLUSIVE

AUGUST 4, 1996   *AUGUST 1, 1999*   *AUGUST 4, 2002*

PROPER 13

FIRST READING: ISAIAH 55:1–5

A reading from Isaiah:

¹Ho, everyone who thirsts, come to the waters;
and you that have no money, come, buy and eat!
Come, buy wine and milk without money and without price.
²Why do you spend your money for that which is not bread,
and your labor for that which does not satisfy?
Listen carefully to me, and eat what is good,
and delight yourselves in rich food.

³Incline your ear, and come to me;
listen, so that you may live.
I will make with you an everlasting covenant,
my steadfast, sure love for David.
⁴See, I made him a witness to the peoples,
a leader and commander for the peoples.
⁵See, you shall call nations that you do not know,
and nations that do not know you shall run to you,
because of the LORD your God, the Holy One of Israel,
for the LORD has glorified you.

PSALMODY: PSALM 145:8–9, 14–21

Psalm 145:8–9, 15–22   LBW/BCP

SECOND READING: ROMANS 9:1–5

A reading from Romans:

¹I am speaking the truth in Christ—I am not lying;
my conscience confirms it by the Holy Spirit—
²I have great sorrow and unceasing anguish in my heart.
³For I could wish that I myself were accursed
and cut off from Christ for the sake of my own people,
my kindred according to the flesh.
⁴They are Israelites, and to them belong the adoption, the glory,
the covenants, the giving of the law, the worship, and the promises;
⁵to them belong the patriarchs,
and from them, according to the flesh, comes the Messiah, who is over all,
God blessed forever. Amen.

GOSPEL: MATTHEW 14:13–21

The Holy Gospel according to Matthew, the fourteenth chapter.

¹³Now when Jesus heard about the beheading of John the Baptist,
he withdrew from there in a boat to a deserted place by himself.
But when the crowds heard it, they followed him on foot from the towns.
¹⁴When he went ashore, he saw a great crowd;
and he had compassion for them and cured their sick.

¹⁵When it was evening, the disciples came to Jesus and said,
"This is a deserted place, and the hour is now late;
send the crowds away so that they may go into the villages
and buy food for themselves."
¹⁶Jesus said to them,
"They need not go away; you give them something to eat."
¹⁷They replied, "We have nothing here but five loaves and two fish."
¹⁸And he said, "Bring them here to me."
¹⁹Then he ordered the crowds to sit down on the grass.
Taking the five loaves and the two fish,
Jesus looked up to heaven, and blessed and broke the loaves,
and gave them to the disciples, and the disciples gave them to the crowds.
²⁰And all ate and were filled;
and they took up what was left over of the broken pieces, twelve baskets full.
²¹And those who ate were about five thousand men,
besides women and children.

The Gospel of the Lord.

✝

AUGUST 11, 1996   AUGUST 8, 1999   AUGUST 11, 2002

PROPER 14

FIRST READING: 1 KINGS 19:9–18

A reading from First Kings:

⁹At Horeb, the mount of God,
Elijah came to a cave, and spent the night there.
Then the word of the LORD came to him, saying,
"What are you doing here, Elijah?"
¹⁰Elijah answered, "I have been very zealous for the LORD, the God of hosts;
for the Israelites have forsaken your covenant, thrown down your altars,
and killed your prophets with the sword.
I alone am left, and they are seeking my life, to take it away."
¹¹The LORD said, "Go out and stand on the mountain before the LORD,
for the LORD is about to pass by."

Now there was a great wind, so strong that it was splitting mountains
and breaking rocks in pieces before the LORD,
but the LORD was not in the wind;
and after the wind an earthquake,
but the LORD was not in the earthquake;
¹²and after the earthquake a fire,
but the LORD was not in the fire;
and after the fire a sound of sheer silence.
¹³When Elijah heard it, he wrapped his face in his mantle
and went out and stood at the entrance of the cave.

Then there came a voice to him that said,
"What are you doing here, Elijah?"
¹⁴He answered,
"I have been very zealous for the LORD, the God of hosts;
for the Israelites have forsaken your covenant, thrown down your altars,
and killed your prophets with the sword.
I alone am left, and they are seeking my life, to take it away."
¹⁵Then the LORD said to him,
"Go, return on your way to the wilderness of Damascus;
when you arrive, you shall anoint Hazael as king over Aram.

[16]Also you shall anoint Jehu son of Nimshi as king over Israel;
and you shall anoint Elisha son of Shaphat of Abel-meholah
as prophet in your place.
[17]Whoever escapes from the sword of Hazael, Jehu shall kill;
and whoever escapes from the sword of Jehu, Elisha shall kill.
[18]Yet I will leave seven thousand in Israel,
all the knees that have not bowed to Baal,
and every mouth that has not kissed him."

PSALMODY: PSALM 85:8–13

SECOND READING: ROMANS 10:5–15

A reading from Romans:

⁵Moses writes concerning the righteousness that comes from the law,
that "the person who does these things will live by them."
⁶But the righteousness that comes from faith says,
"Do not say in your heart, 'Who will ascend into heaven?' "
(that is, to bring Christ down)
⁷"or 'Who will descend into the abyss?' "
(that is, to bring Christ up from the dead).

⁸But what does it say?
"The word is near you,
on your lips and in your heart"
(that is, the word of faith that we proclaim);
⁹because if you confess with your lips that Jesus is Lord
and believe in your heart that God raised him from the dead,
you will be saved.
¹⁰For one believes with the heart and so is justified,
and one confesses with the mouth and so is saved.
¹¹The scripture says, "No one who believes in the Lord will be put to shame."
¹²For there is no distinction between Jew and Greek;
the same Lord is Lord of all and is generous to all who ask for help.
¹³For, "Everyone who calls on the name of the Lord shall be saved."

¹⁴But how are they to call on one in whom they have not believed?
And how are they to believe in one of whom they have never heard?
And how are they to hear without someone to preach?
¹⁵And how are they to preach unless they are sent?
As it is written,
"How beautiful are the feet of those who bring good news!"

The Holy Gospel according to Matthew, the 14th chapter.

²²Jesus made the disciples get into the boat
and go on ahead to the other side of the Sea of Galilee,
while he dismissed the crowds.
²³And after he had dismissed the crowds,
he went up the mountain by himself to pray.
When evening came, he was there alone,
²⁴but by this time the boat, battered by the waves,
was far from the land, for the wind was against them.

²⁵And early in the morning Jesus came walking toward them on the sea.
²⁶But when the disciples saw him walking on the sea,
they were terrified, saying, "It is a ghost!"
And they cried out in fear.
²⁷But immediately Jesus spoke to them and said,
"Take heart, here I am; do not be afraid."

²⁸Peter answered him,
"Lord, if it is you, command me to come to you on the water."
²⁹He said, "Come."
So Peter got out of the boat, started walking on the water,
and came toward Jesus.
³⁰But when Peter noticed the strong wind, he became frightened,
and beginning to sink, he cried out,
"Lord, save me!"
³¹Jesus immediately reached out his hand and caught him, saying to him,
"You of little faith, why did you doubt?"
³²When they got into the boat, the wind ceased.
³³And those in the boat worshiped him, saying,
"Truly you are the Son of God."

The Gospel of the Lord.

✝

SUNDAY BETWEEN
AUGUST 14 AND 20 INCLUSIVE

AUGUST 18, 1996   AUGUST 15, 1999   AUGUST 18, 2002

PROPER 15

FIRST READING: ISAIAH 56:1, 6–8

A reading from Isaiah:

¹Thus says the LORD:
Maintain justice, and do what is right,
for soon my salvation will come,
and my deliverance be revealed.

⁶And the foreigners who join themselves to the LORD,
to minister to the LORD, to love the name of the LORD,
and to be the LORD's servants,
all who keep the sabbath, and do not profane it,
and hold fast my covenant—
⁷these I will bring to my holy mountain,
and make them joyful in my house of prayer;
their burnt offerings and their sacrifices will be accepted on my altar;
for my house shall be called a house of prayer for all peoples.
⁸Thus says the Lord GOD,
who gathers the outcasts of Israel,
I will gather others to them
besides those already gathered.

PSALMODY: PSALM 67

SECOND READING: ROMANS 11:1–2a, 29–32

A reading from Romans:

Paul writes:
[1]I ask, then, has God rejected the chosen people?
By no means! I myself am an Israelite,
a descendant of Abraham, a member of the tribe of Benjamin.
[2]God has not rejected the people whom ages ago God chose.

[29]For the gifts and the calling of God are irrevocable.
[30]Just as you were once disobedient to God
but have now received mercy because of their disobedience,
[31]so they have now been disobedient in order that,
by the mercy shown to you, they too may now receive mercy.
[32]For God has imprisoned all in disobedience in order to be merciful to all.

GOSPEL: MATTHEW 15:[10–20] 21–28

The Holy Gospel according to Matthew, the 15th chapter.

[10]Jesus called the crowd to him and said to them,
"Listen and understand:
11it is not what goes into the mouth that defiles a person,
but it is what comes out of the mouth that defiles."
12Then the disciples approached and said to him,
"Do you know that the Pharisees took offense
when they heard what you said?"
13Jesus answered,
"Every plant that my heavenly Father has not planted will be uprooted.
14Let them alone; they are blind guides of the blind.
And if one blind person guides another, both will fall into a pit."
15But Peter said to him, "Explain this parable to us."
16Then Jesus said, "Are you also still without understanding?
17Do you not see that whatever goes into the mouth enters the stomach,
and goes out into the sewer?
18But what comes out of the mouth proceeds from the heart,
and this is what defiles.
19For out of the heart come evil intentions, murder, adultery,
fornication, theft, false witness, slander.
20These are what defile a person,
but to eat with unwashed hands does not defile."]

21Jesus left that place and went away to the district of Tyre and Sidon.
22Just then a Canaanite woman from that region came out
            and started shouting,
"Have mercy on me, Lord, Son of David;
my daughter is tormented by a demon."
23But he did not answer her at all.
And his disciples came and urged him, saying,
"Send her away, for she keeps shouting after us."
24Jesus answered, "I was sent only to the lost sheep of the house of Israel."
25But she came and knelt before him, saying,
"Lord, help me."
26Jesus answered,
"It is not fair to take the children's food and throw it to the dogs."
27She said, "Yes, Lord,
yet even the dogs eat the crumbs that fall from their masters' table."
28Then Jesus answered her,
"Woman, great is your faith! Let it be done for you as you wish."
And her daughter was healed instantly.

The Gospel of the Lord.

✝

SUNDAY BETWEEN
AUGUST 21 AND 27 INCLUSIVE

AUGUST 25, 1996   *AUGUST 22, 1999*   *AUGUST 25, 2002*

PROPER 16

FIRST READING: ISAIAH 51:1–6

A reading from Isaiah:

[1]Listen to me, you that pursue righteousness, you that seek the LORD.
Look to the rock from which you were hewn,
and to the quarry from which you were dug.
[2]Look to Abraham your father and to Sarah who bore you;
for Abraham was but one when I called him,
but I blessed him and made him many.
[3]For the LORD will comfort Zion,
comfort all its waste places,
and will make its wilderness like Eden,
and its desert like the garden of the LORD;
joy and gladness will be found in Zion,
thanksgiving and the voice of song.

[4]Listen to me, my people,
and give heed to me, my nation;
for a teaching will go out from me,
and my justice for a light to the peoples.
[5]I will bring near my deliverance swiftly,
my salvation has gone out and my arms will rule the peoples;
the coastlands wait for me,
and for my arm they hope.

[6]Lift up your eyes to the heavens,
and look at the earth beneath;
for the heavens will vanish like smoke,
the earth will wear out like a garment,
and those who live on it will die like gnats;
but my salvation will be forever,
and my deliverance will never be ended.

PSALMODY: PSALM 138

SECOND READING: ROMANS 12:1–8

A reading from Romans:

^{1}I appeal to you therefore, brothers and sisters, by the mercies of God,
to present your bodies as a living sacrifice, holy and acceptable to God,
which is your spiritual worship.
^{2}Do not be conformed to this world,
but be transformed by the renewing of your minds,
so that you may discern what is the will of God—
what is good and acceptable and perfect.

^{3}For by the grace given to me I say to everyone among you
not to think of yourself more highly than you ought to think,
but to think with sober judgment,
each according to the measure of faith that God has assigned.
^{4}For as in one body we have many parts,
and not all the parts have the same function,
^{5}so we, who are many, are one body in Christ,
and individually we are parts one of another.
^{6}We have gifts that differ according to the grace given to us:
prophecy, in proportion to faith; ^{7}ministry, in ministering;
the teacher, in teaching; ^{8}the exhorter, in exhortation;
the giver, in generosity; the leader, in diligence;
the compassionate, in cheerfulness.

GOSPEL: MATTHEW 16:13–20

The Holy Gospel according to Matthew, the 16th chapter.

[13]Now when Jesus came into the district of Caesarea Philippi,
he asked his disciples, "Who do people say that the Son-of-Man is?"
[14]And they said,
"Some say John the Baptist, but others Elijah,
and still others Jeremiah or one of the prophets."
[15]Jesus said to them, "But who do you say that I am?"
[16]Simon Peter answered,
"You are the Messiah, the Son of the living God."

[17]And Jesus answered him,
"Blessed are you, Simon son of Jonah!
For flesh and blood has not revealed this to you, but my Father in heaven.
[18]And I tell you, you are Peter, and on this rock I will build my church,
and the gates of Hades will not prevail against it.
[19]I will give you the keys of the dominion of heaven,
and whatever you bind on earth will be bound in heaven,
and whatever you loose on earth will be loosed in heaven."
[20]Then Jesus sternly ordered the disciples not to tell anyone that he was the
Messiah.

The Gospel of the Lord.

✝

Sunday between
August 28 and September 3
Inclusive

SEPTEMBER 1, 1996   AUGUST 29, 1999   SEPTEMBER 1, 2002

PROPER 17

FIRST READING: JEREMIAH 15:15-21

A reading from Jeremiah:

¹⁵O LORD, you know;
remember me and visit me,
and bring down retribution for me on my persecutors.
In your forbearance do not take me away;
know that on your account I suffer insult.
¹⁶Your words were found, and I ate them,
and your words became to me a joy and the delight of my heart;
for I am called by your name, O LORD, God of hosts.
¹⁷I did not sit in the company of merrymakers, nor did I rejoice;
under the weight of your hand I sat alone,
for you had filled me with indignation.
¹⁸Why is my pain unceasing, my wound incurable,
refusing to be healed?
Truly, you are to me like a deceitful brook,
like waters that fail.

¹⁹Therefore thus says the LORD:
If you turn back, I will take you back,
and you shall stand before me.
If you utter what is precious, and not what is worthless,
you shall serve as my mouth.
It is they who will turn to you,
not you who will turn to them.
²⁰And I will make you to this people a fortified wall of bronze;
they will fight against you,
but they shall not prevail over you,
for I am with you to save you and deliver you, says the LORD.
²¹I will deliver you out of the hand of the wicked,
and redeem you from the grasp of the ruthless.

PSALMODY: PSALM 26:1-8

SECOND READING: ROMANS 12:9-21

A reading from Romans:

[9]Let love be genuine;
hate what is evil, hold fast to what is good;
[10]love one another with mutual affection;
outdo one another in showing honor.
[11]Do not lag in zeal, be ardent in spirit, serve the Lord.
[12]Rejoice in hope, be patient in suffering, persevere in prayer.
[13]Contribute to the needs of the saints;
extend hospitality to strangers.

[14]Bless those who persecute you; bless and do not curse them.
[15]Rejoice with those who rejoice, weep with those who weep.
[16]Live in harmony with one another;
do not be haughty, but associate with the lowly;
do not claim to be wiser than you are.
[17]Do not repay anyone evil for evil,
but take thought for what is noble in the sight of all.
[18]If it is possible, so far as it depends on you,
live peaceably with all.

[19]Beloved, never avenge yourselves,
but leave room for the wrath of God;
for it is written,
"Vengeance is mine, I will repay, says the Lord."
[20]No, "if your enemies are hungry, feed them;
if they are thirsty, give them something to drink;
for by doing this you will heap burning coals on their heads."
[21]Do not be overcome by evil, but overcome evil with good.

GOSPEL: MATTHEW 16:21-28

The Holy Gospel according to Matthew, the 16th chapter.

21From that time on,
Jesus began to show his disciples that he must go to Jerusalem
and undergo great suffering at the hands of the elders and chief priests
      and scribes,
and be killed, and on the third day be raised.
22And Peter took Jesus aside and began to rebuke him, saying,
"God forbid it, Lord! This must never happen to you."
23But he turned and said to Peter,
"Get behind me, Satan!
You are a stumbling block to me;
for you are setting your mind not on divine things but on human things."

24Then Jesus told his disciples,
"If any want to become my followers,
let them deny themselves and take up their cross and follow me.
25For those who want to save their life will lose it,
and those who lose their life for my sake will find it.
26For what will it profit them if they gain the whole world but forfeit their life?
Or what will they give in return for their life?

27"For the Son-of-Man is to come with his angels in the glory of his Father,
and then he will repay everyone for what has been done.
28Truly I tell you,
there are some standing here who will not taste death
before they see the Son-of-Man coming in his dominion."

The Gospel of the Lord.

✠

SUNDAY BETWEEN
SEPTEMBER 4 AND 10 INCLUSIVE

SEPTEMBER 8, 1996　　*SEPTEMBER 5, 1999*　　*SEPTEMBER 8, 2002*

PROPER 18

FIRST READING: EZEKIEL 33:7-11

A reading from Ezekiel:

[7]So you, mortal, I have made a sentinel for the house of Israel;
whenever you hear a word from my mouth,
you shall give them warning from me.
[8]If I say to the wicked, "O wicked ones, you shall surely die,"
and you do not speak to warn the wicked to turn from their ways,
the wicked shall die in their iniquity,
but their blood I will require at your hand.
[9]But if you warn the wicked to turn from their ways,
and they do not turn from their ways,
the wicked shall die in their iniquity, but you will have saved your life.

[10]Now you, mortal, say to the house of Israel,
Thus you have said:
"Our transgressions and our sins weigh upon us,
and we waste away because of them; how then can we live?"
[11]Say to them, As I live, says the Lord GOD,
I have no pleasure in the death of the wicked,
but that the wicked turn from their ways and live;
turn back, turn back from your evil ways;
for why will you die, O house of Israel?

PSALMODY: PSALM 119:33-40

SECOND READING: ROMANS 13:8-14

A reading from Romans:

⁸Owe no one anything, except to love one another;
for the one who loves another has fulfilled the law.
⁹The commandments, "You shall not commit adultery;
You shall not murder; You shall not steal; You shall not covet";
and any other commandment, are summed up in this word,
"Love your neighbor as yourself."
¹⁰Love does no wrong to a neighbor;
therefore, love is the fulfilling of the law.

¹¹Besides this, you know what time it is,
how it is now the moment for you to wake from sleep.
For salvation is nearer to us now than when we became believers;
¹²the night is far gone, the day is near.
Let us then lay aside the works of darkness and put on the armor of light;
¹³let us live honorably as in the day, not in reveling and drunkenness,
not in debauchery and licentiousness,
not in quarreling and jealousy.
¹⁴Instead, put on the Lord Jesus Christ,
and make no provision for the flesh, to gratify its desires.

GOSPEL: MATTHEW 18:15-20

The Holy Gospel according to Matthew, the 18th chapter.

Jesus said:
[15]"If another member of the church sins against you,
go and point out the fault when the two of you are alone.
If the member listens to you, you have regained that one.
[16]But if you are not listened to, take one or two others along with you,
so that every word may be confirmed by the evidence of two or three
        witnesses.
[17]If the member refuses to listen to them, tell it to the church;
and if the offender refuses to listen even to the church,
let such a one be to you as a Gentile and a tax collector.

[18]"Truly I tell you, whatever you bind on earth will be bound in heaven,
and whatever you loose on earth will be loosed in heaven.
[19]Again, truly I tell you,
if two of you agree on earth about anything you ask,
it will be done for you by my Father in heaven.

[20]"For where two or three are gathered in my name, I am there among them."

The Gospel of the Lord.

SUNDAY BETWEEN
SEPTEMBER 11 AND 17 INCLUSIVE

SEPTEMBER 15, 1996   SEPTEMBER 12, 1999   SEPTEMBER 15, 2002

PROPER 19

FIRST READING: GENESIS 50:15-21

A reading from Genesis:

15Realizing that their father was dead, Joseph's brothers said,
"What if Joseph still bears a grudge against us
and pays us back in full for all the wrong that we did to him?"
16So they approached Joseph, saying,
"Your father gave this instruction before he died,
17'Say to Joseph: I beg you,
forgive the crime of your brothers and the wrong they did in harming you.'
Now therefore please forgive the crime of the servants of the God of your
      father."
Joseph wept when they spoke to him.
18Then his brothers also wept, fell down before him, and said,
"We are here as your slaves."

19But Joseph said to them, "Do not be afraid!
Am I in the place of God?
20Even though you intended to do harm to me,
God intended it for good, in order to preserve a numerous people,
as God is doing today.
21So have no fear; I myself will provide for you and your little ones."
In this way Joseph reassured them, speaking kindly to them.

PSALMODY: PSALM 103:[1-7] 8-13

SECOND READING: Romans 14:1-12

A reading from Romans:

¹Welcome those who are weak in faith,
but not for the purpose of quarreling over opinions.
²Some believe in eating anything, while the weak eat only vegetables.
³Those who eat must not despise those who abstain,
and those who abstain must not pass judgment on those who eat;
for God has welcomed them.
⁴Who are you to pass judgment on servants of another?
It is before their own lord that they stand or fall.
And they will be upheld, for the Lord is able to make them stand.

⁵Some judge one day to be better than another,
while others judge all days to be alike.
Let all be fully convinced in their own minds.
⁶Those who observe the day, observe it in honor of the Lord.
Also those who eat, eat in honor of the Lord,
since they give thanks to God;
while those who abstain, abstain in honor of the Lord and give thanks to God.

⁷We do not live to ourselves, and we do not die to ourselves.
⁸If we live, we live to the Lord,
and if we die, we die to the Lord;
so then, whether we live or whether we die, we are the Lord's.
⁹For to this end Christ died and lived again,
so that he might be Lord of both the dead and the living.

¹⁰Why do you pass judgment on your brother or sister?
Or you, why do you despise your brother or sister?
For we will all stand before the judgment seat of God.
¹¹For it is written,
"As I live, says the Lord, every knee shall bow to me,
and every tongue shall give praise to God."
¹²So then, each of us will be accountable to God.

The Holy Gospel according to Matthew, the 18th chapter.

[21]Peter came and said to Jesus,
"Lord, if another member of the church sins against me,
how often should I forgive? As many as seven times?"
[22]Jesus said to him,
"Not seven times, but, I tell you, seventy-seven times.

[23]"For this reason the dominion of heaven may be compared to a king
who wished to settle accounts with his slaves.
[24]When he began the reckoning,
one who owed him ten thousand talents was brought to him;
[25]and, as he could not pay, his lord ordered him to be sold,
together with his wife and children and all his possessions,
and payment to be made.
[26]So the slave fell on his knees before him, saying,
'Have patience with me, and I will pay you everything.'
[27]And out of pity for him, the lord of that slave released him
and forgave him the debt.

[28]But that same slave, as he went out,
came upon one of his fellow slaves who owed him a hundred denarii;
and seizing him by the throat, he said, 'Pay what you owe.'
[29]Then his fellow slave fell down and pleaded with him,
'Have patience with me, and I will pay you.'
[30]But he refused;
then he went and threw him into prison until he would pay the debt.
[31]When his fellow slaves saw what had happened, they were greatly distressed,
and they went and reported to their lord all that had taken place.
[32]Then his lord summoned him and said to him,
'You wicked slave!
I forgave you all that debt because you pleaded with me.
[33]Should you not have had mercy on your fellow slave, as I had mercy on you?'
[34]And in anger his lord handed him over to be tortured
until he would pay his entire debt.

[35]"So my heavenly Father will also do to every one of you,
if you do not forgive your brother or sister from your heart."

The Gospel of the Lord.

✠

SUNDAY BETWEEN
SEPTEMBER 18 AND 24 INCLUSIVE

SEPTEMBER 22, 1996   *SEPTEMBER 19, 1999*   *SEPTEMBER 22, 2002*

PROPER 20

FIRST READING: JONAH 3:10—4:11

A reading from Jonah:

[10]When God saw what the people of Ninevah did,
how they turned from their evil ways,
God had second thoughts about the calamity
that God said would be done to them;
and God did not do it.

[4:1]But this was very displeasing to Jonah, and he became angry.
[2]He prayed to the LORD and said,
"O LORD! Is not this what I said while I was still in my own country?
That is why I fled to Tarshish at the beginning;
for I knew that you are a gracious God and merciful,
slow to anger, and abounding in steadfast love,
and ready to relent from punishing.
[3]And now, O LORD, please take my life from me,
for it is better for me to die than to live."
[4]And the LORD said, "Is it right for you to be angry?"
[5]Then Jonah went out of the city and sat down east of the city,
and made a booth for himself there.
He sat under it in the shade, waiting to see what would become of the city.

[6]The LORD God appointed a bush, and made it come up over Jonah,
to give shade over his head, to save him from his discomfort;
so Jonah was very happy about the bush.
[7]But when dawn came up the next day,
God appointed a worm that attacked the bush, so that it withered.
[8]When the sun rose, God prepared a sultry east wind,
and the sun beat down on the head of Jonah so that he was faint
and asked that he might die.
He said, "It is better for me to die than to live."

[9]But God said to Jonah,
"Is it right for you to be angry about the bush?"
And he said, "Yes, angry enough to die."
[10]Then the LORD said,
"You are concerned about the bush, for which you did not labor
and which you did not grow;
it came into being in a night and perished in a night.
[11]And should I not be concerned about Nineveh, that great city,
in which there are more than a hundred and twenty thousand persons
who do not know their right hand from their left, and also many animals?"

PSALMODY: PSALM 145:1-8

SECOND READING: PHILIPPIANS 1:21-30

A reading from Philippians:

21For to me, living is Christ and dying is gain.
22If I am to live in the flesh, that means fruitful labor for me;
and I do not know which I prefer.
23I am hard pressed between the two:
my desire is to depart and be with Christ, for that is far better;
24but to remain in the flesh is more necessary for you.
25Since I am convinced of this, I know that I will remain
and continue with all of you for your progress and joy in faith,
26so that I may share abundantly in your boasting in Christ Jesus
when I come to you again.

27Only, live your life in a manner worthy of the gospel of Christ,
so that, whether I come and see you or am absent and hear about you,
I will know that you are standing firm in one spirit,
striving side by side with one mind for the faith of the gospel,
28and are in no way intimidated by your opponents.
For them this is evidence of their destruction, but of your salvation.
And this is God's doing.
29For God has graciously granted you the privilege
not only of believing in Christ,
but of suffering for Christ as well—
30since you are having the same struggle that you saw I had
and now hear that I still have.

GOSPEL: MATTHEW 20:1-16

The Holy Gospel according to Matthew, the 20th chapter.

Jesus said:
[1]"The dominion of heaven is like a landowner
who went out early in the morning to hire laborers for his vineyard.
[2]After agreeing with the laborers for the usual daily wage,
he sent them into his vineyard.
[3]When he went out about nine o'clock,
he saw others standing idle in the marketplace;
[4]and he said to them,
'You also go into the vineyard, and I will pay you whatever is right.'
So they went.

[5]"When he went out again about noon and about three o'clock, he did
     the same.
[6]And about five o'clock he went out and found others standing around;
and he said to them,
'Why are you standing here idle all day?'
[7]They said to him, 'Because no one has hired us.'
He said to them, 'You also go into the vineyard.'

[8]"When evening came, the owner of the vineyard said to his manager,
'Call the laborers and give them their pay,
beginning with the last and then going to the first.'
[9]When those hired about five o'clock came,
each of them received the usual daily wage.
[10]Now when the first came, they thought they would receive more;
but each of them also received the usual daily wage.
[11]And when they received it,
they grumbled against the landowner, [12]saying,
'These last worked only one hour, and you have made them equal to us
who have borne the burden of the day and the scorching heat.'
[13]But he replied to one of them,
'Friend, I am doing you no wrong;
did you not agree with me for the usual daily wage?
[14]Take what belongs to you and go;
I choose to give to this last the same as I give to you.
[15]Am I not allowed to do what I choose with what belongs to me?
 Or are you envious because I am generous?'

[16]"So the last will be first, and the first will be last."

The Gospel of the Lord.

✠

S U N D A Y   B E T W E E N
S E P T E M B E R   25   A N D   O C T O B E R   1
I N C L U S I V E

SEPTEMBER 29, 1996　　　SEPTEMBER 26, 1999　　　SEPTEMBER 29, 2002

PROPER 21

FIRST READING: EZEKIEL 18:1-4, 25-32

A reading from Ezekiel:

[1]The word of the LORD came to me:
[2]What do you mean by repeating this proverb concerning the land of Israel,
"The parents have eaten sour grapes,
and the children's teeth are set on edge"?
[3]As I live, says the Lord GOD,
this proverb shall no more be used by you in Israel.
[4]Know that all lives are mine;
the life of the parent as well as the life of the child is mine:
it is only the person who sins that shall die. . . .

[25]Yet you say, "The way of the Lord is unfair."
Hear now, O house of Israel: Is my way unfair?
Is it not your ways that are unfair?
[26]When the righteous turn away from their righteousness and commit iniquity,
they shall die for it;
for the iniquity that they have committed they shall die.
[27]Again, when the wicked turn away from the wickedness they have committed
and do what is lawful and right,
they shall save their life.
[28]Because they considered and turned away from all the transgressions
that they had committed,
they shall surely live; they shall not die.
[29]Yet the house of Israel says, "The way of the Lord is unfair."
O house of Israel, are my ways unfair?
Is it not your ways that are unfair?

[30]Therefore I will judge you, O house of Israel,
all of you according to your ways, says the Lord GOD.
Repent and turn from all your transgressions;
otherwise iniquity will be your ruin.
[31]Cast away from you all the transgressions that you have committed
        against me,
and get yourselves a new heart and a new spirit!
Why will you die, O house of Israel?
[32]For I have no pleasure in the death of anyone, says the Lord GOD.
Turn, then, and live.

PSALMODY: PSALM 25:1-9

Psalm 25:1–8   LBW/BCP

SECOND READING: PHILIPPIANS 2:1-13

A reading from Philippians:

¹If then there is any encouragement in Christ,
any consolation from love, any sharing in the Spirit,
any compassion and sympathy,
²make my joy complete:
be of the same mind, having the same love,
being in full accord and of one mind.
³Do nothing from selfish ambition or conceit,
but in humility regard others as better than yourselves.
⁴Let each of you look not to your own interests,
but to the interests of others.

⁵Let the same mind be in you that was in Christ Jesus,
⁶who, although being in the form of God,
did not regard equality with God as something to be exploited,
⁷but relinquished it all, taking the form of a slave,
being born in human likeness.
And being found in human form, ⁸he humbled himself
and became obedient to the point of death—
even death on a cross.

⁹Therefore God also highly exalted him
and gave him the name that is above every name,
¹⁰so that at the name of Jesus every knee should bend,
in heaven and on earth and under the earth,
¹¹and every tongue should confess that Jesus Christ is Lord,
to the glory of God, the Father.

¹²Therefore, my beloved, just as you have always obeyed me,
not only in my presence, but much more now in my absence,
work out your own salvation with fear and trembling;
¹³for it is God who is at work in you,
enabling you both to will and to work for God's good pleasure.

GOSPEL: Matthew 21:23-32

The Holy Gospel according to Matthew, the 21st chapter.

[23]When Jesus entered the temple, the chief priests and the elders of the people
came to him as he was teaching, and said,
"By what authority are you doing these things,
and who gave you this authority?"
[24]Jesus said to them, "I will also ask you one question;
if you tell me the answer,
then I will also tell you by what authority I do these things.
[25]Did the baptism of John come from heaven, or was it of human origin?"
And they argued with one another,
"If we say, 'From heaven,' he will say to us,
'Why then did you not believe him?'
[26]But if we say, 'Of human origin,' we are afraid of the crowd;
for all regard John as a prophet."
[27]So they answered Jesus, "We do not know."
And he said to them,
"Neither will I tell you by what authority I am doing these things.

[28]"What do you think? A man had two sons;
he went to the first and said,
'Son, go and work in the vineyard today.'
[29]He answered, 'I will not'; but later he changed his mind and went.
[30]The father went to the second and said the same;
and he answered, 'I go, sir'; but he did not go.
[31]Which of the two did the will of his father?"
They said, "The first."
Jesus said to them, "Truly I tell you,
the tax collectors and the prostitutes are going into the dominion of God
        ahead of you.
[32]For John came to you in the way of righteousness
and you did not believe him,
but the tax collectors and the prostitutes believed him;
and even after you saw it,
you did not change your minds and believe him."

The Gospel of the Lord.

✠

SUNDAY BETWEEN
OCTOBER 2 AND 8 INCLUSIVE

OCTOBER 6, 1996   OCTOBER 3, 1999   OCTOBER 6, 2002

PROPER 22

FIRST READING: ISAIAH 5:1-7

A reading from Isaiah:

¹Let me sing for my beloved
my love-song concerning my beloved's vineyard:
"My beloved had a vineyard on a very fertile hill.
²My beloved dug it and cleared it of stones,
and planted it with choice vines;
built a watchtower in the midst of it,
and hewed out a wine vat in it,
and expected it to yield grapes, but it yielded wild grapes."

³And now, inhabitants of Jerusalem and people of Judah,
judge between me and my vineyard.
⁴What more was there to do for my vineyard that I have not done in it?
When I expected it to yield grapes, why did it yield wild grapes?

⁵And now I will tell you what I will do to my vineyard.
I will remove its hedge, and it shall be devoured;
I will break down its wall, and it shall be trampled down.
⁶I will make it a waste;
it shall not be pruned or hoed,
and it shall be overgrown with briers and thorns;
I will also command the clouds that they rain no rain upon it.

⁷For the vineyard of the LORD of hosts is the house of Israel,
and the people of Judah are God's pleasant planting;
for the LORD expected justice, but saw bloodshed;
righteousness, but heard a cry!

PSALMODY: PSALM 80:7-15   *Psalm 80:7–14*   LBW/BCP

SECOND READING: PHILIPPIANS 3:4b-14

A reading from Philippians:

Paul writes:
⁴ᵇIf anyone else has reason to be confident in the flesh, I have more:
⁵circumcised on the eighth day,
a member of the people of Israel, of the tribe of Benjamin,
a Hebrew born of Hebrews; as to the law, a Pharisee;
⁶as to zeal, a persecutor of the church;
as to righteousness under the law, blameless.

⁷Yet whatever gains I had,
these I have come to regard as loss because of Christ.
⁸More than that, I regard everything as loss
because of the surpassing value of knowing Christ Jesus my Lord.
For his sake I have suffered the loss of all things,
and I regard them as rubbish,
in order that I may gain Christ ⁹and be found in him,
not having a righteousness of my own that comes from the law,
but one that comes through faith in Christ,
the righteousness from God based on faith.

¹⁰I want to know Christ and the power of his resurrection
and the sharing of his sufferings by becoming like him in his death,
¹¹if somehow I may attain the resurrection from the dead.
¹²Not that I have already obtained this or have already reached the goal
but I press on to make it my own,
because Christ Jesus has made me his own.
¹³Beloved, I do not consider that I have made it my own;
but this one thing I do:
forgetting what lies behind and straining forward to what lies ahead,
¹⁴I press on toward the goal
for the prize of the heavenly call of God in Christ Jesus.

The Holy Gospel according to Matthew, the 21st chapter.

Jesus said:
33"Listen to another parable.
There was a landowner who planted a vineyard,
put a fence around it, dug a wine press in it, and built a watchtower.
Then he leased it to tenants and went to another country.
34When the harvest time had come,
he sent his slaves to the tenants to collect his produce.
35But the tenants seized his slaves and beat one, killed another,
        and stoned another.
36Again he sent other slaves, more than the first;
and they treated them in the same way.
37Finally he sent his son to them, saying,
'They will respect my son.'
38But when the tenants saw the son, they said to themselves,
'This is the heir;
come, let us kill him and get his inheritance.'
39So they seized him, threw him out of the vineyard, and killed him.

40"Now when the owner of the vineyard comes,
what will he do to those tenants?"
41They said to Jesus,
"The owner will put those wretches to a miserable death,
and lease the vineyard to other tenants
who will give him the produce at the harvest time."

42Jesus said to them, "Have you never read in the scriptures:
'The stone that the builders rejected has become the cornerstone;
this was the Lord's doing,
and it is amazing in our eyes'?
43Therefore I tell you,
the dominion of God will be taken away from you
and given to a people that produces the fruits of it.
44The one who falls on this stone will be broken to pieces;
and it will crush anyone on whom it falls."

45When the chief priests and the Pharisees heard his parables,
they realized that he was speaking about them.
46They wanted to arrest him,
but they feared the crowds, because the people regarded him as a prophet.

The Gospel of the Lord.

✝

Sunday between
October 9 and 15 inclusive

OCTOBER 13, 1996   OCTOBER 10, 1999   OCTOBER 13, 2002

PROPER 23

FIRST READING: Isaiah 25:1-9

A reading from Isaiah:

¹O Lord, you are my God;
I will exalt you, I will praise your name;
for you have done wonderful things,
plans formed of old, faithful and sure.
²For you have made the city a heap,
the fortified city a ruin;
the palace of aliens is a city no more,
it will never be rebuilt.
³Therefore strong peoples will glorify you;
cities of ruthless nations will fear you.
⁴For you have been a refuge to the poor,
a refuge to the needy in their distress,
a shelter from the rainstorm and a shade from the heat.
When the blast of the ruthless was like a winter rainstorm,
⁵the noise of aliens like heat in a dry place,
you subdued the heat with the shade of clouds;
the song of the ruthless was stilled.

⁶On this mountain the Lord of hosts will make for all peoples
a feast of rich food, a feast of well-aged wines,
of rich food filled with marrow, of well-aged wines strained clear.
⁷And the Lord will destroy on this mountain
the shroud that is cast over all peoples,
the sheet that is spread over all nations;
the Lord will swallow up death forever.
⁸Then the Lord God will wipe away the tears from all faces,
and the disgrace of the chosen people God will take away from all the earth,
for the Lord has spoken.
⁹It will be said on that day,
Lo, this is our God, for whom we have waited, so that God might save us.
This is the Lord for whom we have waited;
let us be glad and rejoice in the salvation of the Lord.

PSALMODY: Psalm 23

SECOND READING: PHILIPPIANS 4:1-9

A reading from Philippians:

¹My brothers and sisters,
whom I love and long for, my joy and crown,
stand firm in the Lord in this way, my beloved.

²I urge Euodia and I urge Syntyche to be of the same mind in the Lord.
³Yes, and I ask you also, my loyal companion,
help these women,
for they have struggled beside me in the work of the gospel,
together with Clement and the rest of my co-workers,
whose names are in the book of life.

⁴Rejoice in the Lord always; again I will say, Rejoice.
⁵Let your gentleness be known to everyone.
The Lord is near.
⁶Do not worry about anything,
but in everything by prayer and supplication with thanksgiving
let your requests be made known to God.
⁷And the peace of God, which surpasses all understanding,
will guard your hearts and your minds in Christ Jesus.

⁸Finally, beloved, whatever is true, whatever is honorable,
whatever is just, whatever is pure,
whatever is pleasing, whatever is commendable,
if there is any excellence and if there is anything worthy of praise,
think about these things.
⁹Keep on doing the things that you have learned and received
and heard and seen in me,
and the God of peace will be with you.

GOSPEL: MATTHEW 22:1-14

The Holy Gospel according to Matthew, the 22nd chapter.

¹Once more Jesus spoke to them in parables, saying:
²"The dominion of heaven may be compared to a king
who gave a wedding banquet for his son.
³He sent his slaves to call those who had been invited to the wedding banquet,
but they would not come.
⁴Again he sent other slaves, saying,
'Tell those who have been invited:
Look, I have prepared my dinner,
my oxen and my fat calves have been slaughtered,
and everything is ready;
come to the wedding banquet.'
⁵But they made light of it and went away,
one to his farm, another to his business,
⁶while the rest seized his slaves, mistreated them, and killed them.
⁷The king was enraged.
He sent his troops, destroyed those murderers, and burned their city.

⁸"Then the king said to his slaves,
'The wedding is ready, but those invited were not worthy.
⁹Go therefore into the main streets,
and invite everyone you find to the wedding banquet.'
¹⁰Those slaves went out into the streets and gathered all whom they found,
both good and bad; so the wedding hall was filled with guests.

¹¹"But when the king came in to see the guests,
he noticed a man there who was not wearing a wedding robe,
¹²and he said to him,
'Friend, how did you get in here without a wedding robe?'
And he was speechless.
¹³Then the king said to the attendants,
'Bind him hand and foot, and throw him into the outer darkness,
where there will be weeping and gnashing of teeth.'

¹⁴"For many are called, but few are chosen."

The Gospel of the Lord.

✝

SUNDAY BETWEEN
OCTOBER 16 AND 22 INCLUSIVE

OCTOBER 20, 1996   OCTOBER 17, 1999   OCTOBER 20, 2002

PROPER 24

FIRST READING: ISAIAH 45:1-7

A reading from Isaiah:

¹Thus says the LORD to Cyrus, the LORD's anointed,
whose right hand I have grasped to subdue nations before him
and strip rulers of their robes,
to open doors before Cyrus—
and the gates shall not be closed:
²I will go before you and level the mountains,
I will break in pieces the doors of bronze
and cut through the bars of iron,
³I will give you the treasures of darkness
and riches hidden in secret places,
so that you may know that it is I, the LORD,
the God of Israel, who call you by your name.
⁴For the sake of my servant Jacob, and Israel my chosen,
I call you by your name,
I surname you, though you do not know me.
⁵I am the LORD, and there is no other;
besides me there is no god.
I arm you, though you do not know me,
⁶so that they may know,
from the rising of the sun and from the west,
that there is no one besides me;
I am the LORD, and there is no other.
⁷I form light and create darkness,
I make weal and create woe;
I the LORD do all these things.

PSALMODY: PSALM 96:1-9 [10-13]

SECOND READING: 1 THESSALONIANS 1:1-10

A reading from First Thessalonians:

[1]Paul, Silvanus, and Timothy,
To the church of the Thessalonians
in God, the Father, and the Lord Jesus Christ:
Grace to you and peace.

[2]We always give thanks to God for all of you and mention you in our prayers,
constantly [3]remembering before our God and Father
your work of faith and labor of love and steadfastness of hope
in our Lord Jesus Christ.
[4]For we know, brothers and sisters beloved by God, that God has chosen you,
[5]because our message of the gospel came to you not in word only,
but also in power and in the Holy Spirit and with full conviction;
just as you know what kind of persons we proved to be among you
            for your sake.
[6]And you became imitators of us and of the Lord,
for in spite of persecution
you received the word with joy inspired by the Holy Spirit,
[7]so that you became an example to all the believers in Macedonia
            and in Achaia.

[8]For the word of the Lord has sounded forth from you
not only in Macedonia and Achaia,
but in every place your faith in God has become known,
so that we have no need to speak about it.
[9]For the people of those regions report about us
what kind of welcome we had among you,
and how you turned to God from idols, to serve a living and true God,
[10]and to wait for God's Son from heaven, whom God raised from the dead—
Jesus, who rescues us from the wrath that is coming.

The Holy Gospel according to Matthew, the 22nd chapter.

[15]The Pharisees went and plotted to entrap Jesus in what he said.
[16]So they sent their disciples to Jesus, along with the Herodians, saying,
"Teacher, we know that you are sincere,
and teach the way of God in accordance with truth,
and show deference to no one; for you do not regard people with partiality.
[17]Tell us, then, what you think.
Is it lawful to pay taxes to the emperor, or not?"
[18]But Jesus, aware of their malice, said,
"Why are you putting me to the test, you hypocrites?
[19]Show me the coin used for the tax."
And they brought him a denarius.
[20]Then he said to them, "Whose head is this, and whose title?"
[21]They answered, "The emperor's."

Then Jesus said to them,
"Give therefore to the emperor the things that are the emperor's,
and to God the things that are God's."
[22]When they heard this, they were amazed;
and they left him and went away.

The Gospel of the Lord.

✝

SUNDAY BETWEEN
OCTOBER 23 AND 29 INCLUSIVE

OCTOBER 27, 1996   *OCTOBER 24, 1999*   *OCTOBER 27, 2002*

PROPER 25

FIRST READING: LEVITICUS 19:1-2, 15-18

A reading from Leviticus:

¹The LORD spoke to Moses, saying:
²Speak to all the congregation of the people of Israel and say to them:
You shall be holy, for I the LORD your God am holy.

¹⁵You shall not render an unjust judgment;
you shall not be partial to the poor or defer to the great:
with justice you shall judge your neighbor.
¹⁶You shall not go around as a slanderer among your people,
and you shall not profit by the blood of your neighbor: I am the LORD.
¹⁷You shall not hate in your heart anyone of your kin;
you shall reprove your neighbor, or you will incur guilt yourself.
¹⁸You shall not take vengeance or bear a grudge against any of your people,
but you shall love your neighbor as yourself: I am the LORD.

PSALMODY: PSALM 1

SECOND READING: 1 Thessalonians 2:1-8

A reading from First Thessalonians:

[1]You yourselves know, brothers and sisters,
that our coming to you was not in vain,
[2]but though we had already suffered
and been shamefully mistreated at Philippi, as you know,
we had courage in our God to declare to you the gospel of God
in spite of great opposition.
[3]For our appeal does not spring from deceit or impure motives or trickery,
[4]but just as we have been approved by God
to be entrusted with the message of the gospel,
even so we speak, not to please mortals,
but to please God who tests our hearts.

[5]As you know and as God is our witness,
we never came with words of flattery or with a pretext for greed;
[6]nor did we seek praise from mortals, whether from you or from others,
[7]though we might have made demands as apostles of Christ.
But we were gentle among you,
like a nursing mother tenderly caring for her own children.
[8]So deeply do we care for you that we are determined to share with you
not only the gospel of God but also our own selves,
because you have become very dear to us.

GOSPEL: MATTHEW 22:34-46

The Holy Gospel according to Matthew, the 22nd chapter.

[34]When the Pharisees heard that Jesus had silenced the Sadducees,
they gathered together,
[35]and one of them, a lawyer, asked Jesus a question to test him.
[36]"Teacher, which commandment in the law is the greatest?"
[37]He said to him,
" 'You shall love the Lord your God with all your heart,
and with all your soul, and with all your mind.'
[38]This is the greatest and first commandment.
[39]And a second is like it:
'You shall love your neighbor as yourself.'
[40]On these two commandments hang all the law and the prophets."

[41]Now while the Pharisees were gathered together,
Jesus asked them this question:
[42]"What do you think of the Messiah? Whose son is he?"
They said to him, "The son of David."
[43]Jesus said to them,
"How is it then that David by the Spirit calls him Lord, saying,
[44]'The Lord said to my Lord,
"Sit at my right hand,
until I put your enemies under your feet" '?
[45]If David thus calls him Lord, how can he be his son?"
[46]No one was able to give Jesus an answer,
nor from that day did anyone dare to ask him any more questions.

The Gospel of the Lord.

✠

SUNDAY BETWEEN
OCTOBER 30 AND NOVEMBER 5
INCLUSIVE

NOVEMBER 3, 1996   *OCTOBER 31, 1999*   *NOVEMBER 3, 2002*

PROPER 26

FIRST READING: MICAH 3:5-12

A reading from Micah:

⁵Thus says the LORD concerning the prophets who lead my people astray,
who cry "Peace" when they have something to eat,
but declare war against those who put nothing into their mouths.
⁶Therefore it shall be night to you, without vision,
and darkness to you, without revelation.
The sun shall go down upon the prophets,
and the day shall be dark over them;
⁷the seers shall be disgraced,
and the diviners put to shame;
they shall all cover their lips, for there is no answer from God.
⁸But as for me, I am filled with power, with the spirit of the LORD,
and with justice and might,
to declare to Jacob their transgression and to Israel their sin.

⁹Hear this, you rulers of the house of Jacob
and chiefs of the house of Israel,
who abhor justice and pervert all equity,
¹⁰who build Zion with blood and Jerusalem with wrong!
¹¹Its rulers give judgment for a bribe,
its priests teach for a price,
its prophets give oracles for money;
yet they lean upon the LORD and say,
"Surely the LORD is with us!
No harm shall come upon us."
¹²Therefore because of you Zion shall be plowed as a field;
Jerusalem shall become a heap of ruins,
and the mountain of the house a wooded height.

PSALMODY: PSALM 43

SECOND READING: 1 THESSALONIANS 2:9-13

A reading from First Thessalonians:

⁹You remember our labor and toil, brothers and sisters;
we worked night and day,
so that we might not burden any of you
while we proclaimed to you the gospel of God.
¹⁰You are witnesses, and God also,
how pure, upright, and blameless our conduct was toward you believers.
¹¹As you know, we dealt with each one of you like a father with his children,
¹²urging and encouraging you and pleading that you lead a life worthy of God,
who calls you into God's own dominion and glory.

¹³We also constantly give thanks to God for this,
that when you received the word of God that you heard from us,
you accepted it not as a human word but as what it really is,
God's word, which is also at work in you believers.

GOSPEL: MATTHEW 23:1-12

The Holy Gospel according to Matthew, the 23rd chapter.

¹Jesus said to the crowds and to his disciples,
²"The scribes and the Pharisees sit on Moses' seat;
³therefore, do whatever they teach you and follow it;
but do not do as they do, for they do not practice what they teach.
⁴They tie up heavy burdens, hard to bear,
and lay them on the shoulders of others;
but they themselves are unwilling to lift a finger to move them.
⁵They do all their deeds to be seen by others;
for they make their phylacteries broad and their fringes long.
⁶They love to have the place of honor at banquets
and the best seats in the synagogues,
⁷and to be greeted with respect in the marketplaces,
and to have people call them rabbi.
⁸But you are not to be called rabbi,
for you have one teacher, and you are all students.
⁹And call no one your father on earth,
for you have one Father—the one in heaven.
¹⁰Nor are you to be called instructors,
for you have one instructor, the Messiah.

¹¹"The greatest among you will be your servant.
¹²All who exalt themselves will be humbled,
and all who humble themselves will be exalted."

The Gospel of the Lord.

SUNDAY BETWEEN
NOVEMBER 6 AND 12 INCLUSIVE

NOVEMBER 10, 1996   NOVEMBER 7, 1999   NOVEMBER 10, 2002

PROPER 27

FIRST READING: AMOS 5:18-24   *Alternate Reading: Wisdom of Solomon 6:12-16 (p. 418)*

A reading from Amos:

[18]Alas for you who desire the day of the LORD!
Why do you want the day of the LORD?
It is darkness, not light;
[19]as if someone fled from a lion, and was met by a bear;
or went into the house and rested a hand against the wall,
and was bitten by a snake.
[20]Is not the day of the LORD darkness, not light,
and gloom with no brightness in it?

[21]I hate, I despise your festivals,
and I take no delight in your solemn assemblies.
[22]Even though you offer me your burnt offerings and grain offerings,
I will not accept them;
and the offerings of well-being of your fatted animals
I will not look upon.
[23]Take away from me the noise of your songs;
I will not listen to the melody of your harps.
[24]But let justice roll down like waters,
and righteousness like an ever-flowing stream.

PSALMODY: PSALM 70   *Alternate Psalmody: Wisdom of Solomon 6:17–20*

SECOND READING: 1 THESSALONIANS 4:13-18

A reading from First Thessalonians:

¹³We do not want you to be uninformed, brothers and sisters,
about those who have died,
so that you may not grieve as others do who have no hope.
¹⁴For since we believe that Jesus died and rose again,
even so, through Jesus, God will bring with him those who have died.
¹⁵For this we declare to you by the word of the Lord,
that we who are alive, who are left until the coming of the Lord,
will by no means precede those who have died.
¹⁶For that very Lord, with a cry of command,
with the archangel's call and with the sound of God's trumpet,
will descend from heaven, and the dead in Christ will rise first.
¹⁷Then we who are alive, who are left,
will be caught up in the clouds together with them to meet the Lord in the air;
and so we will be with the Lord forever.

¹⁸Therefore encourage one another with these words.

GOSPEL: MATTHEW 25:1-13

The Holy Gospel according to Matthew, the 25th chapter.

Jesus said:
[1]"Then the dominion of heaven will be like this.
Ten bridesmaids took their lamps and went to meet the bridegroom.
[2]Five of them were foolish, and five were wise.
[3]When the foolish took their lamps, they took no oil with them;
[4]but the wise took flasks of oil with their lamps.
[5]As the bridegroom was delayed, all of them became drowsy and slept.

[6]"But at midnight there was a shout,
'Look! Here is the bridegroom! Come out to meet him.'
[7]Then all those bridesmaids got up and trimmed their lamps.
[8]The foolish said to the wise,
'Give us some of your oil, for our lamps are going out.'
[9]But the wise replied,
'No! there will not be enough for you and for us;
you had better go to the dealers and buy some for yourselves.'
[10]And while they went to buy it, the bridegroom came,
and those who were ready went with him into the wedding banquet;
and the door was shut.
[11]Later the other bridesmaids came also, saying,
'Sir, sir, open to us.'
[12]But he replied, 'Truly I tell you, I do not know you.'

[13]"Keep awake therefore, for you know neither the day nor the hour."

The Gospel of the Lord.

$$\maltese$$

SUNDAY BETWEEN
NOVEMBER 13 AND 19 INCLUSIVE

NOVEMBER 17, 1996   *NOVEMBER 14, 1999*   *NOVEMBER 17, 2002*

PROPER 28

FIRST READING: ZEPHANIAH 1:7, 12-18

A reading from Zephaniah:

⁷Be silent before the Lord GOD!
For the day of the LORD is at hand;
the LORD has prepared a sacrifice
and has consecrated those who are called.

¹²At that time I will search Jerusalem with lamps,
and I will punish the people who rest complacently on their dregs,
those who say in their hearts,
"The LORD will not do good, nor will the LORD do harm."
¹³Their wealth shall be plundered, and their houses laid waste.
Though they build houses, they shall not inhabit them;
though they plant vineyards, they shall not drink wine from them.

¹⁴The great day of the LORD is near,
near and hastening fast;
the sound of the day of the LORD is bitter,
the warrior cries aloud there.
¹⁵That day will be a day of wrath,
a day of distress and anguish,
a day of ruin and devastation,
a day of darkness and gloom,
a day of clouds and thick darkness,
¹⁶a day of trumpet blast and battle cry
against the fortified cities and against the lofty battlements.

¹⁷I will bring such distress upon people
that they shall walk like the blind;
because they have sinned against the LORD,
their blood shall be poured out like dust, and their flesh like dung.
¹⁸Neither their silver nor their gold
will be able to save them on the day of the LORD's wrath;
in the fire of the LORD's passion the whole earth shall be consumed;
for a full, a terrible end the LORD will make of all the inhabitants of the earth.

PSALMODY: PSALM 90:1-8 [9–11] 12

SECOND READING: 1 THESSALONIANS 5:1-11

A reading from First Thessalonians:

¹Now concerning the times and the seasons, brothers and sisters,
you do not need to have anything written to you.
²For you yourselves know very well
that the day of the Lord will come like a thief in the night.
³When they say, "There is peace and security,"
then sudden destruction will come upon them,
as labor pains come upon a pregnant woman,
and there will be no escape!

⁴But you, beloved,
are not in darkness, for that day to surprise you like a thief;
⁵for you are all children of light and children of the day;
we are not of the night or of darkness.
⁶So then let us not fall asleep as others do,
but let us keep awake and be sober;
⁷for those who sleep sleep at night,
and those who are drunk get drunk at night.
⁸But since we belong to the day, let us be sober,
and put on the breastplate of faith and love,
and for a helmet the hope of salvation.
⁹For God has destined us not for wrath
but for obtaining salvation through our Lord Jesus Christ,
¹⁰who died for us,
so that whether we are awake or asleep we may live with him.
¹¹Therefore encourage one another and build up each other,
as indeed you are doing.

The Holy Gospel according to Matthew, the 25th chapter.

Jesus said:
¹⁴"For it is as if a man, going on a journey,
summoned his slaves and entrusted his property to them;
¹⁵to one he gave five talents, to another two, to another one,
to each according to his ability.
Then he went away.

¹⁶"The one who had received the five talents went off at once
and traded with them, and made five more talents.
¹⁷In the same way, the one who had the two talents made two more talents.
¹⁸But the one who had received the one talent went off
and dug a hole in the ground and hid his master's money.

¹⁹"After a long time the master of those slaves came
and settled accounts with them.
²⁰Then the one who had received the five talents came forward,
bringing five more talents, saying,
'Master, you handed over to me five talents;
see, I have made five more talents.'
²¹His master said to him,
'Well done, good and trustworthy slave;
you have been trustworthy in a few things,
I will put you in charge of many things;
enter into the joy of your master.'
²²And the one with the two talents also came forward, saying,
'Master, you handed over to me two talents;
see, I have made two more talents.'
²³His master said to him,
'Well done, good and trustworthy slave;
you have been trustworthy in a few things,
I will put you in charge of many things;
enter into the joy of your master.'

²⁴"Then the one who had received the one talent also came forward, saying,
'Master, I knew that you were a harsh man,
reaping where you did not sow, and gathering where you did not scatter seed;
²⁵so I was afraid, and I went and hid your talent in the ground.
Here you have what is yours.'

[26]But his master replied, 'You wicked and lazy slave!
You knew, did you, that I reap where I did not sow,
and gather where I did not scatter?
[27]Then you ought to have invested my money with the bankers,
and on my return I would have received what was my own with interest.
[28]So take the talent from him, and give it to the one with the ten talents.

[29]"'For to all those who have, more will be given,
and they will have an abundance;
but from those who have nothing, even what they have will be taken away.
[30]As for this worthless slave, throw him into the outer darkness,
where there will be weeping and gnashing of teeth.'"

The Gospel of the Lord.

✝

THE REIGN OF CHRIST
Last Sunday after Pentecost†

NOVEMBER 24, 1996   *NOVEMBER 21, 1999*   *NOVEMBER 24, 2002*

PROPER 29

FIRST READING: Ezekiel 34:11-16, 20-24

A reading from Ezekiel:

¹¹Thus says the Lord GOD:
I myself will search for my sheep, and will seek them out.
¹²As shepherds seek out their flocks when they are among their scattered
       sheep,
so I will seek out my sheep.
I will rescue them from all the places to which they have been scattered
on a day of clouds and thick darkness.
¹³I will bring them out from the peoples and gather them from the countries,
and will bring them into their own land;
and I will feed them on the mountains of Israel,
by the watercourses, and in all the inhabited parts of the land.
¹⁴I will feed them with good pasture,
and the mountain heights of Israel shall be their pasture;
there they shall lie down in good grazing land,
and they shall feed on rich pasture on the mountains of Israel.
¹⁵I myself will be the shepherd of my sheep,
and I will make them lie down, says the Lord GOD.
¹⁶I will seek the lost, and I will bring back the strayed,
and I will bind up the injured, and I will strengthen the weak,
but the fat and the strong I will destroy.
I will feed them with justice.

²⁰Therefore, thus says the Lord GOD to them:
I myself will judge between the fat sheep and the lean sheep.
²¹Because you pushed with flank and shoulder,
and butted at all the weak animals with your horns
until you scattered them far and wide,
²²I will save my flock, and they shall no longer be ravaged;
and I will judge between sheep and sheep.

---

†*Sunday between November 20 and 26 inclusive*

[23]I will set up over them one shepherd, my servant David,
and he shall feed them:
he shall feed them and be their shepherd.
[24]And I, the LORD, will be their God,
and my servant David shall be ruler among them;
I, the LORD, have spoken.

PSALMODY: PSALM 95:1-7a

SECOND READING: EPHESIANS 1:15-23

A reading from Ephesians:

¹⁵I have heard of your faith in the Lord Jesus
and your love toward all the saints,
and for this reason ¹⁶I do not cease to give thanks for you
as I remember you in my prayers.
¹⁷I pray that the God of our Lord Jesus Christ, the Father of glory,
may give you a spirit of wisdom and revelation, as you come to know God,
¹⁸so that, with the eyes of your heart enlightened,
you may know what is the hope to which God has called you,
what are the riches of God's glorious inheritance among the saints,
¹⁹and what is the immeasurable greatness of God's power for us who believe,
according to the working of God's great power.

²⁰God put this power to work in Christ
when God raised him from the dead
and seated him at the right hand of Power in the heavenly places,
²¹far above all rule and authority and power and dominion,
and above every name that is named,
not only in this age but also in the age to come.
²²And God has put all things under the feet of Christ
and has made him the head over all things for the church,
²³which is the body of Christ, the fullness of the one who fills all in all.

GOSPEL: MATTHEW 25:31-46

The Holy Gospel according to Matthew, the 25th chapter.

Jesus said:
³¹"When the Son-of-Man comes in his glory, and all the angels with him,
then he will sit on the throne of his glory.
³²All the nations will be gathered before him,
and he will separate people one from another
as a shepherd separates the sheep from the goats,
³³and he will put the sheep at his right hand and the goats at the left.

³⁴"Then the king will say to those at his right hand,
'Come, you that are blessed by my Father,
inherit the dominion prepared for you from the foundation of the world;
³⁵for I was hungry and you gave me food,
I was thirsty and you gave me something to drink,
I was a stranger and you welcomed me,
³⁶I was naked and you gave me clothing,
I was sick and you took care of me,
I was in prison and you visited me.'
³⁷Then the righteous will answer him,

'Lord, when was it that we saw you hungry and gave you food,
or thirsty and gave you something to drink?
[38]And when was it that we saw you a stranger and welcomed you,
or naked and gave you clothing?
[39]And when was it that we saw you sick or in prison and visited you?'
[40]And the king will answer them,
'Truly I tell you,
just as you did it to one of the least of these who are members of my family,
you did it to me.'

[41]"Then he will say to those at his left hand,
'You that are accursed,
depart from me into the eternal fire prepared for the devil and the devil's angels;
[42]for I was hungry and you gave me no food,
I was thirsty and you gave me nothing to drink,
[43]I was a stranger and you did not welcome me,
naked and you did not give me clothing,
sick and in prison and you did not visit me.'
[44]Then they also will answer,
'Lord, when was it that we saw you hungry or thirsty
or a stranger or naked or sick or in prison,
and did not take care of you?'
[45]Then he will answer them,
'Truly I tell you,
just as you did not do it to one of the least of these,
you did not do it to me.'
[46]And these will go away into eternal punishment,
but the righteous into eternal life."

The Gospel of the Lord.

✝

LESSER FESTIVALS
AND OCCASIONS

St. Andrew, Apostle

NOVEMBER 30

FIRST READING: Ezekiel 3:16–21

A reading from Ezekiel:

¹⁶At the end of seven days, the word of the LORD came to me:
¹⁷Mortal, I have made you a sentinel for the house of Israel;
whenever you hear a word from my mouth,
you shall give them warning from me.
¹⁸If I say to the wicked, "You shall surely die,"
and you give them no warning,
or speak to warn the wicked from their wicked way, in order to save their life,
those wicked persons shall die for their iniquity;
but their blood I will require at your hand.
¹⁹But if you warn the wicked,
and they do not turn from their wickedness, or from their wicked way,
they shall die for their iniquity; but you will have saved your life.

²⁰Again, if the righteous turn from their righteousness and commit iniquity,
and I lay a stumbling block before them, they shall die;
because you have not warned them, they shall die for their sin,
and their righteous deeds that they have done shall not be remembered;
but their blood I will require at your hand.
²¹If, however, you warn the righteous not to sin, and they do not sin,
they shall surely live, because they took warning;
and you will have saved your life.

PSALMODY: Psalm 19:1–6

SECOND READING: Romans 10:10–18

A reading from Romans:

¹⁰One believes with the heart and so is justified,
and one confesses with the mouth and so is saved.
¹¹The scripture says,
"No one who believes in the Lord will be put to shame."

¹²For there is no distinction between Jew and Greek;
the same Lord is Lord of all and is generous to all who ask for help.
¹³For, "Everyone who calls on the name of the Lord shall be saved."

¹⁴But how are they to call on one in whom they have not believed?
And how are they to believe in one of whom they have never heard?
And how are they to hear without someone to preach?
¹⁵And how are they to preach unless they are sent?
As it is written,
"How beautiful are the feet of those who bring good news!"
¹⁶But not all have obeyed the good news; for Isaiah says,
"Lord, who has believed our message?"
¹⁷So faith comes from what is heard,
and what is heard comes through the word of Christ.
¹⁸But I ask, have they not heard? Indeed they have; for
"Their voice has gone out to all the earth,
and their words to the ends of the world."

GOSPEL: JOHN 1:35–42

The Holy Gospel according to John, the first chapter.

³⁵The next day John again was standing with two of his disciples,
³⁶and as he watched Jesus walk by, he exclaimed,
"Look, here is the Lamb of God!"
³⁷The two disciples heard him say this, and they followed Jesus.
³⁸When Jesus turned and saw them following, he said to them,
"What are you looking for?"
They said to him,
"Rabbi" (which translated means Teacher),
"where are you staying?"
³⁹He said to them, "Come and see."

They came and saw where Jesus was staying,
and they remained with him that day.
It was about four o'clock in the afternoon.
⁴⁰One of the two who heard John speak and followed him
was Andrew, Simon Peter's brother.
⁴¹Andrew first found his brother Simon and said to him,
"We have found the Messiah" (which is translated Anointed).
⁴²He brought Simon to Jesus, who looked at him and said,
"You are Simon son of John.
You are to be called Cephas" (which is translated Peter).

The Gospel of the Lord.

St. Thomas, Apostle

DECEMBER 21

FIRST READING: JUDGES 6:36–40

A reading from Judges:

³⁶Gideon said to God,
"In order to see whether you will deliver Israel by my hand, as you have said,
³⁷I am going to lay a fleece of wool on the threshing floor;
if there is dew on the fleece alone, and it is dry on all the ground,
then I shall know that you will deliver Israel by my hand, as you have said."
³⁸And it was so.
When Gideon rose early next morning and squeezed the fleece,
he wrung enough dew from the fleece to fill a bowl with water.

³⁹Then Gideon said to God, "Do not let your anger burn against me,
let me speak one more time;
let me, please, make trial with the fleece just once more;
let it be dry only on the fleece, and on all the ground let there be dew."
⁴⁰And God did so that night.
It was dry on the fleece only, and on all the ground there was dew.

PSALMODY: PSALM 136:1–4, 23–26

SECOND READING: EPHESIANS 4:11–16

A reading from Ephesians:

¹¹The gifts of Christ were that some would be apostles,
some prophets, some evangelists, some pastors and teachers,
¹²to equip the saints for the work of ministry,
for building up the body of Christ,
¹³until all of us come to the unity of the faith
and of the knowledge of the Son of God,
to maturity, to the measure of the full stature of Christ.

¹⁴We must no longer be children,
tossed to and fro and blown about by every wind of doctrine,
by people's trickery, by their craftiness in deceitful scheming.
¹⁵But speaking the truth in love,
we must grow up in every way into the one who is the head, into Christ,

¹⁶from whom the whole body,
joined and knit together by every ligament with which it is equipped,
as each part is working properly,
promotes the body's growth in building itself up in love.

GOSPEL: JOHN 14:1–7

The Holy Gospel according to John, the 14th chapter.

Jesus said:
¹"Do not let your hearts be troubled.
Believe in God, believe also in me.
²In my Father's house there are many dwelling places.
If it were not so, would I have told you that I go to prepare a place for you?
³And if I go and prepare a place for you,
I will come again and will take you to myself,
so that where I am, there you may be also.
⁴And you know the way to the place where I am going."

⁵Thomas said to Jesus, "Lord, we do not know where you are going.
How can we know the way?"
⁶Jesus said to him, "I am the way, and the truth, and the life.
No one comes to the Father except through me.
⁷If you know me, you will know my Father also.
From now on you do know and have seen my Father."

The Gospel of the Lord.

St. Stephen, Deacon and Martyr

DECEMBER 26

FIRST READING: 2 CHRONICLES 24:17–22

A reading from Second Chronicles:

[17]Now after the death of Jehoiada the officials of Judah came
and did obeisance to the king;
then the king listened to them.
[18]They abandoned the house of the LORD, the God of their ancestors,
and served the sacred poles and the idols.
And wrath came upon Judah and Jerusalem for this guilt of theirs.
[19]Yet the LORD sent prophets among them to bring them back to the LORD;
they testified against them, but they would not listen.

[20]Then the spirit of God took possession of Zechariah
son of the priest Jehoiada;
he stood above the people and said to them,
"Thus says God:
Why do you transgress the commandments of the LORD
so that you cannot prosper?
Because you have forsaken the LORD, the LORD has also forsaken you."
[21]But they conspired against Zechariah,
and by command of the king
they stoned him to death in the court of the house of the LORD.
[22]King Joash did not remember the kindness that Jehoiada,
Zechariah's father, had shown him, but killed his son.
As he was dying, he said, "May the LORD see and avenge!"

PSALMODY: PSALM 17:1–9, 15   *Psalm 17:1–9, 16*   LBW/BCP

SECOND READING: ACTS 6:8—7:2a, 51–60

A reading from Acts:

[8]Stephen, full of grace and power,
did great wonders and signs among the people.
[9]Then some of those who belonged to the synagogue of the Freed Slaves
        (as it was called),
Cyrenians, Alexandrians, and others of those from Cilicia and Asia,
stood up and argued with Stephen.

¹⁰But they could not withstand the wisdom and the Spirit with which he spoke.
¹¹Then they secretly instigated some men to say,
"We have heard him speak blasphemous words against Moses and God."

¹²They stirred up the people as well as the elders and the scribes;
then they suddenly confronted Stephen, seized him,
and brought him before the council.
¹³They set up false witnesses who said,
"This man never stops saying things against this holy place and the law;
¹⁴for we have heard him say that this Jesus of Nazareth will destroy this place
and will change the customs that Moses handed on to us."
¹⁵And all who sat in the council looked intently at him,
and they saw that his face was like the face of an angel.
⁷:¹Then the high priest asked him,
"Are these things so?"

²ᵃAnd Stephen replied: "Brothers and fathers, listen to me.
⁵¹"You are stiff-necked and uncircumcised in heart and ears.
You are forever opposing the Holy Spirit, just as your ancestors used to do.
⁵²Which of the prophets did your ancestors not persecute?
They killed those who foretold the coming of the Righteous One,
and now you have become his betrayers and murderers.
⁵³You are the ones that received the law as ordained by angels,
and yet you have not kept it."

⁵⁴When they heard these things, they became enraged
and ground their teeth at Stephen.
⁵⁵But filled with the Holy Spirit,
he gazed into heaven and saw the glory of God
and Jesus standing at the right hand of God.
⁵⁶"Look," he said,
"I see the heavens opened
and the Son-of-Man standing at the right hand of God!"

⁵⁷But they covered their ears,
and with a loud shout all rushed together against him.
⁵⁸Then they dragged Stephen out of the city and began to stone him;
and the witnesses laid their coats at the feet of a young man named Saul.
⁵⁹While they were stoning Stephen, he prayed,
"Lord Jesus, receive my spirit."
⁶⁰Then he knelt down and cried out in a loud voice,
"Lord, do not hold this sin against them."
When he had said this, he died.

The Holy Gospel according to Matthew, the 23rd chapter.

Jesus said:
[34]"Therefore I send you prophets, sages, and scribes,
some of whom you will kill and crucify,
and some you will flog in your synagogues and pursue from town to town,
[35]so that upon you may come all the righteous blood shed on earth,
from the blood of righteous Abel to the blood of Zechariah son of Barachiah,
whom you murdered between the sanctuary and the altar.
[36]Truly I tell you, all this will come upon this generation.

[37]"Jerusalem, Jerusalem,
the city that kills the prophets and stones those who are sent to it!
How often have I desired to gather your children together
as a hen gathers her brood under her wings,
and you were not willing!
[38]See, your house is left to you, desolate.
[39]For I tell you, you will not see me again until you say,
'Blessed is the one who comes in the name of the Lord.' "

The Gospel of the Lord.

St. John, Apostle and Evangelist

DECEMBER 27

FIRST READING: Genesis 1:1–5, 26–31

A reading from Genesis:

¹In the beginning when God created the heavens and the earth,
²the earth was a formless void
and darkness covered the face of the deep,
while a wind from God swept over the face of the waters.
³Then God said, "Let there be light"; and there was light.
⁴And God saw that the light was good;
and God separated the light from the darkness.
⁵God called the light Day, and the darkness God called Night.
And there was evening and there was morning, the first day.

²⁶Then God said,
"Let us make humankind in our image, according to our likeness;
and let them have dominion over the fish of the sea,
and over the birds of the air, and over the cattle,
and over all the wild animals of the earth,
and over every creeping thing that creeps upon the earth."

²⁷So God created humankind in the divine image,
in the image of God humankind was created;
male and female God created them.
²⁸God blessed them, and God said to them,
"Be fruitful and multiply, and fill the earth and subdue it;
and have dominion over the fish of the sea
and over the birds of the air
and over every living thing that moves upon the earth."

²⁹God said,
"See, I have given you every plant yielding seed that is upon the face
        of all the earth,
and every tree with seed in its fruit;
you shall have them for food.
³⁰And to every beast of the earth, and to every bird of the air,
and to everything that creeps on the earth,
everything that has the breath of life,
I have given every green plant for food."

And it was so.

³¹God saw everything that had been made,
and indeed, it was very good.
And there was evening and there was morning, the sixth day.

PSALMODY: PSALM 116:12–19   *Psalm 116:10–17*   LBW/BCP

SECOND READING: 1 JOHN 1:1—2:2

A reading from First John:

¹We declare to you what was from the beginning,
what we have heard, what we have seen with our eyes,
what we have looked at and touched with our hands,
concerning the word of life—
²this life was revealed, and we have seen it and testify to it,
and declare to you the eternal life that was with the Father
and was revealed to us—
³we declare to you what we have seen and heard
so that you also may have communion with us;
and truly our communion is with the Father and with Jesus Christ, the Son.
⁴We are writing these things so that our joy may be complete.

⁵This is the message we have heard from Jesus Christ and proclaim to you,
that God is light and in God there is no darkness at all.
⁶If we say that we have communion with God while we are walking in darkness,
we lie and do not do what is true;
⁷but if we walk in the light as God is in the light,
we have communion with one another,
and the blood of Jesus, God's Son, cleanses us from all sin.
⁸If we say that we have no sin, we deceive ourselves,
and the truth is not in us.
⁹If we confess our sins,
God who is faithful and just will forgive us our sins
and cleanse us from all unrighteousness.
¹⁰If we say that we have not sinned, we make God a liar,
and God's word is not in us.

²:¹My little children,
I am writing these things to you so that you may not sin.
But if anyone does sin, we have an advocate with the Father,
Jesus Christ the righteous,
²who is the atoning sacrifice for our sins,
and not for ours only but also for the sins of the whole world.

The Holy Gospel according to John, the 21st chapter.

[20]Peter turned and saw the disciple whom Jesus loved following them;
he was the one who had reclined next to Jesus at the supper and had said,
"Lord, who is it that is going to betray you?"
[21]When Peter saw him, he said to Jesus,
"Lord, what about this man?"
[22]Jesus said to Peter,
"If it is my will that he remain until I come, what is that to you?
Follow me!"
[23]So the rumor spread in the community that this disciple would not die.
Yet Jesus did not say to Peter that this disciple would not die, but,
"If it is my will that he remain until I come, what is that to you?"

[24]This is the disciple who is testifying to these things
and has written them, and we know that his testimony is true.
[25]But there are also many other things that Jesus did;
if every one of them were written down,
I suppose that the world itself could not contain the books that would be
       written.

The Gospel of the Lord.

THE HOLY INNOCENTS, MARTYRS

DECEMBER 28

FIRST READING: JEREMIAH 31:15–17

A reading from Jeremiah:

¹⁵Thus says the LORD:
A voice is heard in Ramah,
lamentation and bitter weeping.
Rachel is weeping for her children;
she refuses to be comforted for her children,
because they are no more.
¹⁶Thus says the LORD:
Keep your voice from weeping, and your eyes from tears;
for there is a reward for your work, says the LORD:
they shall come back from the land of the enemy;
¹⁷there is hope for your future, says the LORD:
your children shall come back to their own country.

PSALMODY: PSALM 124

SECOND READING: 1 PETER 4:12–19

A reading from First Peter:

¹²Beloved, do not be surprised at the fiery ordeal
that is taking place among you to test you,
as though something strange were happening to you.
¹³But rejoice insofar as you are sharing Christ's sufferings,
so that you may also be glad and shout for joy when his glory is revealed.
¹⁴If you are reviled for the name of Christ, you are blessed,
because the spirit of glory, which is the Spirit of God, is resting on you.
¹⁵But let none of you suffer as a murderer, a thief,
a criminal, or even as a mischief maker.

¹⁶Yet if any of you suffers as a Christian, do not consider it a disgrace,
but glorify God because you bear this name.
¹⁷For the time has come for judgment to begin with the household of God;

if it begins with us,
what will be the end for those who do not obey the gospel of God?
[18]And
"If it is hard for the righteous to be saved,
what will become of the ungodly and the sinners?"
[19]Therefore, let those suffering in accordance with God's will
entrust themselves to a faithful Creator, while continuing to do good.

GOSPEL: MATTHEW 2:13–18

The Holy Gospel according to Matthew, the second chapter.

[13]Now after the magi had left,
an angel of the Lord appeared to Joseph in a dream and said,
"Get up, take the child and his mother, and flee to Egypt,
and remain there until I tell you;
for Herod is about to search for the child, to destroy him."
[14]Then Joseph got up, took the child and his mother by night,
and went to Egypt,
[15]and remained there until the death of Herod.
This was to fulfill what had been spoken by the Lord through the prophet,
"Out of Egypt I have called my son."

[16]When Herod saw that he had been tricked by the magi,
he was infuriated,
and he sent and killed all the children in and around Bethlehem
who were two years old or under,
according to the time that he had learned from the magi.
[17]Then was fulfilled what had been spoken through the prophet Jeremiah:
[18]"A voice was heard in Ramah,
wailing and loud lamentation,
Rachel weeping for her children;
she refused to be consoled, because they are no more."

The Gospel of the Lord.

THE NAME OF JESUS

JANUARY 1

FIRST READING: NUMBERS 6:22–27

A reading from Numbers:

²²The LORD spoke to Moses, saying:
²³Speak to Aaron and his sons, saying,
Thus you shall bless the Israelites:
You shall say to them,
²⁴The LORD bless you and keep you;
²⁵the LORD's face shine upon you, and be gracious to you;
²⁶the LORD look upon you with favor, and give you peace.

²⁷So they shall put my name on the Israelites, and I will bless them.

PSALMODY: PSALM 8

SECOND READING: GALATIANS 4:4–7
Or Philippians 2:5-11, following

A reading from Galatians:

⁴When the fullness of time had come,
God sent the Son, born of a woman, born under the law,
⁵in order to redeem those who were under the law,
so that we might receive adoption as children.
⁶And because you are children,
God has sent the Spirit of the Son into our hearts,
crying, "Abba! Father!"
⁷So you are no longer a slave but a child,
and if a child then also an heir, through God.

A reading from Philippians:

⁵Let the same mind be in you that was in Christ Jesus,
⁶who, although being in the form of God,
did not regard equality with God as something to be exploited,
⁷but relinquished it all, taking the form of a slave, being born in human likeness.
And being found in human form,
⁸he humbled himself and became obedient to the point of death—
even death on a cross.

⁹Therefore God also highly exalted him
and gave him the name that is above every name,
¹⁰so that at the name of Jesus every knee should bend,
in heaven and on earth and under the earth,
¹¹and every tongue should confess that Jesus Christ is Lord,
to the glory of God, the Father.

GOSPEL: LUKE 2:15–21

The Holy Gospel according to Luke, the second chapter.

¹⁵When the angels had left them and gone into heaven,
the shepherds said to one another,
"Let us go now to Bethlehem
and see this thing that has taken place,
which the Lord has made known to us."
¹⁶So they went with haste and found Mary and Joseph,
and the child lying in the manger.
¹⁷When they saw this,
they made known what had been told them about this child;
¹⁸and all who heard it were amazed at what the shepherds told them.
¹⁹But Mary treasured all these words and pondered them in her heart.
²⁰The shepherds returned,
glorifying and praising God for all they had heard and seen,
as it had been told them.

²¹After eight days had passed, it was time to circumcise the child;
and he was called Jesus,
the name given by the angel before he was conceived in the womb.

The Gospel of the Lord.

THE CONFESSION OF ST. PETER

JANUARY 18

FIRST READING: ACTS 4:8–13

A reading from Acts:

[8]Peter, filled with the Holy Spirit, said to the authorities,
"Rulers of the people and elders,
[9]if we are questioned today because of a good deed
done to someone who was sick
and are asked how this man has been healed,
[10]let it be known to all of you, and to all the people of Israel,
that this man is standing before you in good health
by the name of Jesus Christ of Nazareth,
whom you crucified, whom God raised from the dead.
[11]This Jesus is 'the stone that was rejected by you, the builders;
it has become the cornerstone.'
[12]There is salvation in no one else,
for there is no other name under heaven given among mortals
by which we must be saved."

[13]Now when they saw the boldness of Peter and John
and realized that they were uneducated and ordinary men,
they were amazed and recognized them as companions of Jesus.

PSALMODY: PSALM 18:1–6, 16–19　　　　　　　*Psalm 18:1–7, 17–20*　LBW/BCP

SECOND READING: 1 Corinthians 10:1–5

A reading from First Corinthians:

¹I do not want you to be unaware, brothers and sisters,
that our ancestors were all under the cloud,
and all passed through the sea,
²and all were baptized into Moses in the cloud and in the sea,
³and all ate the same spiritual food,
⁴and all drank the same spiritual drink.
For they drank from the spiritual rock that followed them,
and the rock was Christ.
⁵Nevertheless, God was not pleased with most of them,
and they were struck down in the wilderness.

GOSPEL: Matthew 16:13–19

The Holy Gospel according to Matthew, the 16th chapter.

¹³Now when Jesus came into the district of Caesarea Philippi,
he asked his disciples, "Who do people say that the Son-of-Man is?"
¹⁴And they said,
"Some say John the Baptist, but others Elijah,
and still others Jeremiah or one of the prophets."
¹⁵Jesus said to them, "But who do you say that I am?"
¹⁶Simon Peter answered,
"You are the Messiah, the Son of the living God."

¹⁷And Jesus answered him,
"Blessed are you, Simon son of Jonah!
For flesh and blood has not revealed this to you,
but my Father in heaven.
¹⁸And I tell you, you are Peter,
and on this rock I will build my church,
and the gates of Hades will not prevail against it.
¹⁹I will give you the keys of the dominion of heaven,
and whatever you bind on earth will be bound in heaven,
and whatever you loose on earth will be loosed in heaven."

The Gospel of the Lord.

✝

THE CONVERSION OF ST. PAUL

JANUARY 25

FIRST READING: ACTS 9:1–22

A reading from Acts:

¹Saul, still breathing threats and murder against the disciples of the Lord,
went to the high priest
²and asked him for letters to the synagogues at Damascus,
so that if he found any who belonged to the Way, men or women,
he might bring them bound to Jerusalem.

³Now as he was going along and approaching Damascus,
suddenly a light from heaven flashed around him.
⁴He fell to the ground and heard a voice saying to him,
"Saul, Saul, why do you persecute me?"
⁵He asked, "Who are you, Lord?"
The reply came, "I am Jesus, whom you are persecuting.
⁶But get up and enter the city,
and you will be told what you are to do."
⁷The men who were traveling with him stood speechless
because they heard the voice but saw no one.
⁸Saul got up from the ground,
and though his eyes were open, he could see nothing;
so they led him by the hand and brought him into Damascus.
⁹For three days he was without sight, and neither ate nor drank.

¹⁰Now there was a disciple in Damascus named Ananias.
The Lord said to him in a vision, "Ananias."
He answered, "Here I am, Lord."
¹¹The Lord said to him,
"Get up and go to the street called Straight,
and at the house of Judas look for a man of Tarsus named Saul.
At this moment he is praying,
¹²and he has seen in a vision a man named Ananias come in
and lay his hands on him so that he might regain his sight."
¹³But Ananias answered,
"Lord, I have heard from many about this man,
how much evil he has done to your saints in Jerusalem;
¹⁴and here he has authority from the chief priests
to bind all who invoke your name."

¹⁵But the Lord said to Ananias,
"Go, for he is an instrument whom I have chosen
to bring my name before Gentiles and rulers and before the people of Israel;
¹⁶I myself will show him how much he must suffer for the sake of my name."

¹⁷So Ananias went and entered the house.
He laid his hands on Saul and said,
"Brother Saul, the Lord Jesus, who appeared to you on your way here,
has sent me so that you may regain your sight
and be filled with the Holy Spirit."
¹⁸And immediately something like scales fell from his eyes,
and his sight was restored.
Then he got up and was baptized,
¹⁹and after taking some food, he regained his strength.

For several days Saul was with the disciples in Damascus,
²⁰and immediately he began to proclaim Jesus in the synagogues, saying,
"He is the Son of God."
²¹All who heard him were amazed and said,
"Is not this the man who made havoc in Jerusalem
among those who invoked this name?
And has he not come here
for the purpose of bringing them bound before the chief priests?"
²²Saul became increasingly more powerful
and confounded the Jewish people who lived in Damascus
by proving that Jesus was the Messiah.

PSALMODY: PSALM 67

SECOND READING: GALATIANS 1:11–24

A reading from Galatians:

¹¹I want you to know, brothers and sisters,
that the gospel that was proclaimed by me is not of human origin;
¹²for I did not receive it from a human source,
nor was I taught it,
but I received it through a revelation of Jesus Christ.

¹³You have heard, no doubt, of my earlier life in Judaism.
I was violently persecuting the church of God and was trying to destroy it.
¹⁴I advanced in Judaism beyond many among my people of the same age,
for I was far more zealous for the traditions of my ancestors.

¹⁵But when God, who had set me apart before I was born
and called me through grace,
was pleased ¹⁶to reveal the Son of God to me,

so that I might proclaim Christ among the Gentiles,
I did not confer with any human being,
[17]nor did I go up to Jerusalem to those who were already apostles before me,
but I went away at once into Arabia,
and afterwards I returned to Damascus.
[18]Then after three years I did go up to Jerusalem to visit Cephas
and stayed with him fifteen days;
[19]but I did not see any other apostle except James the Lord's brother.
[20]In what I am writing to you, before God, I do not lie!
[21]Then I went into the regions of Syria and Cilicia,
[22]and I was still unknown by sight to the churches of Judea that are in Christ;
[23]they only heard it said,
"He who formerly was persecuting us
is now proclaiming the faith he once tried to destroy."
[24]And they glorified God because of me.

GOSPEL: Luke 21:10–19

The Holy Gospel according to Luke, the 21st chapter.

[10]Jesus said,
"Nation will rise against nation, and country against country;
[11]there will be great earthquakes,
and in various places famines and plagues;
and there will be dreadful portents and great signs from heaven.

[12]"But before all this occurs, they will arrest you and persecute you;
they will hand you over to synagogues and prisons,
and you will be brought before rulers and governors because of my name.
[13]This will give you an opportunity to testify.
[14]So make up your minds not to prepare your defense in advance;
[15]for I will give you words and a wisdom
that none of your opponents will be able to withstand or contradict.
[16]You will be betrayed even by parents and family,
by relatives and friends;
and they will put some of you to death.
[17]You will be hated by all because of my name.
[18]But not a hair of your head will perish.
[19]By your endurance you will gain your souls."

The Gospel of the Lord.

THE PRESENTATION OF OUR LORD

FEBRUARY 2

FIRST READING: MALACHI 3:1–4

A reading from Malachi:

¹See, I am sending my messenger to prepare the way before me,
and the Lord whom you seek will suddenly come to the temple.
Indeed, the messenger of the covenant in whom you delight
is coming, says the LORD of hosts.
²But who can endure the day of his coming,
and who can stand when he appears?

For he is like a refiner's fire and like fullers' soap;
³he will sit as a refiner and purifier of silver,
and will purify the descendants of Levi
and refine them like gold and silver,
until they present offerings to the LORD in righteousness.
⁴Then the offering of Judah and Jerusalem will be pleasing to the LORD
as in the days of old and as in former years.

PSALMODY: PSALM 84 or PSALM 24:7–10

SECOND READING: HEBREWS 2:14–18

A reading from Hebrews:

¹⁴Since, therefore, the children share flesh and blood,
Jesus himself likewise shared the same things,
so that through death he might destroy the one who has the power of death,
that is, the devil,
¹⁵and free those who all their lives were held in slavery by the fear of death.

¹⁶For it is clear that Jesus did not come to help angels,
but the descendants of Abraham.
¹⁷Therefore Jesus had to become like his brothers and sisters in every respect,
so that he might be a merciful and faithful high priest in the service of God,
to make a sacrifice of atonement for the sins of the people.
¹⁸Because Jesus himself was tested by what he suffered,
he is able to help those who are being tested.

GOSPEL: LUKE 2:22–40

The Holy Gospel according to Luke, the second chapter.

²²When the time came for their purification according to the law of Moses,
Mary and Joseph brought Jesus up to Jerusalem to present him to the Lord
²³(as it is written in the law of the Lord,
"Every firstborn male shall be designated as holy to the Lord"),
²⁴and they offered a sacrifice according to what is stated in the law of the Lord,
"a pair of turtledoves or two young pigeons."

²⁵Now there was a man in Jerusalem whose name was Simeon;
this man was righteous and devout,
looking forward to the consolation of Israel,
and the Holy Spirit rested on him.
²⁶It had been revealed to him by the Holy Spirit
that he would not see death before he had seen the Lord's Messiah.
²⁷Guided by the Spirit, Simeon came into the temple;
and when the parents brought in the child Jesus,
to do for him what was customary under the law,
²⁸Simeon took Jesus in his arms and praised God, saying,
²⁹"Lord, now you are dismissing your servant in peace,
according to your word;
³⁰for my eyes have seen your salvation,
³¹which you have prepared in the presence of all peoples,
³²a light for revelation to the Gentiles
and for glory to your people Israel."
³³And the child's father and mother were amazed at what was being said about him.

³⁴Then Simeon blessed them and said to his mother Mary,
"This child is destined for the falling and the rising of many in Israel,
and to be a sign that will be opposed
³⁵so that the inner thoughts of many will be revealed—
and a sword will pierce your own soul too."

³⁶There was also a prophet,
Anna the daughter of Phanuel, of the tribe of Asher.
She was of a great age,
having lived with her husband seven years after her marriage,
³⁷then as a widow to the age of eighty-four.
She never left the temple
but worshiped there with fasting and prayer night and day.
³⁸At that moment she came, and began to praise God
and to speak about the child to all who were looking for the redemption of
       Jerusalem.

³⁹When the parents had finished everything required by the law of the Lord,
they returned to Galilee, to their own town of Nazareth.
⁴⁰The child grew and became strong, filled with wisdom;
and the favor of God was upon him.

The Gospel of the Lord.

✝

St. Matthias, Apostle

FEBRUARY 24

FIRST READING: Isaiah 66:1–2

A reading from Isaiah:

¹Thus says the LORD:
Heaven is my throne and the earth is my footstool;
what is the house that you would build for me,
and what is my resting place?
²All these things my hand has made,
and so all these things are mine, says the LORD.
But this is the one to whom I will look,
to the humble and contrite in spirit,
who trembles at my word.

PSALMODY: Psalm 56

SECOND READING: Acts 1:15–26

A reading from Acts:

¹⁵In those days Peter stood up among the believers
(together the crowd numbered about one hundred twenty persons)
and said,
¹⁶"Friends, the scripture had to be fulfilled,
which the Holy Spirit through David foretold concerning Judas,
who became a guide for those who arrested Jesus—
¹⁷for he was numbered among us and was allotted his share in this ministry."
¹⁸(Now this man acquired a field with the reward of his wickedness;
and falling headlong, he burst open in the middle
and all his bowels gushed out.
¹⁹This became known to all the residents of Jerusalem,
so that the field was called in their language Hakeldama,
that is, Field of Blood.)

²⁰"For it is written in the book of Psalms,
'Let his homestead become desolate,
and let there be no one to live in it';
and 'Let another take his position of overseer.'

²¹"So one of the men who have accompanied us
during all the time that the Lord Jesus went in and out among us,
²²beginning from the baptism of John
until the day when Jesus was taken up from us—
one of these must become a witness with us to his resurrection."
²³So they proposed two,
Joseph called Barsabbas, who was also known as Justus, and Matthias.
²⁴Then they prayed and said,
"Lord, you know everyone's heart.
Show us which one of these two you have chosen
²⁵to take the place in this ministry and apostleship
from which Judas turned aside to go to his own place."
²⁶And they cast lots for them, and the lot fell on Matthias;
and he was added to the eleven apostles.

GOSPEL: LUKE 6:12–16

The Holy Gospel according to Luke, the sixth chapter.

¹²During those days Jesus went out to the mountain to pray;
and he spent the night in prayer to God.
¹³And when day came, he called his disciples and chose twelve of them,
whom he also named apostles:
¹⁴Simon, whom he named Peter, and his brother Andrew,
and James, and John, and Philip, and Bartholomew,
¹⁵and Matthew, and Thomas, and James son of Alphaeus,
and Simon, who was called the Zealot,
¹⁶and Judas son of James, and Judas Iscariot, who became a traitor.

The Gospel of the Lord.

The Annunciation of Our Lord

MARCH 25

FIRST READING: Isaiah 7:10–14

A reading from Isaiah:

¹⁰The LORD spoke to Ahaz, saying,
¹¹Ask a sign of the LORD your God;
let it be deep as Sheol or high as heaven.
¹²But Ahaz said, I will not ask,
and I will not put the LORD to the test.
¹³Then Isaiah said:
"Hear then, O house of David!
Is it too little for you to weary mortals, that you weary my God also?
¹⁴Therefore this very Lord will give you a sign.
Look, the young woman is with child and shall bear a son,
and shall name him Immanuel."

PSALMODY: Psalm 45 or Psalm 40:5–10   *Psalm 40:5–11*   LBW/BCP

SECOND READING: Hebrews 10:4–10

A reading from Hebrews:

⁴It is impossible for the blood of bulls and goats to take away sins.
⁵Consequently, when Christ came into the world, he said,
"Sacrifices and offerings you have not desired,
but a body you have prepared for me;
⁶in burnt offerings and sin offerings you have taken no pleasure.
⁷Then I said, 'See, God, I have come to do your will, O God'
(in the scroll of the book it is written of me)."
⁸When Christ said above,
"You have neither desired nor taken pleasure in sacrifices
and offerings and burnt offerings and sin offerings"
(these are offered according to the law),
⁹then he added, "See, I have come to do your will."
Christ abolishes the first in order to establish the second.
¹⁰And it is by God's will that we have been sanctified
through the offering of the body of Jesus Christ once for all.

The Holy Gospel according to Luke, the first chapter.

[26]In the sixth month the angel Gabriel was sent by God
to a town in Galilee called Nazareth,
[27]to a virgin woman engaged to a man
whose name was Joseph, of the house of David.
The virgin's name was Mary.
[28]And the angel came to her and said,
"Greetings, favored one! The Lord is with you."
[29]But she was much perplexed by the angel's words
and pondered what sort of greeting this might be.

[30]The angel said to her,
"Do not be afraid, Mary, for you have found favor with God.
[31]And now, you will conceive in your womb and bear a son,
and you will name him Jesus.
[32]He will be great, and will be called the Son of the Most High,
and the Lord God will give to him the throne of his ancestor David.
[33]He will reign over the house of Jacob forever,
and of his dominion there will be no end."
[34]Mary said to the angel,
"How can this be, since I am a virgin?"
[35]The angel said to her,
"The Holy Spirit will come upon you,
and the power of the Most High will overshadow you;
therefore the child to be born will be holy;
he will be called Son of God.
[36]And now, your relative Elizabeth in her old age has also conceived a son;
and this is the sixth month for her who was said to be barren.
[37]For nothing will be impossible with God."

[38]Then Mary said, "Here am I, the servant of the Lord;
let it be with me according to your word."

Then the angel departed from her.

The Gospel of the Lord.

✠

St. Mark, Evangelist

APRIL 25

FIRST READING: Isaiah 52:7–10

A reading from Isaiah:

7How beautiful upon the mountains
are the feet of the messenger who announces peace,
who brings good news,
who announces salvation,
who says to Zion, "Your God reigns."
8Listen! Your sentinels lift up their voices,
together they sing for joy;
for in plain sight they see the return of the LORD to Zion.
9Break forth together into singing, you ruins of Jerusalem;
for the LORD has comforted the chosen people
and has redeemed Jerusalem.
10The holy arm of the LORD is bared before the eyes of all the nations;
and all the ends of the earth shall see the salvation of our God.

PSALMODY: Psalm 57

SECOND READING: 2 Timothy 4:6–11, 18

A reading from Second Timothy:

6As for me, I am already being poured out as a libation,
and the time of my departure has come.
7I have fought the good fight,
I have finished the race,
I have kept the faith.
8From now on there is reserved for me the crown of righteousness,
which the Lord, the righteous judge, will give me on that day,
and not only to me
but also to all who have longed for the Lord's appearing.

9Do your best to come to me soon,
10for Demas, in love with this present world,
has deserted me and gone to Thessalonica;
Crescens has gone to Galatia, Titus to Dalmatia.

¹¹Only Luke is with me.
Get Mark and bring him with you,
for he is useful in my ministry.

¹⁸The Lord will rescue me from every evil attack
and save me for the dominion of heaven.
To the Lord be the glory forever and ever. Amen.

GOSPEL: MARK 1:1–15

The Holy Gospel according to Mark, the first chapter.

¹The beginning of the good news of Jesus Christ, the Son of God.
²As it is written in the prophet Isaiah,
"See, I am sending my messenger ahead of you,
who will prepare your way;
³the voice of one crying out in the wilderness:
'Prepare the way of the Lord,
make straight the paths of the Lord,'"
⁴John the baptizer appeared in the wilderness,
proclaiming a baptism of repentance for the forgiveness of sins.
⁵And people from the whole Judean countryside
and all the people of Jerusalem were going out to him,
and were baptized by him in the river Jordan, confessing their sins.
⁶Now John was clothed with camel's hair, with a leather belt around his waist,
and he ate locusts and wild honey.
⁷He proclaimed, "The one who is more powerful than I is coming after me,
the thong of whose sandals I am not worthy to stoop down and untie.
⁸I have baptized you with water;
but the one who is coming will baptize you with the Holy Spirit."

⁹In those days Jesus came from Nazareth of Galilee
and was baptized by John in the Jordan.
¹⁰And just as he was coming up out of the water,
he saw the heavens torn apart and the Spirit descending like a dove on him.
¹¹And a voice came from heaven,
"You are my Son, the Beloved; with you I am well pleased."

¹²And the Spirit immediately drove Jesus out into the wilderness.
¹³He was in the wilderness forty days, tempted by Satan;
and he was with the wild beasts; and the angels waited on him.

¹⁴Now after John was arrested, Jesus came to Galilee,
proclaiming the good news of God, ¹⁵and saying,
"The time is fulfilled, and the dominion of God has come near;
repent, and believe in the good news."

The Gospel of the Lord.

St. Philip and St. James, Apostles

MAY 1

FIRST READING: Isaiah 30:18–21

A reading from Isaiah:

¹⁸The LORD waits to be gracious to you;
therefore the LORD will rise up to show mercy to you.
For the LORD is a God of justice;
blessed are all those who wait for the LORD.

¹⁹Truly, O people in Zion, inhabitants of Jerusalem,
you shall weep no more.
The LORD will surely be gracious to you at the sound of your cry;
hearing it, God will answer you.
²⁰Though the Lord may give you the bread of adversity
and the water of affliction,
yet your Teacher will not hide away any more,
but your eyes shall see your Teacher.
²¹And when you turn to the right or when you turn to the left,
your ears shall hear a word behind you, saying,
"This is the way; walk in it."

PSALMODY: Psalm 44:1–3, 20–26

SECOND READING: 2 Corinthians 4:1–6

A reading from Second Corinthians:

¹Since it is by God's mercy that we are engaged in this ministry,
we do not lose heart.
²We have renounced the shameful things that one hides;
we refuse to practice cunning or to falsify God's word;
but by the open statement of the truth
we commend ourselves to the conscience of everyone in the sight of God.
³And even if our gospel is veiled,
it is veiled to those who are perishing.
⁴In their case the god of this world has blinded the minds of the unbelievers,
to keep them from seeing the light of the gospel of the glory of Christ,
who is the image of God.

⁵For we do not proclaim ourselves;
we proclaim Jesus Christ as Lord
and ourselves as your slaves for Jesus' sake.
⁶For it is the God who said, "Let light shine out of darkness,"
who has shone in our hearts
to give the light of the knowledge of the glory of God
in the face of Jesus Christ.

GOSPEL: JOHN 14:8–14

The Holy Gospel according to John, the 14th chapter.

⁸Philip said to Jesus,
"Lord, show us the Father, and we will be satisfied."
⁹Jesus said to him,
"Have I been with you all this time, Philip,
and you still do not know me?
Whoever has seen me has seen the Father.
How can you say, 'Show us the Father'?
¹⁰Do you not believe that I am in the Father and the Father is in me?
The words that I say to you I do not speak on my own;
but it is the Father who dwells in me who does these works.
¹¹Believe me that I am in the Father and the Father is in me;
but if you do not, then believe me because of the works themselves.

¹²"Very truly, I tell you,
the one who believes in me will also do the works that I do and,
in fact, will do greater works than these,
because I am going to the Father.
¹³I will do whatever you ask in my name,
so that the Father may be glorified in the Son.
¹⁴If in my name you ask me for anything, I will do it."

The Gospel of the Lord.

$$\dagger$$

THE VISITATION

MAY 31

FIRST READING: 1 SAMUEL 2:1–10

A reading from First Samuel:

[1]Hannah prayed and said,
"My heart exults in the LORD;
my strength is exalted in my God.
My mouth derides my enemies,
because I rejoice in my victory.

[2]"There is no Holy One like the LORD,
no one besides you;
there is no Rock like our God.
[3]Talk no more so very proudly,
let not arrogance come from your mouth;
for the LORD is a God of knowledge,
by whom actions are weighed.
[4]The bows of the mighty are broken,
but the feeble gird on strength.
[5]Those who were full have hired themselves out for bread,
but those who were hungry are fat with spoil.
The barren has borne seven,
but she who has many children is forlorn.
[6]The LORD kills and brings to life;
the LORD brings down to Sheol and raises up.
[7]The LORD makes poor and makes rich;
the LORD brings low, and also exalts.
[8]The LORD raises up the poor from the dust,
and lifts the needy from the ash heap,
to make them sit with rulers and inherit a seat of honor.
For the pillars of the earth are the LORD's,
and on them God has set the world.

[9]"The LORD will guard the feet of the faithful ones,
but the wicked shall be cut off in darkness;
for not by might does one prevail.
[10]The LORD! The adversaries of the LORD shall be shattered;
the Most High will thunder in heaven.
The LORD will judge the ends of the earth,

giving strength to the chosen king,
and exalting the power of God's anointed."

PSALMODY: PSALM 113

SECOND READING: ROMANS 12:9–16b

A reading from Romans:

[9]Let love be genuine;
hate what is evil, hold fast to what is good;
[10]love one another with mutual affection;
outdo one another in showing honor.
[11]Do not lag in zeal, be ardent in spirit, serve the Lord.
[12]Rejoice in hope, be patient in suffering, persevere in prayer.
[13]Contribute to the needs of the saints;
extend hospitality to strangers.

[14]Bless those who persecute you; bless and do not curse them.
[15]Rejoice with those who rejoice, weep with those who weep.
[16]Live in harmony with one another;
do not be haughty, but associate with the lowly.

The Holy Gospel according to Luke, the first chapter.

³⁹In those days Mary set out
and went with haste to a Judean town in the hill country,
⁴⁰where she entered the house of Zechariah and greeted Elizabeth.
⁴¹When Elizabeth heard Mary's greeting, the child leaped in her womb.
And Elizabeth was filled with the Holy Spirit
⁴²and exclaimed with a loud cry,
"Blessed are you among women, and blessed is the fruit of your womb.
⁴³And why has this happened to me,
that the mother of my Lord comes to me?
⁴⁴For as soon as I heard the sound of your greeting,
the child in my womb leaped for joy.
⁴⁵And blessed is she who believed
that there would be a fulfillment of what was spoken to her by the Lord."

⁴⁶And Mary said,
"My soul magnifies the Lord,
⁴⁷and my spirit rejoices in God my Savior,
⁴⁸who has looked with favor on me, a lowly servant.
Surely, from now on all generations will call me blessed;
⁴⁹for the Mighty One has done great things for me:
holy is the name of the Lord,
⁵⁰whose mercy is for the God-fearing from generation to generation.
⁵¹The arm of the Lord is filled with strength,
scattering the proud in the thoughts of their hearts.
⁵²God has brought down the powerful from their thrones,
and lifted up the lowly;
⁵³God has filled the hungry with good things,
and sent the rich away empty.
⁵⁴God has helped Israel, the Lord's servant, in remembrance of mercy,
⁵⁵according to the promise God made to our ancestors,
to Abraham and to his descendants forever."

⁵⁶And Mary remained with her about three months
and then returned to her home.

⁵⁷Now the time came for Elizabeth to give birth,
and she bore a son.

The Gospel of the Lord.

✝

St. Barnabas, Apostle

JUNE 11

FIRST READING: Isaiah 42:5–12

A reading from Isaiah:

5Thus says God, the LORD,
who created the heavens and stretched them out,
who spread out the earth and what comes from it,
who gives breath to the people upon it
and spirit to those who walk in it:
6I am the LORD, I have called you in righteousness,
I have taken you by the hand and kept you;
I have given you as a covenant to the people,
a light to the nations,
7to open the eyes that are blind,
to bring out the prisoners from the dungeon,
from the prison those who sit in darkness.
8I am the LORD, that is my name;
my glory I give to no other,
nor my praise to idols.
9See, the former things have come to pass,
and new things I now declare;
before they spring forth,
I tell you of them.

10Sing to the LORD a new song,
the praise of God from the end of the earth!
Let the sea roar and all that fills it,
the coastlands and their inhabitants.
11Let the desert and its towns lift up their voice,
the villages that Kedar inhabits;
let the inhabitants of Sela sing for joy,
let them shout from the tops of the mountains.
12Let them give glory to the LORD,
and declare the praise of God in the coastlands.

PSALMODY: Psalm 112

SECOND READING: ACTS 11:19–30; 13:1–3

A reading from Acts:

¹⁹Now those who were scattered because of the persecution
      that took place over Stephen
traveled as far as Phoenicia, Cyprus, and Antioch,
and they spoke the word to no one except Jews.
²⁰But among them were some from Cyprus and Cyrene who,
on coming to Antioch, spoke to the Hellenists also,
proclaiming the Lord Jesus.
²¹The hand of the Lord was with them,
and a great number became believers and turned to the Lord.
²²News of this came to the ears of the church in Jerusalem,
and they sent Barnabas to Antioch.

²³When Barnabas came and saw the grace of God, he rejoiced,
and he exhorted them all to remain faithful to the Lord with steadfast devotion;
²⁴for he was a good man, full of the Holy Spirit and of faith.
And a great many people were brought to the Lord.
²⁵Then Barnabas went to Tarsus to look for Saul,
²⁶and when he had found him, he brought him to Antioch.
So it was that for an entire year
they met with the church and taught a great many people,
and it was in Antioch that the disciples were first called "Christians."

²⁷At that time prophets came down from Jerusalem to Antioch.
²⁸One of them named Agabus stood up and predicted by the Spirit
that there would be a severe famine over all the world;
and this took place during the reign of Claudius.
²⁹The disciples determined that according to their ability,
each would send relief to the believers living in Judea;
³⁰this they did, sending it to the elders by Barnabas and Saul.

¹³:¹Now in the church at Antioch there were prophets and teachers:
Barnabas, Simeon who was called Niger,
Lucius of Cyrene, Manaen a member of the court of Herod the ruler, and Saul.
²While they were worshiping the Lord and fasting,
the Holy Spirit said,
"Set apart for me Barnabas and Saul for the work to which I have called them."
³Then after fasting and praying
they laid their hands on them and sent them off.

GOSPEL: MATTHEW 10:7–16

The Holy Gospel according to Matthew, the tenth chapter.

Jesus said:
[7]"As you go, proclaim the good news,
'The dominion of heaven has come near.'
[8]Cure the sick, raise the dead, cleanse those with leprosy, cast out demons.
You received without payment; give without payment.
[9]Take no gold, or silver, or copper in your belts,
[10]no bag for your journey, or two tunics, or sandals, or a staff;
for laborers deserve their food.

[11]"Whatever town or village you enter, find out who in it is worthy,
and stay there until you leave.
[12]As you enter the house, greet it.
[13]If the house is worthy, let your peace come upon it;
but if it is not worthy, let your peace return to you.
[14]If anyone will not welcome you or listen to your words,
shake off the dust from your feet as you leave that house or town.
[15]Truly I tell you,
it will be more tolerable for the land of Sodom and Gomorrah
        on the day of judgment
than for that town.

[16]"See, I am sending you out like sheep into the midst of wolves;
so be wise as serpents and innocent as doves."

The Gospel of the Lord.

✠

THE NATIVITY OF
ST. JOHN THE BAPTIST

JUNE 24

FIRST READING: MALACHI 3:1-4

A reading from Malachi:

¹See, I am sending my messenger to prepare the way before me,
and the Lord whom you seek will suddenly come to the temple.
Indeed, the messenger of the covenant in whom you delight
is coming, says the LORD of hosts.
²But who can endure the day of his coming,
and who can stand when he appears?

For he is like a refiner's fire and like fullers' soap;
³he will sit as a refiner and purifier of silver,
and will purify the descendants of Levi
and refine them like gold and silver,
until they present offerings to the LORD in righteousness.
⁴Then the offering of Judah and Jerusalem will be pleasing to the LORD
as in the days of old and as in former years.

PSALMODY: PSALM 141

SECOND READING: ACTS 13:13-26

A reading from Acts:

¹³Paul and his companions set sail from Paphos
and came to Perga in Pamphylia.
John, however, left them and returned to Jerusalem;
¹⁴but they went on from Perga and came to Antioch in Pisidia.
And on the sabbath day they went into the synagogue and sat down.
¹⁵After the reading of the law and the prophets,
the officials of the synagogue sent them a message, saying,
"Brothers, if you have any word of exhortation for the people, give it."

¹⁶So Paul stood up and with a gesture began to speak:
"You Israelites, and others who fear God, listen.
¹⁷The God of this people Israel chose our ancestors
and made the people great during their stay in the land of Egypt,

and with uplifted arm led them out of it.
[18]For about forty years God put up with them in the wilderness.
[19]After destroying seven nations in the land of Canaan,
God gave them their land as an inheritance
[20]for about four hundred fifty years.
After that God gave them judges until the time of the prophet Samuel.
[21]Then they asked for a king;
and God gave them Saul son of Kish, a man of the tribe of Benjamin,
who reigned for forty years.
[22]When he was removed, God made David their king.
In testifying about him God said,
'I have found David, son of Jesse, to be a man after my heart,
who will carry out all my wishes.'
[23]Of this man's posterity God has brought to Israel a Savior,
Jesus, as God promised;
[24]before his coming John had already proclaimed a baptism of repentance
to all the people of Israel.
[25]And as John was finishing his work, he said,
'What do you suppose that I am? I am not he.
No, but one is coming after me;
I am not worthy to untie the thong of the sandals on his feet.'

[26]"My brothers, you descendants of Abraham's family,
and others who fear God,
to us the message of this salvation has been sent."

GOSPEL: LUKE 1:57-67 [68-80]

The Holy Gospel according to Luke, the first chapter.

[57]Now the time came for Elizabeth to give birth, and she bore a son.
[58]Her neighbors and relatives heard that the Lord had shown great mercy to her,
and they rejoiced with her.

[59]On the eighth day they came to circumcise the child,
and they were going to name him Zechariah after his father.
[60]But his mother said, "No; he is to be called John."
[61]They said to her, "None of your relatives has this name."
[62]Then they began motioning to his father
to find out what name he wanted to give him.
[63]He asked for a writing tablet and wrote,
"His name is John."
And all of them were amazed.
[64]Immediately his mouth was opened and his tongue freed,
and he began to speak, praising God.
[65]Fear came over all their neighbors,
and all these things were talked about
throughout the entire hill country of Judea.

^{66}All who heard them pondered them and said,
"What then will this child become?"
For, indeed, the hand of the Lord was with him.

^{67}Then his father Zechariah was filled with the Holy Spirit
and spoke this prophecy:
[^{68}"Blessed be the Lord God of Israel,
who has looked favorably on the chosen people and redeemed them.
^{69}God has raised up a mighty savior for us
in the house of David, the servant of the Lord,
^{70}as God spoke through the mouth of the holy prophets from of old,
^{71}that we would be saved from our enemies
and from the hand of all who hate us.
^{72}Thus God has shown the mercy promised to our ancestors,
and has remembered the holy covenant,
^{73}the oath sworn to our ancestor Abraham,
to grant us ^{74}that we, being rescued from the hands of our enemies,
might serve God without fear,
^{75}in holiness and righteousness
before the Lord all our days.

^{76}"And you, child, will be called the prophet of the Most High;
for you will go before the Lord to prepare the way,
^{77}to give knowledge of salvation to the people
by the forgiveness of their sins.
^{78}By the tender mercy of our God,
the dawn from on high will break upon us,
^{79}to give light to those who sit in darkness and in the shadow of death,
to guide our feet into the way of peace."

^{80}The child grew and became strong in spirit,
and he was in the wilderness until the day he appeared publicly to Israel.]

The Gospel of the Lord.

ST. PETER AND ST. PAUL, APOSTLES

JUNE 29

FIRST READING: EZEKIEL 34:11-16

A reading from Ezekiel:

¹¹Thus says the Lord GOD:
I myself will search for my sheep, and will seek them out.
¹²As shepherds seek out their flocks
when they are among their scattered sheep,
so I will seek out my sheep.
I will rescue them from all the places to which they have been scattered
on a day of clouds and thick darkness.
¹³I will bring them out from the peoples and gather them from the countries,
and will bring them into their own land;
and I will feed them on the mountains of Israel,
by the watercourses, and in all the inhabited parts of the land.
¹⁴I will feed them with good pasture,
and the mountain heights of Israel shall be their pasture;
there they shall lie down in good grazing land,
and they shall feed on rich pasture on the mountains of Israel.
¹⁵I myself will be the shepherd of my sheep,
and I will make them lie down, says the Lord GOD.
¹⁶I will seek the lost, and I will bring back the strayed,
and I will bind up the injured, and I will strengthen the weak,
but the fat and the strong I will destroy.
I will feed them with justice.

PSALMODY: PSALM 87:1-3, 5-7   *Psalm 87:1–2, 4–6*   LBW/BCP

SECOND READING: 1 Corinthians 3:16-23

A reading from First Corinthians:

[16]Do you not know that you are God's temple
and that God's Spirit dwells in you?
[17]Anyone who destroys God's temple will be destroyed by God.
For God's temple is holy, and you are that temple.

[18]Do not deceive yourselves.
If you think that you are wise in this age,
you should become fools so that you may become wise.
[19]For the wisdom of this world is foolishness with God.
For it is written,
"God catches the wise in their craftiness,"
[20]and again,
"The Lord knows the thoughts of the wise,
that they are futile."
[21]So let no one boast about human leaders.
For all things are yours,
[22]whether Paul or Apollos or Cephas
or the world or life or death or the present or the future—
all belong to you,
[23]and you belong to Christ,
and Christ belongs to God.

The Holy Gospel according to Mark, the eighth chapter.

27Jesus went on with his disciples to the villages of Caesarea Philippi;
and on the way he asked his disciples,
"Who do people say that I am?"
28And they answered him,
"John the Baptist; and others, Elijah;
and still others, one of the prophets."
29Jesus asked them, "But who do you say that I am?"
Peter answered him, "You are the Messiah."
30And he sternly ordered them not to tell anyone about him.

31Then he began to teach them
that the Son-of-Man must undergo great suffering,
and be rejected by the elders, the chief priests, and the scribes,
and be killed, and after three days rise again.
32He said all this quite openly.
And Peter took him aside and began to rebuke him.
33But turning and looking at his disciples, Jesus rebuked Peter and said,
"Get behind me, Satan!
For you are setting your mind not on divine things but on human things."

34Jesus called the crowd with his disciples, and said to them,
"If any want to become my followers,
let them deny themselves and take up their cross and follow me.
35For those who want to save their life will lose it,
and those who lose their life for my sake, and for the sake of the gospel,
will save it."

The Gospel of the Lord.

St. Mary Magdalene

JULY 22

FIRST READING: Ruth 1:6-18

Or Exodus 2:1-10, following

A reading from Ruth:

⁶Naomi started to return with her daughters-in-law Orpah and Ruth
        from the country of Moab,
for she had heard in the country of Moab
that the L ORD had considered the chosen people
and given them food.
⁷So she set out from the place where she had been living,
she and her two daughters-in-law,
and they went on their way to go back to the land of Judah.
⁸But Naomi said to her two daughters-in-law,
"Go back each of you to your mother's house.
May the L ORD deal kindly with you,
as you have dealt with the dead and with me.
⁹The L ORD grant that you may find security,
each of you in the house of your husband."
Then she kissed them, and they wept aloud.

¹⁰They said to her, "No, we will return with you to your people."
¹¹But Naomi said,
"Turn back, my daughters, why will you go with me?
Do I still have sons in my womb that they may become your husbands?
¹²Turn back, my daughters, go your way,
for I am too old to have a husband.
Even if I thought there was hope for me,
even if I should have a husband tonight and bear sons,
¹³would you then wait until they were grown?
Would you then refrain from marrying?
No, my daughters, it has been far more bitter for me than for you,
because the hand of the L ORD has turned against me."

¹⁴Then they wept aloud again.
Orpah kissed her mother-in-law, but Ruth clung to her.

¹⁵So Naomi said,
"See, your sister-in-law has gone back to her people and to her deities;
return after your sister-in-law."
¹⁶But Ruth said,
"Do not press me to leave you
or to turn back from following you!
Where you go, I will go;
where you lodge, I will lodge;
your people shall be my people,
and your God my God.
¹⁷Where you die, I will die—
there will I be buried.
May the LORD do thus and so to me,
and more as well,
if even death parts me from you!"
¹⁸When Naomi saw that Ruth was determined to go with her,
she said no more to her.

OR: EXODUS 2:1-10

A reading from Exodus:

¹Now a man from the house of Levi went and married a Levite woman.
²The woman conceived and bore a son;
and when she saw that he was a fine baby, she hid him three months.
³When she could hide him no longer she got a papyrus basket for him,
and plastered it with bitumen and pitch;
she put the child in it and placed it among the reeds on the bank of the river.
⁴His sister stood at a distance, to see what would happen to him.

⁵The daughter of Pharaoh came down to bathe at the river,
while her attendants walked beside the river.
She saw the basket among the reeds and sent her maid to bring it.
⁶When she opened it, she saw the child.
He was crying, and she took pity on him,
"This must be one of the Hebrews' children," she said.
⁷Then his sister said to Pharaoh's daughter,
"Shall I go and get you a nurse from the Hebrew women
to nurse the child for you?"
⁸Pharaoh's daughter said to her, "Yes."
So the girl went and called the child's mother.
⁹Pharaoh's daughter said to her,
"Take this child and nurse it for me, and I will give you your wages."
So the woman took the child and nursed it.

¹⁰When the child grew up, she brought him to Pharaoh's daughter,
and she took him as her son.
She named him Moses, "because," she said,
"I drew him out of the water."

PSALMODY: P<small>SALM</small> 73:23-28

Psalm 73:23–29 LBW/BCP

SECOND READING: A<small>CTS</small> 13:26-33a

A reading from Acts:

Paul spoke in the synagogue:
²⁶"My brothers, you descendants of Abraham's family,
and others who fear God,
to us the message of this salvation has been sent.
²⁷Because the residents of Jerusalem and their leaders did not recognize Jesus
or understand the words of the prophets that are read every sabbath,
they fulfilled those words by condemning him.
²⁸Even though they found no cause for a sentence of death,
they asked Pilate to have him killed.
²⁹When they had carried out everything that was written about him,
they took him down from the tree and laid him in a tomb.

³⁰"But God raised Jesus from the dead;
³¹and for many days he appeared to those who came up with him
from Galilee to Jerusalem,
and they are now his witnesses to the people.
³²And we bring you the good news that what God promised to our ancestors
^{33a}this God has fulfilled for us, their children, by raising Jesus."

GOSPEL: JOHN 20:1-2, 11-18

The Holy Gospel according to John, the 20th chapter.

¹Early on the first day of the week, while it was still dark,
Mary Magdalene came to the tomb
and saw that the stone had been removed from the tomb.
²So she ran and went to Simon Peter and the other disciple,
the one whom Jesus loved, and said to them,
"They have taken the Lord out of the tomb,
and we do not know where they have laid him."

¹¹Mary stood weeping outside the tomb.
As she wept, she bent over to look into the tomb;
¹²and she saw two angels in white,
sitting where the body of Jesus had been lying,
one at the head and the other at the feet.
¹³They said to her, "Woman, why are you weeping?"
She said to them,
"They have taken away my Lord, and I do not know where they have laid him."
¹⁴When she had said this, she turned around and saw Jesus standing there,
but she did not know that it was Jesus.
¹⁵Jesus said to her,
"Woman, why are you weeping? Whom are you looking for?"
Supposing him to be the gardener, she said to him,
"Sir, if you have carried him away, tell me where you have laid him,
and I will take him away."

¹⁶Jesus said to her, "Mary!"
She turned and said to him in Hebrew,
"Rabbouni!" (which means Teacher).
¹⁷Jesus said to her,
"Do not hold on to me, because I have not yet ascended to the Father.
But go to my brothers and say to them,
'I am ascending to my Father and your Father, to my God and your God.'"
¹⁸Mary Magdalene went and announced to the disciples,
"I have seen the Lord";
and she told them that Jesus had said these things to her.

The Gospel of the Lord.

✝

S T .   J A M E S   T H E   E L D E R ,   A P O S T L E

JULY 25

FIRST READING: 1 KINGS 19:9-18

A reading from First Kings:

⁹At Horeb, the mount of God,
Elijah came to a cave, and spent the night there.
Then the word of the LORD came to him, saying,
"What are you doing here, Elijah?"
¹⁰Elijah answered, "I have been very zealous for the LORD, the God of hosts;
for the Israelites have forsaken your covenant, thrown down your altars,
and killed your prophets with the sword.
I alone am left, and they are seeking my life, to take it away."
¹¹The LORD said, "Go out and stand on the mountain before the LORD,
for the LORD is about to pass by."

Now there was a great wind, so strong that it was splitting mountains
and breaking rocks in pieces before the LORD,
but the LORD was not in the wind;
and after the wind an earthquake,
but the LORD was not in the earthquake;
¹²and after the earthquake a fire,
but the LORD was not in the fire;
and after the fire a sound of sheer silence.
¹³When Elijah heard it, he wrapped his face in his mantle
and went out and stood at the entrance of the cave.

Then there came a voice to him that said,
"What are you doing here, Elijah?"
¹⁴He answered,
"I have been very zealous for the LORD, the God of hosts;
for the Israelites have forsaken your covenant, thrown down your altars,
and killed your prophets with the sword.
I alone am left, and they are seeking my life, to take it away."
¹⁵Then the LORD said to him,
"Go, return on your way to the wilderness of Damascus;
when you arrive, you shall anoint Hazael as king over Aram.
¹⁶Also you shall anoint Jehu son of Nimshi as king over Israel;
and you shall anoint Elisha son of Shaphat of Abel-meholah
as prophet in your place.

¹⁷Whoever escapes from the sword of Hazael, Jehu shall kill;
and whoever escapes from the sword of Jehu, Elisha shall kill.
¹⁸Yet I will leave seven thousand in Israel,
all the knees that have not bowed to Baal,
and every mouth that has not kissed him."

PSALMODY: PSALM 7:1-10   *Psalm 7:1–11* LBW/BCP

SECOND READING: ACTS 11:27—12:3a

A reading from Acts:

²⁷At that time when Barnabas and Saul were in Antioch,
prophets came down from Jerusalem to Antioch.
²⁸One of them named Agabus stood up and predicted by the Spirit
that there would be a severe famine over all the world;
and this took place during the reign of Claudius.
²⁹The disciples determined that according to their ability,
each would send relief to the believers living in Judea;
this they did, sending it to the elders by Barnabas and Saul.

^{12:1}About that time
King Herod laid violent hands upon some who belonged to the church.
²He had James, the brother of John, killed with the sword.
^{3a}After Herod saw that it pleased the Jewish leaders, he proceeded to arrest
Peter also.

GOSPEL: MARK 10:35-45

The Holy Gospel according to Mark, the tenth chapter.

35James and John, the sons of Zebedee, came forward to Jesus and said to him,
 "Teacher, we want you to do for us whatever we ask of you."
36And Jesus said to them, "What is it you want me to do for you?"
37And they said to him,
"Grant us to sit, one at your right hand and one at your left, in your glory."
38But Jesus said to them,
"You do not know what you are asking.
Are you able to drink the cup that I drink,
or be baptized with the baptism that I am baptized with?"
39They replied, "We are able."
Then Jesus said to them,
"The cup that I drink you will drink;
and with the baptism with which I am baptized, you will be baptized;
40but to sit at my right hand or at my left is not mine to grant,
but it is for those for whom it has been prepared."

41When the ten heard this, they began to be angry with James and John.
42So Jesus called them and said to them,
"You know that among the Gentiles
those whom they recognize as their rulers are domineering,
and their great ones are tyrants over them.
43But it is not so among you;
but whoever wishes to become great among you must be your servant,
44and whoever wishes to be first among you must be slave of all.
45For the Son-of-Man came not to be served but to serve,
and to give his life a ransom for many."

The Gospel of the Lord.

✠

MARY, MOTHER OF OUR LORD

AUGUST 15

FIRST READING: ISAIAH 61:7-11

A reading from Isaiah:

⁷Because their shame was double,
and dishonor was proclaimed as their lot,
therefore they shall possess a double portion;
everlasting joy shall be theirs.

⁸For I the LORD love justice,
I hate robbery and wrongdoing;
I will faithfully give them their recompense,
and I will make an everlasting covenant with them.
⁹Their descendants shall be known among the nations,
and their offspring among the peoples;
all who see them shall acknowledge
that they are a people whom the LORD has blessed.
¹⁰I will greatly rejoice in the LORD,
my whole being shall exult in my God;
for God has clothed me with the garments of salvation
and has covered me with the robe of righteousness,
as a bridegroom decks himself with a garland,
and as a bride adorns herself with her jewels.
¹¹For as the earth brings forth its shoots,
and as a garden causes what is sown in it to spring up,
so the Lord GOD will cause righteousness and praise
to spring up before all the nations.

PSALMODY: PSALM 45:10-15

Psalm 45:11–16 LBW/BCP

SECOND READING: GALATIANS 4:4-7

A reading from Galatians:

⁴When the fullness of time had come,
God sent the Son, born of a woman, born under the law,
⁵in order to redeem those who were under the law,
so that we might receive adoption as children.
⁶And because you are children,

God has sent the Spirit of the Son into our hearts,
crying, "Abba! Father!"
[7]So you are no longer a slave but a child,
and if a child then also an heir, through God.

GOSPEL: LUKE 1:46-55

The Holy Gospel according to Luke, the first chapter.

[46]And Mary said,
"My soul magnifies the Lord,
[47]and my spirit rejoices in God my Savior,
[48]who has looked with favor on me, a lowly servant.
Surely, from now on all generations will call me blessed;
[49]for the Mighty One has done great things for me:
holy is the name of the Lord,
[50]whose mercy is for the God-fearing from generation to generation.
[51]The arm of the Lord is filled with strength,
scattering the proud in the thoughts of their hearts.
[52]God has brought down the powerful from their thrones,
and lifted up the lowly;
[53]God has filled the hungry with good things,
and sent the rich away empty.
[54]God has helped Israel, the Lord's servant, in remembrance of mercy,
[55]according to the promise God made to our ancestors,
to Abraham and to his descendants forever."

The Gospel of the Lord.

St. Bartholomew, Apostle

AUGUST 24

FIRST READING: Exodus 19:1-6

A reading from Exodus:

¹On the third new moon after the Israelites had gone out of the land of Egypt,
on that very day, they came into the wilderness of Sinai.
²They had journeyed from Rephidim, entered the wilderness of Sinai,
and camped in the wilderness;
Israel camped there in front of the mountain.
³Then Moses went up to God;
the Lord called to him from the mountain, saying,
"Thus you shall say to the house of Jacob, and tell the Israelites:
⁴You have seen what I did to the Egyptians,
and how I bore you on eagles' wings and brought you to myself.
⁵Now therefore, if you obey my voice and keep my covenant,
you shall be my treasured possession out of all the peoples.
Indeed, the whole earth is mine,
⁶but you shall be for me a realm of priests and a holy nation.
These are the words that you shall speak to the Israelites."

PSALMODY: Psalm 12

SECOND READING: 1 Corinthians 12:27-31a

A reading from First Corinthians:

²⁷Now you are the body of Christ and individually members of it.
²⁸And God has appointed in the church first apostles,
second prophets, third teachers;
then deeds of power, then gifts of healing,
forms of assistance, forms of leadership, various kinds of tongues.
²⁹Are all apostles? Are all prophets? Are all teachers?
Do all work miracles? Do all possess gifts of healing?
³⁰Do all speak in tongues? Do all interpret?
³¹ᵃBut strive for the greater gifts.

GOSPEL: John 1:43-51

The Holy Gospel according to John, the first chapter.

⁴³The next day Jesus decided to go to Galilee.
He found Philip and said to him, "Follow me."
⁴⁴Now Philip was from Bethsaida, the city of Andrew and Peter.
⁴⁵Philip found Nathanael and said to him,
"We have found him about whom Moses in the law and also the prophets
       wrote,
Jesus son of Joseph from Nazareth."
⁴⁶Nathanael said to him, "Can anything good come out of Nazareth?"
Philip said to him, "Come and see."

⁴⁷When Jesus saw Nathanael coming toward him, he said of him,
"Here is truly an Israelite in whom there is no deceit!"
⁴⁸Nathanael asked him, "Where did you get to know me?"
Jesus answered, "I saw you under the fig tree before Philip called you."
⁴⁹Nathanael replied,
"Rabbi, you are the Son of God! You are the King of Israel!"
⁵⁰Jesus answered,
"Do you believe because I told you that I saw you under the fig tree?
You will see greater things than these."
⁵¹And Jesus said to him,
"Very truly, I tell you, you will see heaven opened
and the angels of God ascending and descending upon the Son-of-Man."

The Gospel of the Lord.

H O L Y C R O S S D A Y

SEPTEMBER 14

FIRST READING: NUMBERS 21:4b-9

A reading from Numbers:

From Mount Hor the Israelites set out,
[4b]but the people became impatient on the way.
[5]They spoke against God and against Moses,
"Why have you brought us up out of Egypt to die in the wilderness?
For there is no food and no water, and we detest this miserable food."
[6]Then the LORD sent poisonous serpents among the people,
and they bit the people, so that many Israelites died.

[7]The people came to Moses and said,
"We have sinned by speaking against the LORD and against you;
pray to the LORD to take away the serpents from us."
So Moses prayed for the people.
[8]And the LORD said to Moses,
"Make a poisonous serpent, and set it on a pole;
and everyone who is bitten shall look at it and live."
[9]So Moses made a serpent of bronze, and put it upon a pole;
and whenever a serpent bit someone,
that person would look at the serpent of bronze and live.

PSALMODY: PSALM 98:1-4 or PSALM 78:1-2, 34-38   *Psalm 98:1–5* LBW/BCP

SECOND READING: 1 CORINTHIANS 1:18-24

A reading from First Corinthians:

[18]The message about the cross is foolishness to those who are perishing,
but to us who are being saved it is the power of God.
[19]For it is written,
"I will destroy the wisdom of the wise,
and the discernment of the discerning I will thwart."
[20]Where is the one who is wise?
Where is the scribe?
Where is the debater of this age?
Has not God made foolish the wisdom of the world?

²¹For since, in the wisdom of God,
the world did not know God through wisdom,
God decided, through the foolishness of our proclamation,
to save those who believe.
²²For Jews demand signs and Greeks desire wisdom,
²³but we proclaim Christ crucified,
a stumbling block to Jews and foolishness to Gentiles,
²⁴but to those who are the called, both Jews and Greeks,
Christ the power of God and the wisdom of God.

GOSPEL: JOHN 3:13-17

The Holy Gospel according to John, the third chapter.

Jesus said:
¹³"No one has ascended into heaven
except the one who descended from heaven,
the Son-of-Man.
¹⁴And just as Moses lifted up the serpent in the wilderness,
so must the Son-of-Man be lifted up,
¹⁵that whoever believes in him may have eternal life.

¹⁶"For God loved the world in this way,
that God gave the Son, the only begotten one,
so that everyone who believes in him may not perish
but may have eternal life.
¹⁷Indeed, God did not send the Son into the world to condemn the world,
but in order that the world might be saved through him."

The Gospel of the Lord.

$$\dagger$$

St. Matthew, Apostle
and Evangelist

SEPTEMBER 21

FIRST READING: EZEKIEL 2:8—3:11

A reading from Ezekiel:

⁸You, mortal, hear what I say to you;
do not be rebellious like that rebellious house;
open your mouth and eat what I give you.
⁹I looked, and a hand was stretched out to me,
and a written scroll was in it.
¹⁰The LORD spread it before me;
it had writing on the front and on the back,
and written on it were words of lamentation and mourning and woe.

3:1The LORD said to me, O mortal, eat what is offered to you;
eat this scroll, and go, speak to the house of Israel.
²So I opened my mouth, and the LORD gave me the scroll to eat.
³The LORD said to me, Mortal, eat this scroll that I give you
and fill your stomach with it.
Then I ate it; and in my mouth it was as sweet as honey.

⁴The LORD said to me: Mortal, go to the house of Israel
and speak my very words to them.
⁵For you are not sent to a people of obscure speech and difficult language,
but to the house of Israel—
⁶not to many peoples of obscure speech and difficult language,
whose words you cannot understand.
Surely, if I sent you to them, they would listen to you.
⁷But the house of Israel will not listen to you,
for they are not willing to listen to me;
because all the house of Israel have a hard forehead and a stubborn heart.
⁸See, I have made your face hard against their faces,
and your forehead hard against their foreheads.
⁹Like the hardest stone, harder than flint, I have made your forehead;
do not fear them or be dismayed at their looks,
for they are a rebellious house.
¹⁰The LORD said to me: Mortal, all my words that I shall speak to you
receive in your heart and hear with your ears;
¹¹then go to the exiles, to your people, and speak to them.

Say to them, "Thus says the Lord GOD";
whether they hear or refuse to hear.

PSALMODY: PSALM 119:33-40

SECOND READING: EPHESIANS 2:4-10

A reading from Ephesians:

⁴God, who is rich in mercy,
out of the great love with which God loved us
⁵even when we were dead through our trespasses,
made us alive together with Christ—by grace you have been saved.
With Christ ⁶God raised us up
and enthroned us in the heavenly places in Christ Jesus,
⁷so that in the ages to come
might be shown the immeasurable riches of God's grace
in kindness toward us in Christ Jesus.
⁸For by grace you have been saved through faith,
and this is not your own doing;
it is the gift of God—
⁹not the result of works, so that no one may boast.
¹⁰For we are what God has made us,
created in Christ Jesus for good works,
which God prepared beforehand to be our way of life.

The Holy Gospel according to Matthew, the ninth chapter.

[9]As Jesus was walking along,
he saw a man called Matthew sitting at the tax booth;
and he said to him, "Follow me."
And he got up and followed him.

[10]And as Jesus sat at dinner in the house,
many tax collectors and sinners came
and were sitting with him and his disciples.
[11]When the Pharisees saw this, they said to his disciples,
"Why does your teacher eat with tax collectors and sinners?"
[12]But when he heard this, he said,
"Those who are well have no need of a physician,
but those who are sick.
[13]Go and learn what this means,
'I desire mercy, not sacrifice.'
For I have come to call not the righteous but sinners."

The Gospel of the Lord.

St. Michael and All Angels

FIRST READING: DANIEL 10:10-14; 12:1-3

A reading from Daniel:

¹⁰A hand touched me and roused me to my hands and knees.
¹¹A voice said to me, "Daniel, greatly beloved,
pay attention to the words that I am going to speak to you.
Stand on your feet, for I have now been sent to you."
So while these words were spoken to me, I stood up trembling.
¹²Then the voice said to me, "Do not fear, Daniel,
for from the first day that you set your mind to gain understanding
and to humble yourself before your God,
your words have been heard, and I have come because of your words.
¹³But the ruler of the realm of Persia opposed me twenty-one days.
So Michael, one of the chief rulers, came to help me,
and I left him there with the ruler of the dominion of Persia,
¹⁴and have come to help you understand what is to happen to your people
at the end of days.
For there is a further vision for those days.

¹²:¹"At that time Michael, the great ruler,
the protector of your people, shall arise.
There shall be a time of anguish,
such as has never occurred since nations first came into existence.
But at that time your people shall be delivered,
everyone who is found written in the book.
²Many of those who sleep in the dust of the earth shall awake,
some to everlasting life, and some to shame and everlasting contempt.
³Those who are wise shall shine like the brightness of the sky,
and those who lead many to righteousness,
like the stars forever and ever."

PSALMODY: PSALM 103:1-5, 20-22

SECOND READING: REVELATION 12:7-12

A reading from Revelation:

⁷War broke out in heaven;
Michael and the angels fought against the dragon.
The dragon and its angels fought back,
⁸but they were defeated, and there was no longer any place for them in heaven.
⁹The great dragon was thrown down,
that ancient serpent, who is called the Devil and Satan,
the deceiver of the whole world—
the dragon was thrown down to the earth, together with its angels.

¹⁰Then I heard a loud voice in heaven, proclaiming,
"Now have come the salvation and the power
and the dominion of our God and the authority of the Messiah of God,
for the accuser of our comrades has been thrown down,
who accuses them day and night before our God.
¹¹But they have conquered the accuser by the blood of the Lamb
and by the word of their testimony,
for they did not cling to life even in the face of death.
¹²Rejoice then, you heavens and those who dwell in them!
But woe to the earth and the sea,
for the devil has come down to you with great wrath,
because the devil knows that its time is short!"

GOSPEL: LUKE 10:17-20

The Holy Gospel according to Luke, the tenth chapter.

¹⁷The seventy returned with joy, saying,
"Lord, in your name even the demons submit to us!"
¹⁸Jesus said to them,
"I watched Satan fall from heaven like a flash of lightning.
¹⁹See, I have given you authority to tread on snakes and scorpions,
and over all the power of the enemy;
and nothing will hurt you.
²⁰Nevertheless, do not rejoice at this,
that the spirits submit to you,
but rejoice that your names are written in heaven."

The Gospel of the Lord.

✠

St. Luke, Evangelist

OCTOBER 18

FIRST READING: Isaiah 43:8-13

Or Isaiah 35:5-8, following

A reading from Isaiah:

⁸Bring forth the people who are blind, yet have eyes,
who are deaf, yet have ears!
⁹Let all the nations gather together, and let the peoples assemble.
Who among them declared this,
and foretold to us the former things?
Let them bring their witnesses to justify them,
and let them hear and say, "It is true."
¹⁰You are my witnesses, says the LORD,
and my servant whom I have chosen,
so that you may know and believe me
and understand that I am the one.
Before me no deity was formed, nor shall there be any after me.
¹¹I, I am the LORD,
and besides me there is no savior.
¹²I declared and saved and proclaimed,
when there was no strange deity among you;
and you are my witnesses, says the LORD.
¹³I am God, and also henceforth I am the one;
there is no one who can deliver from my hand;
I work and who can hinder it?

OR: Isaiah 35:5-8

A reading from Isaiah:

⁵Then the eyes of the blind shall be opened,
and the ears of the deaf unstopped;
⁶then the lame shall leap like a deer,
and the tongue of the speechless sing for joy.
For waters shall break forth in the wilderness,
and streams in the desert;
⁷the burning sand shall become a pool,
and the thirsty ground springs of water;

the haunt of jackals shall become a swamp,
the grass shall become reeds and rushes.

⁸A highway shall be there,
and it shall be called the Holy Way;
the unclean shall not travel on it,
but it shall be for God's people;
no traveler, not even fools, shall go astray.

PSALMODY: PSALM 124

SECOND READING: 2 TIMOTHY 4:5-11

A reading from Second Timothy:

⁵As for you, always be sober, endure suffering,
do the work of an evangelist, carry out your ministry fully.

⁶As for me, I am already being poured out as a libation,
and the time of my departure has come.
⁷I have fought the good fight,
I have finished the race,
I have kept the faith.
⁸From now on there is reserved for me the crown of righteousness,
which the Lord, the righteous judge, will give me on that day,
and not only to me but also to all who have longed for the Lord's appearing.

⁹Do your best to come to me soon,
¹⁰for Demas, in love with this present world,
has deserted me and gone to Thessalonica;
Crescens has gone to Galatia, Titus to Dalmatia.
¹¹Only Luke is with me.
Get Mark and bring him with you, for he is useful in my ministry.

The Holy Gospel according to Luke, the first and twenty-fourth chapters.

Luke writes:
[1]Since many have undertaken to set down an orderly account
of the events that have been fulfilled among us,
[2]just as they were handed on to us
by those who from the beginning were eyewitnesses and servants of the word,
[3]I too decided, after investigating everything carefully from the very first,
to write an orderly account for you, most excellent Theophilus,
[4]so that you may know the truth concerning the things
about which you have been instructed.

And again Luke writes:
[24:44]Jesus said:
"These are my words that I spoke to you while I was still with you—
that everything written about me in the law of Moses,
the prophets, and the psalms must be fulfilled."
[45]Then Jesus opened their minds to understand the scriptures,
[46]and said to them, "Thus it is written,
that the Messiah is to suffer and to rise from the dead on the third day,
[47]and that repentance and forgiveness of sins is to be proclaimed in his name
to all nations, beginning from Jerusalem.
[48]You are witnesses of these things.
[49]And see, I am sending upon you what my Father promised;
so stay here in the city until you have been clothed with power from on high."

[50]Then Jesus led them out as far as Bethany,
and, lifting up his hands, he blessed them.
[51]While he was blessing them,
he withdrew from them and was carried up into heaven.
[52]And they worshiped him, and returned to Jerusalem with great joy;
[53]and they were continually in the temple blessing God.

The Gospel of the Lord.

St. Simon and St. Jude, Apostles

OCTOBER 28

FIRST READING: JEREMIAH 26:[1-6] 7-16

A reading from Jeremiah:

[¹At the beginning of the reign of King Jehoiakim son of Josiah of Judah,
this word came from the LORD:
²Thus says the LORD:
Stand in the court of the LORD's house,
and speak to all the cities of Judah that come to worship in the house
      of the LORD;
speak to them all the words that I command you;
do not hold back a word.
³It may be that they will listen, all of them,
and will turn from their evil way,
that I may change my mind about the disaster
that I intend to bring on them because of their evil doings.
⁴You shall say to them:
Thus says the LORD: If you will not listen to me,
to walk in my law that I have set before you,
⁵and to heed the words of my servants the prophets
whom I send to you urgently—
though you have not heeded—
⁶then I will make this house like Shiloh,
and I will make this city a curse for all the nations of the earth.]

⁷The priests and the prophets and all the people
heard Jeremiah speaking these words in the house of the LORD.
⁸And when Jeremiah had finished speaking
all that the LORD had commanded him to speak to all the people,
then the priests and the prophets and all the people laid hold of him,
saying, "You shall die!
⁹Why have you prophesied in the name of the LORD, saying,
'This house shall be like Shiloh,
and this city shall be desolate, without inhabitant'?"
And all the people gathered around Jeremiah in the house of the LORD.

¹⁰When the officials of Judah heard these things,
they came up from the king's house to the house of the LORD
and took their seat in the entry of the New Gate of the house of the LORD.

[11]Then the priests and the prophets said to the officials and to all the people,
"This man deserves the sentence of death
because he has prophesied against this city,
as you have heard with your own ears."

[12]Then Jeremiah spoke to all the officials and all the people, saying,
"It is the LORD who sent me to prophesy
against this house and this city all the words you have heard.
[13]Now therefore amend your ways and your doings,
and obey the voice of the LORD your God,
and the LORD will have second thoughts about the disaster
that was pronounced against you.
[14]But as for me, here I am in your hands.
Do with me as seems good and right to you.
[15]Only know for certain that if you put me to death,
you will be bringing innocent blood upon yourselves
and upon this city and its inhabitants,
for in truth the LORD sent me to you to speak all these words in your ears."

[16]Then the officials and all the people said to the priests and the prophets,
"This man does not deserve the sentence of death,
for he has spoken to us in the name of the LORD our God."

PSALMODY: PSALM 11

SECOND READING: 1 JOHN 4:1-6

A reading from First John:

[1]Beloved, do not believe every spirit,
but test the spirits to see whether they are from God;
for many false prophets have gone out into the world.
[2]By this you know the Spirit of God:
every spirit that confesses that Jesus Christ has come in the flesh is from God,
[3]and every spirit that does not confess Jesus is not from God.
And this is the spirit of the antichrist,
of which you have heard that it is coming;
and now it is already in the world.

[4]Little children, you are from God, and have conquered them;
for the one who is in you is greater than the one who is in the world.
[5]They are from the world;
therefore what they say is from the world, and the world listens to them.

⁶We are from God.
Whoever knows God listens to us,
and whoever is not from God does not listen to us.
From this we know the spirit of truth and the spirit of error.

GOSPEL: JOHN 14:21-27

The Holy Gospel according to John, the 14th chapter.

Jesus said:
²¹"They who have my commandments and keep them are those who love me;
and those who love me will be loved by my Father,
and I will love them and reveal myself to them."
²²Judas (not Iscariot) said to Jesus,
"Lord, how is it that you will reveal yourself to us, and not to the world?"
²³Jesus answered him,
"Those who love me will keep my word, and my Father will love them,
and we will come to them and make our home with them.
²⁴Whoever does not love me does not keep my words;
and the word that you hear is not mine, but is from the Father who sent me.

²⁵"I have said these things to you while I am still with you.
²⁶But the Advocate, the Holy Spirit, whom the Father will send in my name,
will teach you everything,
and remind you of all that I have said to you.
²⁷Peace I leave with you; my peace I give to you.
I do not give to you as the world gives.
Do not let your hearts be troubled, and do not let them be afraid."

The Gospel of the Lord.

✠

R E F O R M A T I O N   D A Y

OCTOBER 31

REFORMATION SUNDAY: OCTOBER 27, 1996   OCTOBER 31, 1999   OCTOBER 27, 2002

FIRST READING: JEREMIAH 31:31-34

A reading from Jeremiah:

³¹The days are surely coming, says the LORD,
when I will make a new covenant with the house of Israel
        and the house of Judah.
³²It will not be like the covenant that I made with their ancestors
when I took them by the hand to bring them out of the land of Egypt—
a covenant that they broke, though I was married to them, says the LORD.

³³But this is the covenant that I will make with the house of Israel
after those days, says the LORD:
I will put my law within them,
and I will write it on their hearts;
and I will be their God, and they shall be my people.
³⁴No longer shall they teach one another,
or say to each other, "Know the LORD,"
for they shall all know me,
from the least of them to the greatest, says the LORD;
for I will forgive their iniquity, and remember their sin no more.

PSALMODY: PSALM 46

SECOND READING: ROMANS 3:19-28

A reading from Romans:

¹⁹Now we know that whatever the law says,
it speaks to those who are under the law,
so that every mouth may be silenced,
and the whole world may be held accountable to God.
²⁰For "no human being will be justified in the sight of God"
by deeds prescribed by the law,
for through the law comes the knowledge of sin.

²¹But now, apart from law, the righteousness of God has been disclosed,
and is attested by the law and the prophets,
²²the righteousness of God through faith in Jesus Christ for all who believe.
For there is no distinction,
²³since all have sinned and fall short of the glory of God;
²⁴they are now justified by God's grace as a gift,
through the redemption that is in Christ Jesus,
²⁵whom God put forward as a sacrifice of atonement by his blood,
effective through faith.
This was to show God's righteousness,
because in divine forbearance
God had passed over the sins previously committed;
²⁶it was to prove at the present time that God is righteous
and that God justifies the one who has faith in Jesus.

²⁷Then what becomes of boasting?
It is excluded.
By what law? By that of works?
No, but by the law of faith.
²⁸For we hold that a person is justified by faith apart from works
          prescribed by the law.

GOSPEL: JOHN 8:31-36

The Holy Gospel according to John, the eighth chapter.

³¹Jesus said to the Judeans who had believed in him,
"If you continue in my word, you are truly my disciples;
³²and you will know the truth,
and the truth will make you free."
³³They answered him,
"We are descendants of Abraham and have never been slaves to anyone.
What do you mean by saying, 'You will be made free'?"

³⁴Jesus answered them,
"Very truly, I tell you, everyone who commits sin is a slave to sin.
³⁵The slave does not have a permanent place in the household;
the son has a place there forever.

³⁶"So if the Son makes you free, you will be free indeed."

The Gospel of the Lord.

ALL SAINTS DAY

NOVEMBER 1

ALL SAINTS SUNDAY: NOVEMBER 3, 1996   NOVEMBER 7, 1999   NOVEMBER 3, 2002

FIRST READING: REVELATION 7:9-17

A reading from Revelation:

[9]I looked, and there was a great multitude that no one could count,
from every nation, from all tribes and peoples and languages,
standing before the throne and before the Lamb,
robed in white, with palm branches in their hands.
[10]They cried out in a loud voice, saying,
"Salvation belongs to our God who is seated on the throne, and to the Lamb!"

[11]And all the angels stood around the throne
and around the elders and the four living creatures,
and they fell on their faces before the throne and worshiped God, [12]singing,
"Amen! Blessing and glory and wisdom
and thanksgiving and honor and power and might
be to our God forever and ever! Amen."

[13]Then one of the elders addressed me, saying,
"Who are these, robed in white, and where have they come from?"
[14]I said to him, "Sir, you are the one that knows."
Then he said to me,
"These are they who have come out of the great ordeal;
they have washed their robes and made them white in the blood of the Lamb.
[15]For this reason they are before the throne of God,
and worship God day and night within the temple,
and the one who is seated on the throne will shelter them.
[16]They will hunger no more, and thirst no more;
the sun will not strike them, nor any scorching heat;
[17]for the Lamb at the center of the throne will be their shepherd,
and will guide them to springs of the water of life,
and God will wipe away every tear from their eyes."

PSALMODY: PSALM 34:1-10, 22

Psalm 34:1–9, 22   LBW/BCP

SECOND READING: 1 JOHN 3:1-3

A reading from First John:

[1]See what love the Father has given us,
that we should be called children of God;
and that is what we are.
The reason the world does not know us is that it did not know God.
[2]Beloved, we are God's children now;
what we will be has not yet been revealed.
What we do know is this:
when it is revealed, we will be like God,
for we will see God as God is.
[3]And all who have this hope in God purify themselves,
just as the Son is pure.

GOSPEL: MATTHEW 5:1-12

The Holy Gospel according to Matthew, the fifth chapter.

[1]When Jesus saw the crowds, he went up the mountain and sat down,
and his disciples came to him.

[2]Then Jesus began to speak, and taught them, saying:
[3]Blessed are the poor in spirit, for theirs is the dominion of heaven.
[4]Blessed are those who mourn, for they will be comforted.
[5]Blessed are the meek, for they will inherit the earth.
[6]Blessed are those who hunger and thirst for righteousness,
        for they will be filled.
[7]Blessed are the merciful, for they will receive mercy.
[8]Blessed are the pure in heart, for they will see God.
[9]Blessed are the peacemakers, for they will be called children of God.

[10]"Blessed are those who are persecuted for righteousness' sake,
for theirs is the dominion of heaven.
[11]Blessed are you when people revile you and persecute you
and utter all kinds of evil against you falsely on my account.
[12]Rejoice and be glad, for your reward is great in heaven,
for in the same way they persecuted the prophets who were before you."

The Gospel of the Lord.

NEW YEAR'S EVE

DECEMBER 31

FIRST READING: ECCLESIASTES 3:1-13

A reading from Ecclesiastes:

¹For everything there is a season, and a time for every matter under heaven:
²a time to be born, and a time to die;
a time to plant, and a time to pluck up what is planted;
³a time to kill, and a time to heal;
a time to break down, and a time to build up;
⁴a time to weep, and a time to laugh;
a time to mourn, and a time to dance;
⁵a time to throw away stones, and a time to gather stones together;
a time to embrace, and a time to refrain from embracing;
⁶a time to seek, and a time to lose;
a time to keep, and a time to throw away;
⁷a time to tear, and a time to sew;
a time to keep silence, and a time to speak;
⁸a time to love, and a time to hate;
a time for war, and a time for peace.

⁹What gain have the workers from their toil?
¹⁰I have seen the business that God has given to everyone to be busy with.
¹¹God has made everything suitable for its time;
moreover God has put a sense of past and future into their minds,
yet they cannot find out what God has done from the beginning to the end.
¹²I know that there is nothing better for them than to be happy
and enjoy themselves as long as they live;
¹³moreover, it is God's gift
that all should eat and drink and take pleasure in all their toil.

PSALMODY: PSALM 8

SECOND READING: REVELATION 21:1-6a

A reading from Revelation:

¹I saw a new heaven and a new earth;
for the first heaven and the first earth had passed away,
and the sea was no more.
²And I saw the holy city, the new Jerusalem,
coming down out of heaven from God,
prepared as a bride adorned for her husband.
³And I heard a loud voice from the throne saying,
"See, the home of God is among mortals.
God will dwell with them as their God;
they will be God's people,
and that very God will be with them,
⁴and will wipe every tear from their eyes.
Death will be no more;
mourning and crying and pain will be no more,
for the first things have passed away."

⁵And the one who was seated on the throne said,
"See, I am making all things new,"
and also said,
"Write this, for these words are trustworthy and true."
⁶ᵃThen the one seated on the throne said to me,
"It is done! I am the Alpha and the Omega, the beginning and the end."

GOSPEL: MATTHEW 25:31-46

The Holy Gospel according to Matthew, the 25th chapter.

Jesus said:
³¹"When the Son-of-Man comes in his glory, and all the angels with him,
then he will sit on the throne of his glory.
³²All the nations will be gathered before him,
and he will separate people one from another
as a shepherd separates the sheep from the goats,
³³and he will put the sheep at his right hand and the goats at the left.

³⁴"Then the king will say to those at his right hand,
'Come, you that are blessed by my Father,
inherit the dominion prepared for you from the foundation of the world;
³⁵for I was hungry and you gave me food,
I was thirsty and you gave me something to drink,
I was a stranger and you welcomed me,
³⁶I was naked and you gave me clothing,
I was sick and you took care of me,
I was in prison and you visited me.'
³⁷Then the righteous will answer him,

'Lord, when was it that we saw you hungry and gave you food,
or thirsty and gave you something to drink?
38And when was it that we saw you a stranger and welcomed you,
or naked and gave you clothing?
39And when was it that we saw you sick or in prison and visited you?'
40And the king will answer them,
'Truly I tell you,
just as you did it to one of the least of these who are members of my family,
you did it to me.'

41"Then he will say to those at his left hand,
'You that are accursed,
depart from me into the eternal fire prepared for the devil and the devil's angels;
42for I was hungry and you gave me no food,
I was thirsty and you gave me nothing to drink,
43I was a stranger and you did not welcome me,
naked and you did not give me clothing,
sick and in prison and you did not visit me.'
44Then they also will answer,
'Lord, when was it that we saw you hungry or thirsty
or a stranger or naked or sick or in prison,
and did not take care of you?'
45Then he will answer them,
'Truly I tell you,
just as you did not do it to one of the least of these,
you did not do it to me.'
46And these will go away into eternal punishment,
but the righteous into eternal life."

The Gospel of the Lord.

✠

DAY OF THANKSGIVING

CANADA: OCTOBER 14, 1996   OCTOBER 11, 1999   OCTOBER 14, 2002
U.S.A.:   NOVEMBER 28, 1996   NOVEMBER 25, 1999   NOVEMBER 28, 2002

FIRST READING: Deuteronomy 8:7-18

A reading from Deuteronomy:

⁷The Lord your God is bringing you into a good land,
a land with flowing streams,
with springs and underground waters welling up in valleys and hills,
⁸a land of wheat and barley, of vines and fig trees and pomegranates,
a land of olive trees and honey,
⁹a land where you may eat bread without scarcity,
where you will lack nothing,
a land whose stones are iron and from whose hills you may mine copper.
¹⁰You shall eat your fill
and bless the Lord your God for the good land that the Lord has given you.

¹¹Take care that you do not forget the Lord your God,
by failing to keep the commandments, the ordinances, and the statutes of the Lord,
which I am commanding you today.
¹²When you have eaten your fill and have built fine houses and live in them,
¹³and when your herds and flocks have multiplied,
and your silver and gold is multiplied, and all that you have is multiplied,
¹⁴then do not exalt yourself, forgetting the Lord your God,
who brought you out of the land of Egypt, out of the house of slavery,
¹⁵who led you through the great and terrible wilderness,
an arid wasteland with poisonous snakes and scorpions.
The Lord made water flow for you from flint rock,
¹⁶and fed you in the wilderness with manna that your ancestors did not know,
to humble you and to test you, and in the end to do you good.
¹⁷Do not say to yourself,
"My power and the might of my own hand have gotten me this wealth."
¹⁸But remember the Lord your God,
for it is the Lord who gives you power to get wealth,
in order to confirm, then as today,
the covenant that the Lord swore to your ancestors.

PSALMODY: Psalm 65

SECOND READING: 2 CORINTHIANS 9:6-15

A reading from Second Corinthians:

[6]The point is this: the one who sows sparingly will also reap sparingly,
and the one who sows bountifully will also reap bountifully.
[7]Each of you must give as you have made up your mind,
not reluctantly or under compulsion,
for God loves a cheerful giver.

[8]And God is able to provide you with every blessing in abundance,
so that by always having enough of everything,
you may share abundantly in every good work.
[9]As it is written,
"God scatters abroad, and gives to the poor;
the righteousness of God endures forever."
[10]The one who supplies seed to the sower and bread for food
will supply and multiply your seed for sowing
and increase the harvest of your righteousness.

[11]You will be enriched in every way for your great generosity,
which will produce thanksgiving to God through us;
[12]for the rendering of this ministry not only supplies the needs of the saints
but also overflows with many thanksgivings to God.
[13]Through the testing of this ministry you glorify God
by your obedience to the confession of the gospel of Christ
and by the generosity of your sharing with them and with all others,
[14]while they long for you and pray for you
because of the surpassing grace of God that has been given you.
[15]Thanks be to God for this indescribable gift!

GOSPEL: LUKE 17:11-19

The Holy Gospel according to Luke, the 17th chapter.

[11]On the way to Jerusalem
Jesus was going through the region between Samaria and Galilee.
[12]As he entered a village, ten people who had leprosy approached him.
Keeping their distance, [13]they called out, saying,
"Jesus, Master, have mercy on us!"
[14]When he saw them, he said to them,
"Go and show yourselves to the priests."
And as they went, they were made clean.

[15]Then one of them, when he saw that he was healed,
turned back, praising God with a loud voice.
[16]He prostrated himself at Jesus' feet and thanked him.
And he was a Samaritan.
[17]Then Jesus asked, "Were not ten made clean?
But the other nine, where are they?
[18]Was none of them found to return and give praise to God
except this foreigner?"
[19]Then Jesus said to the Samaritan,
"Get up and go on your way; your faith has made you well."

The Gospel of the Lord.

APPENDIX A

SEMI-CONTINUOUS FIRST READINGS AND PSALMODY

Sunday between
May 29 and June 4 inclusive

(if after Trinity Sunday)

JUNE 2, 2002

PROPER 4

FIRST READING: GENESIS 6:9–22; 7:24; 8:14–19

A reading from Genesis:

⁹These are the descendants of Noah.
Noah was a righteous man, blameless in his generation;
Noah walked with God.
¹⁰And Noah had three sons, Shem, Ham, and Japheth.

¹¹Now the earth was corrupt in God's sight,
and the earth was filled with violence.
¹²And God saw that the earth was corrupt;
for all flesh had corrupted its ways upon the earth.
¹³And God said to Noah,
"I have determined to make an end of all flesh,
for the earth is filled with violence because of them;
now I am going to destroy them along with the earth.
¹⁴Make yourself an ark of cypress wood;
make rooms in the ark, and cover it inside and out with pitch.
¹⁵This is how you are to make it:
the length of the ark three hundred cubits, its width fifty cubits,
and its height thirty cubits.
¹⁶Make a roof for the ark, and finish it to a cubit above;
and put the door of the ark in its side;
make it with lower, second, and third decks.

¹⁷For my part, I am going to bring a flood of waters on the earth,
to destroy from under heaven all flesh in which is the breath of life;
everything that is on the earth shall die.
¹⁸But I will establish my covenant with you;
and you shall come into the ark,
you, your sons, your wife, and your sons' wives with you.
¹⁹And of every living thing, of all flesh,
you shall bring two of every kind into the ark, to keep them alive with you;
they shall be male and female.
²⁰Of the birds according to their kinds,
and of the animals according to their kinds,
of every creeping thing of the ground according to its kind,
two of every kind shall come in to you, to keep them alive.

²¹Also take with you every kind of food that is eaten, and store it up; and it shall serve as food for you and for them."
²²Noah did this; he did all that God commanded him.

⁷:²⁴And the waters swelled on the earth for one hundred fifty days.

⁸:¹⁴In the second month, on the twenty-seventh day of the month, the earth was dry.
¹⁵Then God said to Noah,
¹⁶"Go out of the ark, you and your wife, and your sons and your sons' wives with you.
¹⁷Bring out with you every living thing that is with you of all flesh— birds and animals and every creeping thing that creeps on the earth— so that they may abound on the earth, and be fruitful and multiply on the earth."
¹⁸So Noah went out with his sons and his wife and his sons' wives.
¹⁹And every animal, every creeping thing, and every bird, everything that moves on the earth, went out of the ark by families.

PSALMODY: PSALM 46

Readings continue on p. 203

✝

Sunday between
June 5 and 11 inclusive
(if after Trinity Sunday)

PROPER 5

FIRST READING: Genesis 12:1-9

A reading from Genesis:

[1]The Lord said to Abram,
"Go from your country and your kindred and your father's house
to the land that I will show you.
[2]I will make of you a great nation, and I will bless you,
and make your name great, so that you will be a blessing.
[3]I will bless those who bless you,
and the one who curses you I will curse;
and in you all the families of the earth shall be blessed."

[4]So Abram went, as the Lord had told him; and Lot went with him.
Abram was seventy-five years old when he departed from Haran.
[5]Abram took his wife Sarai and his brother's son Lot,
and all the possessions that they had gathered,
and the persons whom they had acquired in Haran;
and they set forth to go to the land of Canaan.
When they had come to the land of Canaan,
[6]Abram passed through the land to the place at Shechem, to the oak of Moreh.
At that time the Canaanites were in the land.

[7]Then the Lord appeared to Abram, and said,
"To your offspring I will give this land."
So Abram built there an altar to the Lord, who had appeared to him.
[8]From there he moved on to the hill country on the east of Bethel,
and pitched his tent, with Bethel on the west and Ai on the east;
and there Abram built an altar to the Lord and invoked the name of the Lord.
[9]And Abram journeyed on by stages toward the Negeb.

PSALMODY: Psalm 33:1-12

Readings continue on p. 206

✝

SUNDAY BETWEEN
JUNE 12 AND 18 INCLUSIVE
(if after Trinity Sunday)

JUNE 16, 1996   *JUNE 13, 1999*   *JUNE 16, 2002*

PROPER 6

FIRST READING: GENESIS 18:1-15 [21:1-7]

A reading from Genesis:

¹The LORD appeared to Abraham by the oaks of Mamre,
as he sat at the entrance of his tent in the heat of the day.
²Abraham looked up and saw three men standing near him.
When he saw them, he ran from the tent entrance to meet them,
and bowed down to the ground.
³He said, "My lord, if I find favor with you, do not pass by your servant.
⁴Let a little water be brought, and wash your feet,
and rest yourselves under the tree.
⁵Let me bring a little bread, that you may refresh yourselves,
and after that you may pass on—since you have come to your servant."
So they said, "Do as you have said."

⁶And Abraham hastened into the tent to Sarah, and said,
"Make ready quickly three measures of choice flour,
knead it, and make cakes."
⁷Abraham ran to the herd, and took a calf, tender and good,
and gave it to the servant, who hastened to prepare it.
⁸Then he took curds and milk and the calf that he had prepared,
and set it before them;
and he stood by them under the tree while they ate.

⁹They said to him, "Where is your wife Sarah?"
And he said, "There, in the tent."
¹⁰Then one said,
"I will surely return to you in due season,
and your wife Sarah shall have a son."
And Sarah was listening at the tent entrance behind him.

¹¹Now Abraham and Sarah were old, advanced in age;
it had ceased to be with Sarah after the manner of women.
¹²So Sarah laughed to herself, saying,
"After I have grown old, and my husband is old, shall I have pleasure?"
¹³The LORD said to Abraham,
"Why did Sarah laugh, and say, 'Shall I indeed bear a child, now that I am old?'
¹⁴Is anything too wonderful for the LORD?

At the set time I will return to you, in due season,
and Sarah shall have a son."
¹⁵But Sarah denied, saying, "I did not laugh"; for she was afraid.
The LORD said, "Oh yes, you did laugh."

[²¹:¹The LORD dealt with Sarah as the LORD had said,
and the LORD did for Sarah as was promised.
²Sarah conceived and bore Abraham a son in his old age,
at the time of which God had spoken to him.
³Abraham gave the name Isaac to his son whom Sarah bore him.
⁴And Abraham circumcised his son Isaac when he was eight days old,
as God had commanded him.
⁵Abraham was a hundred years old when his son Isaac was born to him.
⁶Now Sarah said,
"God has brought laughter for me;
everyone who hears will laugh with me."
⁷And she said,
"Who would ever have said to Abraham that Sarah would nurse children?
Yet I have borne him a son in his old age."]

PSALMODY: PSALM 116:1-2, 12-19   *Psalm 116:1–2, 10–17*   LBW/BCP

Readings continue on p. 209

✝

S U N D A Y B E T W E E N
J U N E **19** A N D **25** I N C L U S I V E
(if after Trinity Sunday)

JUNE 23, 1996   JUNE 20, 1999   JUNE 23, 2002

PROPER 7

FIRST READING: GENESIS 21:8-21

A reading from Genesis:

[8]The child Isaac grew, and was weaned;
and Abraham made a great feast on the day that Isaac was weaned.
[9]But Sarah saw the son of Hagar the Egyptian,
         whom she had borne to Abraham,
playing with her son Isaac.
[10]So she said to Abraham,
"Cast out this slave with her son;
for the son of this slave shall not inherit along with my son Isaac."
[11]The matter was very distressing to Abraham on account of his son.
[12]But God said to Abraham,
"Do not be distressed because of the boy and because of your slave;
whatever Sarah says to you, do as she tells you,
for it is through Isaac that offspring shall be named for you.
[13]As for the son of the slave, I will make a nation of him also,
because he is your offspring."

[14]So Abraham rose early in the morning, and took bread and a skin of water,
and gave it to Hagar, putting it on her shoulder, along with the child,
and sent her away.
And she departed, and wandered about in the wilderness of Beer-sheba.

[15]When the water in the skin was gone,
Hagar cast the child under one of the bushes.
[16]Then she went and sat down opposite him a good way off,
about the distance of a bowshot;
for she said, "Do not let me look on the death of the child."
And as she sat opposite him, she lifted up her voice and wept.
[17]And God heard the voice of the boy;
and the angel of God called to Hagar from heaven, and said to her,
"What troubles you, Hagar?
Do not be afraid; for God has heard the voice of the boy where he is.
[18]Come, lift up the boy and hold him fast with your hand,
for I will make a great nation of him."

¹⁹Then God opened her eyes and she saw a well of water.
She went, and filled the skin with water, and gave the boy a drink.

²⁰God was with the boy, and he grew up;
he lived in the wilderness, and became an expert with the bow.
²¹He lived in the wilderness of Paran;
and his mother got a wife for him from the land of Egypt.

PSALMODY: Psalm 86:1-10, 16-17

Readings continue on p. 212

SUNDAY BETWEEN
JUNE 26 AND JULY 2 INCLUSIVE

JUNE 30, 1996   JUNE 27, 1999   JUNE 30, 2002

PROPER 8

FIRST READING: GENESIS 22:1-14

A reading from Genesis:

¹God tested Abraham,
and said to him, "Abraham!"
And he said, "Here I am."
²God said,
"Take your son, your only son Isaac, whom you love,
and go to the land of Moriah, and offer him there as a burnt offering
on one of the mountains that I shall show you."

³So Abraham rose early in the morning, saddled his donkey,
and took two of his servants with him, and his son Isaac;
he cut the wood for the burnt offering,
and set out and went to the place in the distance that God had shown him.
⁴On the third day Abraham looked up and saw the place far away.
⁵Then Abraham said to his young men,
"Stay here with the donkey;
the boy and I will go over there;
we will worship, and then we will come back to you."

⁶Abraham took the wood of the burnt offering and laid it on his son Isaac,
and he himself carried the fire and the knife.
So the two of them walked on together.
⁷Isaac said to his father Abraham, "Father!"
And he said, "Here I am, my son."
Isaac said, "The fire and the wood are here,
but where is the lamb for a burnt offering?"
⁸Abraham said,
"It is God who will provide the lamb for a burnt offering, my son."
So the two of them walked on together.

⁹When they came to the place that God had shown him,
Abraham built an altar there and laid the wood in order.
He bound his son Isaac, and laid him on the altar, on top of the wood.
¹⁰Then Abraham reached out his hand and took the knife to kill his son.
¹¹But the angel of the LORD called to him from heaven, and said,
"Abraham, Abraham!"
And he said, "Here I am."

[12]The angel said,
"Do not lay your hand on the boy or do anything to him;
for now I know that you fear God,
since you have not withheld your son, your only son, from me."
[13]And Abraham looked up and saw a ram, caught in a thicket by its horns.
Abraham went and took the ram
and offered it up as a burnt offering instead of his son.
[14]So Abraham called that place "The LORD will provide";
as it is said to this day,
"On the mount of the LORD it shall be provided."

PSALMODY: PSALM 13

Readings continue on p. 215

SUNDAY BETWEEN
JULY 3 AND 9 INCLUSIVE

JULY 7, 1996   JULY 4, 1999   JULY 7, 2002

PROPER 9

FIRST READING: GENESIS 24:34-38, 42-49, 58-67

A reading from Genesis:

The visitor said to Laban,
34"I am Abraham's servant.
35The LORD has greatly blessed my master, and he has become wealthy;
the LORD has given him flocks and herds, silver and gold,
male and female slaves, camels and donkeys.
36And Sarah my master's wife bore a son to my master when she was old;
and Abraham has given him all that he has.
37My master made me swear, saying,
'You shall not take a wife for my son from the daughters of the Canaanites,
in whose land I live;
38but you shall go to my father's house, to my kindred,
and get a wife for my son.'

42"I came today to the spring, and said,
'O LORD, the God of my master Abraham,
if now you will only make successful the way I am going!
43I am standing here by the spring of water;
let the young woman who comes out to draw,
to whom I shall say, "Please give me a little water from your jar to drink,"
44and who will say to me, "Drink, and I will draw for your camels also"—
let her be the woman whom the LORD has appointed for my master's son.'

45"Before I had finished speaking in my heart,
there was Rebekah coming out with her water jar on her shoulder;
and she went down to the spring, and drew.
I said to her, 'Please let me drink.'
46She quickly let down her jar from her shoulder, and said,
'Drink, and I will also water your camels.'
So I drank, and she also watered the camels.
47Then I asked her, 'Whose daughter are you?'
She said, 'The daughter of Bethuel, Nahor's son, whom Milcah bore to him.'
So I put the ring on her nose, and the bracelets on her arms.
48Then I bowed my head and worshiped the LORD,
and blessed the LORD, the God of my master Abraham,
who had led me by the right way

to obtain the daughter of my master's kinsman for his son.
⁴⁹Now then, if you will deal loyally and truly with my master, tell me;
and if not, tell me, so that I may turn either to the right hand or to the left."

⁵⁸And they called Rebekah, and said to her, "Will you go with this man?"
She said, "I will."
⁵⁹So they sent away their sister Rebekah and her nurse
along with Abraham's servant and his men.
⁶⁰And they blessed Rebekah and said to her,
"May you, our sister, become thousands of myriads;
may your offspring gain possession of the gates of their foes."
⁶¹Then Rebekah and her maids rose up, mounted the camels,
        and followed the man;
thus the servant took Rebekah, and went his way.

⁶²Now Isaac had come from Beer-lahai-roi, and was settled in the Negeb.
⁶³Isaac went out in the evening to walk in the field;
and looking up, he saw camels coming.
⁶⁴And Rebekah looked up,
and when she saw Isaac, she slipped quickly from the camel,
⁶⁵and said to the servant,
"Who is the man over there, walking in the field to meet us?"
The servant said, "It is my master."
So she took her veil and covered herself.
⁶⁶And the servant told Isaac all the things that he had done.

⁶⁷Then Isaac brought her into his mother Sarah's tent.
He took Rebekah, and she became his wife; and he loved her.
So Isaac was comforted after his mother's death.

PSALMODY: Psalm 45:10-17 or Song of Solomon 2:8-13   *Psalm 45:11–18*   LBW/BCP

Readings continue on p. 218

SUNDAY BETWEEN
JULY 10 AND 16 INCLUSIVE

JULY 14, 1996   JULY 11, 1999   JULY 14, 2002

PROPER 10

FIRST READING: GENESIS 25:19-34

A reading from Genesis:

19These are the descendants of Isaac, Abraham's son:
Abraham was the father of Isaac,
20and Isaac was forty years old when he married Rebekah,
daughter of Bethuel the Aramean of Paddan-aram,
sister of Laban the Aramean.

21Isaac prayed to the LORD for his wife, because she was barren;
and the LORD granted his prayer, and his wife Rebekah conceived.
22The children struggled together within her; and she said,
"If it is to be this way, why do I live?"
So she went to inquire of the LORD.
23And the LORD said to her,
"Two nations are in your womb,
and two peoples born of you shall be divided;
the one shall be stronger than the other,
the elder shall serve the younger."
24When her time to give birth was at hand, there were twins in her womb.
25The first came out red, all his body like a hairy mantle;
so they named him Esau.
26Afterward his brother came out, with his hand gripping Esau's heel;
so he was named Jacob.
Isaac was sixty years old when she bore them.

27When the boys grew up, Esau was a skillful hunter, a man of the field,
while Jacob was a quiet man, living in tents.
28Isaac loved Esau, because he was fond of game;
but Rebekah loved Jacob.

29Once when Jacob was cooking a stew, Esau came in from the field,
and he was famished.
30Esau said to Jacob,
"Let me eat some of that red stuff, for I am famished!"
(Therefore he was called Edom.)
31Jacob said, "First sell me your birthright."
32Esau said, "I am about to die; of what use is a birthright to me?"

[33]Jacob said, "Swear to me first."
So Esau swore to him, and sold his birthright to Jacob.
[34]Then Jacob gave Esau bread and lentil stew, and he ate and drank, and rose and went his way.
Thus Esau despised his birthright.

PSALMODY: PSALM 119:105-112

Readings continue on p. 221

✠

SUNDAY BETWEEN
JULY 17 AND 23 INCLUSIVE

JULY 21, 1996   *JULY 18, 1999*   *JULY 21, 2002*

PROPER 11

FIRST READING: GENESIS 28:10-19a

A reading from Genesis:

¹⁰Jacob left Beer-sheba and went toward Haran.
¹¹He came to a certain place and stayed there for the night,
because the sun had set.
Taking one of the stones of the place,
Jacob put it under his head and lay down in that place.
¹²And he dreamed that there was a ladder set up on the earth,
the top of it reaching to heaven;
and the angels of God were ascending and descending on it.
¹³And the LORD stood beside him and said,
"I am the LORD, the God of Abraham your father and the God of Isaac;
the land on which you lie I will give to you and to your offspring;
¹⁴and your offspring shall be like the dust of the earth,
and you shall spread abroad to the west and to the east
and to the north and to the south;
and all the families of the earth shall be blessed in you and in your offspring.
¹⁵Know that I am with you and will keep you wherever you go,
and will bring you back to this land;
for I will not leave you until I have done what I have promised you."

¹⁶Then Jacob woke from his sleep and said,
"Surely the LORD is in this place—and I did not know it!"
¹⁷And Jacob was afraid, and said,
"How awesome is this place!
This is none other than the house of God, and this is the gate of heaven."

¹⁸So Jacob rose early in the morning,
and he took the stone that he had put under his head
and set it up for a pillar and poured oil on the top of it.
¹⁹ᵃHe called that place Bethel.

PSALMODY: PSALM 139:1-12, 23-24   *Psalm 139:1–11, 22–23* LBW/BCP

Readings continue on p. 224

✠

SUNDAY BETWEEN
JULY 24 AND 30 INCLUSIVE

JULY 28, 1996   JULY 25, 1999   JULY 28, 2002

PROPER 12

FIRST READING: GENESIS 29:15-28

A reading from Genesis:

[15]Laban said to Jacob,
"Because you are my kinsman, should you therefore serve me for nothing?
Tell me, what shall your wages be?"
[16]Now Laban had two daughters;
the name of the elder was Leah, and the name of the younger was Rachel.
[17]Leah's eyes were lovely, and Rachel was graceful and beautiful.
[18]Jacob loved Rachel; so he said,
"I will serve you seven years for your younger daughter Rachel."
[19]Laban said,
"It is better that I give her to you than that I should give her to any other man;
stay with me."
[20]So Jacob served seven years for Rachel,
and they seemed to him but a few days because of the love he had for her.

[21]Then Jacob said to Laban,
"Give me my wife that I may go in to her, for my time is completed."
[22]So Laban gathered together all the people of the place, and made a feast.
[23]But in the evening he took his daughter Leah and brought her to Jacob;
and he went in to her.
[24](Laban gave his maid Zilpah to his daughter Leah to be her maid.)
[25]When morning came, it was Leah!
And Jacob said to Laban, "What is this you have done to me?
Did I not serve with you for Rachel? Why then have you deceived me?"
[26]Laban said,
"This is not done in our country—giving the younger before the firstborn.
[27]Complete the week of this one,
and we will give you the other also
in return for serving me another seven years."
[28]Jacob did so, and completed her week;
then Laban gave him his daughter Rachel as a wife.

PSALMODY: PSALM 105:1-11, 45b or PSALM 128

Readings continue on p. 227

✝

SUNDAY BETWEEN
JULY 31 AND AUGUST 6 INCLUSIVE

AUGUST 4, 1996   AUGUST 1, 1999   AUGUST 4, 2002

PROPER 13

FIRST READING: GENESIS 32:22-31

A reading from Genesis:

²²The same night Jacob got up and took his two wives, his two female slaves,
and his eleven children, and crossed the ford of the Jabbok.
²³He took them and sent them across the stream,
and likewise everything that he had.
²⁴Jacob was left alone;
and a man wrestled with him until daybreak.

²⁵When the man saw that he did not prevail against Jacob,
he struck him on the hip socket;
and Jacob's hip was put out of joint as he wrestled with him.
²⁶Then the man said, "Let me go, for the day is breaking."
But Jacob said, "I will not let you go, unless you bless me."
²⁷So he said to him, "What is your name?"
And he said, "Jacob."
²⁸Then the man said,
"You shall no longer be called Jacob, but Israel,
for you have striven with God and with humans, and have prevailed."
²⁹Then Jacob asked the man, "Please tell me your name."
But the man said, "Why is it that you ask my name?"
And there the man blessed Jacob.

³⁰So Jacob called the place Peniel, saying,
"For I have seen God face to face, and yet my life is preserved."
³¹The sun rose upon him as he passed Penuel, limping because of his hip.

PSALMODY: PSALM 17:1-7, 15   *Psalm 17:1–17, 16* LBW/BCP

Readings continue on p. 230

✝

SUNDAY BETWEEN
AUGUST 7 AND 13 INCLUSIVE

AUGUST 11, 1996   *AUGUST 8, 1999*   *AUGUST 11, 2002*

PROPER 14

FIRST READING: GENESIS 37:1-4, 12-28

A reading from Genesis:

¹Jacob settled in the land where his father had lived as an alien,
the land of Canaan.
²This is the story of the family of Jacob.

Joseph, being seventeen years old,
was shepherding the flock with his brothers;
he was a helper to the sons of Bilhah and Zilpah, his father's wives;
and Joseph brought a bad report of them to their father.
³Now Israel loved Joseph more than any other of his children,
because he was the son of his old age;
and he had made him a long robe with sleeves.
⁴But when his brothers saw that their father loved him
        more than all his brothers,
they hated him, and could not speak peaceably to him.

¹²Now his brothers went to pasture their father's flock near Shechem.
¹³And Israel said to Joseph,
"Are not your brothers pasturing the flock at Shechem?
Come, I will send you to them."
He answered, "Here I am."
¹⁴So he said to him,
"Go now, see if it is well with your brothers and with the flock;
and bring word back to me."
So he sent Joseph from the valley of Hebron.

Joseph came to Shechem, ¹⁵and a man found him wandering in the fields;
the man asked him, "What are you seeking?"
¹⁶"I am seeking my brothers," he said;
"tell me, please, where they are pasturing the flock."
¹⁷The man said,
"They have gone away, for I heard them say, 'Let us go to Dothan.'"

So Joseph went after his brothers, and found them at Dothan.
¹⁸They saw him from a distance,
and before he came near to them, they conspired to kill him.

¹⁹They said to one another,
"Here comes this dreamer.
²⁰Come now, let us kill him and throw him into one of the pits;
then we shall say that a wild animal has devoured him,
and we shall see what will become of his dreams."
²¹But when Reuben heard it, he delivered Joseph out of their hands, saying,
"Let us not take his life."
²²Reuben said to them,
"Shed no blood; throw him into this pit here in the wilderness,
but lay no hand on him"—
that he might rescue him out of their hand and restore him to his father.

²³So when Joseph came to his brothers,
they stripped him of his robe, the long robe with sleeves that he wore;
²⁴and they took him and threw him into a pit.
The pit was empty; there was no water in it.
²⁵Then they sat down to eat;
and looking up they saw a caravan of Ishmaelites coming from Gilead,
with their camels carrying gum, balm, and resin,
on their way to carry it down to Egypt.
²⁶Then Judah said to his brothers,
"What profit is it if we kill our brother and conceal his blood?
²⁷Come, let us sell him to the Ishmaelites,
and not lay our hands on him, for he is our brother, our own flesh."
And his brothers agreed.
²⁸When some Midianite traders passed by, they drew Joseph up,
lifting him out of the pit,
and sold him to the Ishmaelites for twenty pieces of silver.
And they took Joseph to Egypt.

PSALMODY: PSALM 105:1-6, 16-22, 45b

Readings continue on p. 233

Sunday between
August 14 and 20 inclusive

AUGUST 18, 1996   AUGUST 15, 1999   AUGUST 18, 2002

PROPER 15

FIRST READING: Genesis 45:1-15

A reading from Genesis:

¹Joseph could no longer control himself before all those who stood by him,
and he cried out, "Send everyone away from me."
So no one stayed with him when Joseph made himself known to his brothers.
²And he wept so loudly that the Egyptians heard it,
and the household of Pharaoh heard it.

³Joseph said to his brothers,
"I am Joseph. Is my father still alive?"
But his brothers could not answer him, so dismayed were they at his presence.

⁴Then Joseph said to his brothers, "Come closer to me."
And they came closer.
He said, "I am your brother, Joseph, whom you sold into Egypt.
⁵And now do not be distressed, or angry with yourselves,
because you sold me here;
for God sent me before you to preserve life.
⁶For the famine has been in the land these two years;
and there are five more years in which there will be neither plowing nor
     harvest.
⁷God sent me before you to preserve for you a remnant on earth,
and to keep alive for you many survivors.
⁸So it was not you who sent me here, but God;
God has made me a father to Pharaoh,
and lord of all his house and ruler over all the land of Egypt.
⁹Hurry and go up to my father and say to him,
'Thus says your son Joseph,
God has made me lord of all Egypt; come down to me, do not delay.
¹⁰You shall settle in the land of Goshen,
and you shall be near me, you and your children and your children's children,
as well as your flocks, your herds, and all that you have.
¹¹I will provide for you there—
since there are five more years of famine to come—
so that you and your household, and all that you have,
     will not come to poverty.'

[12]And now your eyes and the eyes of my brother Benjamin see
that it is my own mouth that speaks to you.
[13]You must tell my father how greatly I am honored in Egypt,
and all that you have seen.
Hurry and bring my father down here."
[14]Then Joseph fell upon his brother Benjamin's neck and wept,
while Benjamin wept upon his neck.
[15]And he kissed all his brothers and wept upon them;
and after that his brothers talked with him.

PSALMODY: P<small>SALM</small> 133

Readings continue on p. 236

SUNDAY BETWEEN
AUGUST 21 AND 27 INCLUSIVE

AUGUST 25, 1996   AUGUST 22, 1999   AUGUST 25, 2002

PROPER 16

FIRST READING: EXODUS 1:8—2:10

A reading from Exodus:

⁸Now a new king arose over Egypt, who did not know Joseph.
⁹He said to his people,
"Look, the Israelite people are more numerous and more powerful than we.
¹⁰Come, let us deal shrewdly with them,
or they will increase and, in the event of war,
join our enemies and fight against us and escape from the land."
¹¹Therefore they set taskmasters over them to oppress them with forced labor.
They built supply cities, Pithom and Rameses, for Pharaoh.
¹²But the more they were oppressed, the more they multiplied and spread,
so that the Egyptians came to dread the Israelites.
¹³The Egyptians became ruthless in imposing tasks on the Israelites,
¹⁴and made their lives bitter with hard service in mortar and brick
and in every kind of field labor.
They were ruthless in all the tasks that they imposed on them.

¹⁵The king of Egypt said to the Hebrew midwives,
one of whom was named Shiphrah and the other Puah,
¹⁶"When you act as midwives to the Hebrew women,
and see them on the birthstool, if it is a boy, kill him;
but if it is a girl, she shall live."
¹⁷But the midwives feared God;
they did not do as the king of Egypt commanded them,
but they let the boys live.
¹⁸So the king of Egypt summoned the midwives and said to them,
"Why have you done this, and allowed the boys to live?"
¹⁹The midwives said to Pharaoh,
"Because the Hebrew women are not like the Egyptian women;
for they are vigorous and give birth before the midwife comes to them."

²⁰So God dealt well with the midwives;
and the people multiplied and became very strong.
²¹And because the midwives feared God, God gave them families.
²²Then Pharaoh commanded all his people,
"Every boy that is born to the Hebrews you shall throw into the Nile,
but you shall let every girl live."

¹Now a man from the house of Levi went and married a Levite woman.
²The woman conceived and bore a son;
and when she saw that he was a fine baby, she hid him three months.
³When she could hide him no longer she got a papyrus basket for him,
and plastered it with bitumen and pitch;
she put the child in it and placed it among the reeds on the bank of the river.
⁴His sister stood at a distance, to see what would happen to him.

⁵The daughter of Pharaoh came down to bathe at the river,
while her attendants walked beside the river.
She saw the basket among the reeds and sent her maid to bring it.
⁶When she opened it, she saw the child.
He was crying, and she took pity on him,
"This must be one of the Hebrews' children," she said.
⁷Then his sister said to Pharaoh's daughter,
"Shall I go and get you a nurse from the Hebrew women to nurse the child
for you?"
⁸Pharaoh's daughter said to her, "Yes."
So the girl went and called the child's mother.
⁹Pharaoh's daughter said to her,
"Take this child and nurse it for me, and I will give you your wages."
So the woman took the child and nursed it.

¹⁰When the child grew up, she brought him to Pharaoh's daughter,
and she took him as her son.
She named him Moses,
"because," she said, "I drew him out of the water."

PSALMODY: PSALM 124

Readings continue on p. 239

SUNDAY BETWEEN
AUGUST 28 AND SEPTEMBER 3
INCLUSIVE

FIRST READING: EXODUS 3:1-15

A reading from Exodus:

[1]Moses was keeping the flock of his father-in-law Jethro, the priest of Midian;
he led his flock beyond the wilderness, and came to Horeb,
    the mountain of God.
[2]There the angel of the LORD appeared to Moses in a flame of fire out of a bush;
he looked, and the bush was blazing, yet it was not consumed.
[3]Then Moses said,
"I must turn aside and look at this great sight,
and see why the bush is not burned up."
[4]When the LORD saw that he had turned aside to see,
God called to him out of the bush, "Moses, Moses!"
And he said, "Here I am."
[5]Then God said,
"Come no closer! Remove the sandals from your feet,
for the place on which you are standing is holy ground."
[6]God said further,
"I am the God of your father, the God of Abraham,
the God of Isaac, and the God of Jacob."
And Moses hid his face, for he was afraid to look at God.

[7]Then the LORD said,
"I have observed the misery of my people who are in Egypt;
I have heard their cry on account of their taskmasters.
Indeed, I know their sufferings,
[8]and I have come down to deliver them from the Egyptians,
and to bring them up out of that land to a good and broad land,
a land flowing with milk and honey,
to the country of the Canaanites, the Hittites, the Amorites,
the Perizzites, the Hivites, and the Jebusites.
[9]The cry of the Israelites has now come to me;
I have also seen how the Egyptians oppress them.
[10]So come, I will send you to Pharaoh
to bring my people, the Israelites, out of Egypt."

[11]But Moses said to God,
"Who am I that I should go to Pharaoh, and bring the Israelites out of Egypt?"
[12]God said, "I will be with you;
and this shall be the sign for you that it is I who sent you:
when you have brought the people out of Egypt,
you shall worship God on this mountain."

[13]But Moses said to God,
"If I come to the Israelites and say to them,
'The God of your ancestors has sent me to you,'
and they ask me, 'What is God's name?' what shall I say to them?"
[14]God said to Moses,
"I AM WHO I AM."
God said further,
"Thus you shall say to the Israelites, 'I AM has sent me to you.'"
[15]God also said to Moses,
"Thus you shall say to the Israelites,
'The LORD, the God of your ancestors,
the God of Abraham, the God of Isaac, and the God of Jacob,
has sent me to you':

This is my name forever,
and this my title for all generations."

PSALMODY: PSALM 105:1-6, 23-26, 45c

Readings continue on p. 242

✝

Sunday between
September 4 and 10 inclusive

FIRST READING: EXODUS 12:1-14

A reading from Exodus:

[1]The LORD said to Moses and Aaron in the land of Egypt:
[2]This month shall mark for you the beginning of months;
it shall be the first month of the year for you.
[3]Tell the whole congregation of Israel
that on the tenth of this month they are to take a lamb for each family,
a lamb for each household.
[4]If a household is too small for a whole lamb,
it shall join its closest neighbor in obtaining one;
the lamb shall be divided in proportion to the number of people who eat of it.

[5]Your lamb shall be without blemish, a year-old male;
you may take it from the sheep or from the goats.
[6]You shall keep it until the fourteenth day of this month;
then the whole assembled congregation of Israel shall slaughter it at twilight.
[7]They shall take some of the blood and put it on the two doorposts
and the lintel of the houses in which they eat it.
[8]They shall eat the lamb that same night;
they shall eat it roasted over the fire
with unleavened bread and bitter herbs.
[9]Do not eat any of it raw or boiled in water,
but roasted over the fire, with its head, legs, and inner organs.
[10]You shall let none of it remain until the morning;
anything that remains until the morning you shall burn.

[11]This is how you shall eat it:
your loins girded, your sandals on your feet, and your staff in your hand;
and you shall eat it hurriedly.
It is the passover of the LORD.
[12]For I will pass through the land of Egypt that night,
and I will strike down every firstborn in the land of Egypt,
both human beings and animals;
on all the deities of Egypt I will execute judgments:
I am the LORD.

¹³The blood shall be a sign for you on the houses where you live:
when I see the blood, I will pass over you,
and no plague shall destroy you when I strike the land of Egypt.

¹⁴This day shall be a day of remembrance for you.
You shall celebrate it as a festival to the LORD;
throughout your generations you shall observe it as a perpetual ordinance.

PSALMODY: PSALM 149

Readings continue on p. 245

✚

Sunday between
September 11 and 17 inclusive

SEPTEMBER 15, 1996   *SEPTEMBER 12, 1999*   *SEPTEMBER 15, 2002*

PROPER 19

FIRST READING: Exodus 14:19-31

A reading from Exodus:

¹⁹The angel of God who was going before the Israelite army moved
and went behind them;
and the pillar of cloud moved from in front of them
and took its place behind them.
²⁰It came between the army of Egypt and the army of Israel.
And so the cloud was there with the darkness,
and it lit up the night;
one did not come near the other all night.

²¹Then Moses stretched out his hand over the sea.
The LORD drove the sea back by a strong east wind all night,
and turned the sea into dry land;
and the waters were divided.
²²The Israelites went into the sea on dry ground,
the waters forming a wall for them on their right and on their left.
²³The Egyptians pursued, and went into the sea after them,
all of Pharaoh's horses, chariots, and chariot drivers.
²⁴At the morning watch the LORD in the pillar of fire and cloud
looked down upon the Egyptian army,
and threw the Egyptian army into panic,
²⁵clogging their chariot wheels so that they turned with difficulty.
The Egyptians said,
"Let us flee from the Israelites,
for the LORD is fighting for them against Egypt."

²⁶Then the LORD said to Moses,
"Stretch out your hand over the sea,
so that the water may come back upon the Egyptians,
upon their chariots and chariot drivers."
²⁷So Moses stretched out his hand over the sea,
and at dawn the sea returned to its normal depth.
As the Egyptians fled before it,
the LORD tossed the Egyptians into the sea.
²⁸The waters returned and covered the chariots and the chariot drivers,
the entire army of Pharaoh that had followed them into the sea;

not one of them remained.
29But the Israelites walked on dry ground through the sea,
the waters forming a wall for them on their right and on their left.

30Thus the LORD saved Israel that day from the Egyptians;
and Israel saw the Egyptians dead on the seashore.
31Israel saw the great work that the LORD did against the Egyptians.
So the people feared the LORD
and believed in the LORD and in Moses, the servant of the LORD.

PSALMODY: PSALM 114 or EXODUS 15:1b-11, 20-21

Readings continue on p. 248

✠

SUNDAY BETWEEN
SEPTEMBER 18 AND 24 INCLUSIVE

SEPTEMBER 22, 1996   SEPTEMBER 19, 1999   SEPTEMBER 22, 2002

PROPER 20

FIRST READING: EXODUS 16:2-15

A reading from Exodus:

²The whole congregation of the Israelites complained
against Moses and Aaron in the wilderness.
³The Israelites said to them,
"If only we had died by the hand of the LORD in the land of Egypt,
when we sat by the fleshpots and ate our fill of bread;
for you have brought us out into this wilderness
to kill this whole assembly with hunger."

⁴Then the LORD said to Moses,
"I am going to rain bread from heaven for you,
and each day the people shall go out and gather enough for that day.
In that way I will test them,
whether they will follow my instruction or not.
⁵On the sixth day, when they prepare what they bring in,
it will be twice as much as they gather on other days."

⁶So Moses and Aaron said to all the Israelites,
"In the evening you shall know that it was the LORD
who brought you out of the land of Egypt,
⁷and in the morning you shall see the glory of the LORD,
because your complaining against the LORD has been heard.
For what are we, that you complain against us?"
⁸And Moses said,
"When the LORD gives you meat to eat in the evening
and your fill of bread in the morning,
because the LORD has heard the complaining that you utter—
what are we?
Your complaining is not against us but against the LORD."

⁹Then Moses said to Aaron,
"Say to the whole congregation of the Israelites,
'Draw near to the LORD, for the LORD has heard your complaining.'"
¹⁰And as Aaron spoke to the whole congregation of the Israelites,
they looked toward the wilderness,
and the glory of the LORD appeared in the cloud.

¹¹The LORD spoke to Moses and said,
¹²"I have heard the complaining of the Israelites;
say to them, 'At twilight you shall eat meat,
and in the morning you shall have your fill of bread;
then you shall know that I am the LORD your God.' "

¹³In the evening quails came up and covered the camp;
and in the morning there was a layer of dew around the camp.
¹⁴When the layer of dew lifted,
there on the surface of the wilderness was a fine flaky substance,
as fine as frost on the ground.
¹⁵When the Israelites saw it, they said to one another,
"What is it?" For they did not know what it was.
Moses said to them,
"It is the bread that the LORD has given you to eat."

PSALMODY: PSALM 105:1-6, 37-45

Readings continue on p. 252

✝

SUNDAY BETWEEN
SEPTEMBER 25 AND OCTOBER 1
INCLUSIVE

SEPTEMBER 29, 1996   SEPTEMBER 26, 1999   SEPTEMBER 29, 2002

PROPER 21

FIRST READING: EXODUS 17:1-7

A reading from Exodus:

¹From the wilderness of Sin the whole congregation of the Israelites
journeyed by stages, as the LORD commanded.
They camped at Rephidim, but there was no water for the people to drink.
²The people quarreled with Moses, and said, "Give us water to drink."
Moses said to them,
"Why do you quarrel with me? Why do you test the LORD?"
³But the people thirsted there for water;
and the people complained against Moses and said,
"Why did you bring us out of Egypt,
to kill us and our children and livestock with thirst?"

⁴So Moses cried out to the LORD,
"What shall I do with this people? They are almost ready to stone me."
⁵The LORD said to Moses,
"Go on ahead of the people, and take some of the elders of Israel with you;
take in your hand the staff with which you struck the Nile, and go.
⁶I will be standing there in front of you on the rock at Horeb.
Strike the rock, and water will come out of it,
so that the people may drink."
Moses did so, in the sight of the elders of Israel.
⁷He called the place Massah and Meribah,
because the Israelites quarreled and tested the LORD, saying,
"Is the LORD among us or not?"

PSALMODY: PSALM 78:1-4, 12-16

Readings continue on p. 256

✚

SUNDAY BETWEEN
OCTOBER 2 AND 8 INCLUSIVE

OCTOBER 6, 1996   OCTOBER 3, 1999   OCTOBER 6, 2002

PROPER 22

FIRST READING: EXODUS 20:1-4, 7-9, 12-20

A reading from Exodus:

¹God spoke all these words:

²I am the LORD your God, who brought you out of the land of Egypt,
out of the house of slavery;
³you shall have no other gods before me.
⁴You shall not make for yourself an idol,
whether in the form of anything that is in heaven above,
or that is on the earth beneath,
or that is in the water under the earth.

⁷You shall not make wrongful use of the name of the LORD your God,
for the LORD will not acquit anyone who misuses the divine name.

⁸Remember the sabbath day, and keep it holy.
⁹Six days you shall labor and do all your work.

¹²Honor your father and your mother,
so that your days may be long in the land that the LORD your God is giving you.
¹³You shall not murder.
¹⁴You shall not commit adultery.
¹⁵You shall not steal.
¹⁶You shall not bear false witness against your neighbor.
¹⁷You shall not covet your neighbor's house;
you shall not covet your neighbor's wife,
or male or female slave, or ox, or donkey,
or anything that belongs to your neighbor.

¹⁸When all the people witnessed the thunder and lightning,
the sound of the trumpet, and the mountain smoking,
they were afraid and trembled and stood at a distance,
¹⁹and said to Moses,
"You speak to us, and we will listen;
but do not let God speak to us, or we will die."

[20]Moses said to the people,
"Do not be afraid; for God has come only to test you
and to put the fear of God upon you so that you do not sin."

PSALMODY: Psalm 19

Readings continue on p. 259

✚

S U N D A Y   B E T W E E N
O C T O B E R   9   A N D   1 5   I N C L U S I V E

OCTOBER 13, 1996   *OCTOBER 10, 1999*   *OCTOBER 13, 2002*

PROPER 23

FIRST READING: Exodus 32:1-14

A reading from Exodus:

¹When the people saw that Moses delayed to come down from the mountain,
the people gathered around Aaron, and said to him,
"Come, make gods for us, who shall go before us;
as for this Moses, the man who brought us up out of the land of Egypt,
we do not know what has become of him."
²Aaron said to them,
"Take off the gold rings that are on the ears of your wives, your sons,
      and your daughters, and bring them to me."
³So all the people took off the gold rings from their ears,
and brought them to Aaron.
⁴He took the gold from them, formed it in a mold, and cast an image of a calf;
and they said, "These are your gods, O Israel,
who brought you up out of the land of Egypt!"
⁵When Aaron saw this, he built an altar before it;
and Aaron made proclamation and said,
"Tomorrow shall be a festival to the LORD."
⁶They rose early the next day,
and offered burnt offerings and brought sacrifices of well-being;
and the people sat down to eat and drink, and rose up to revel.

⁷The LORD said to Moses,
"Go down at once!
Your people, whom you brought up out of the land of Egypt,
have acted perversely;
⁸they have been quick to turn aside from the way that I commanded them;
they have cast for themselves an image of a calf,
and have worshiped it and sacrificed to it, and said,
'These are your gods, O Israel, who brought you up out of the land of Egypt!'"
⁹The LORD said to Moses,
"I have seen this people, how stiff-necked they are.
¹⁰Now let me alone,
so that my wrath may burn hot against them and I may consume them;
and of you I will make a great nation."

¹¹But Moses implored the LORD his God, and said,

"O Lord, why does your wrath burn hot against your people,
whom you brought out of the land of Egypt with great power
    and with a mighty hand?
12Why should the Egyptians say,
'It was with evil intent that their god brought them out
to kill them in the mountains,
and to consume them from the face of the earth'?
Turn from your fierce wrath;
change your mind and do not bring disaster on your people.
13Remember Abraham, Isaac, and Israel, your servants,
how you swore to them by your own self, saying to them,
'I will multiply your descendants like the stars of heaven,
and all this land that I have promised I will give to your descendants,
and they shall inherit it forever.' "
14And the Lord relented
from bringing about the disaster that had been planned upon the people.

PSALMODY: Psalm 106:1–6, 19–23

Readings continue on p. 262

SUNDAY BETWEEN
OCTOBER 16 AND 22 INCLUSIVE

OCTOBER 20, 1996   *OCTOBER 17, 1999*   *OCTOBER 20, 2002*

PROPER 24

FIRST READING: EXODUS 33:12-23

A reading from Exodus:

¹²Moses said to the LORD,
"See, you have said to me, 'Bring up this people';
but you have not let me know whom you will send with me.
Yet you have said,
'I know you by name, and you have also found favor in my sight.'
¹³Now if I have found favor in your sight, show me your ways,
so that I may know you and find favor in your sight.
Consider too that this nation is your people."
¹⁴The LORD said, "My presence will go with you, and I will give you rest."
¹⁵And he said to the LORD,
"If your presence will not go, do not carry us up from here.
¹⁶For how shall it be known that I have found favor in your sight,
I and your people, unless you go with us?
In this way, we shall be distinct, I and your people,
from every people on the face of the earth."

¹⁷The LORD said to Moses,
"I will do the very thing that you have asked;
for you have found favor in my sight, and I know you by name."
¹⁸Moses said, "Show me your glory, I pray."
¹⁹And the LORD said,
"I will make all my goodness pass before you,
and will proclaim before you the name, 'The LORD';
and I will be gracious to whom I will be gracious,
and will show mercy on whom I will show mercy.
²⁰But," the LORD said, "you cannot see my face;
for no one shall see me and live."

[21]And the LORD continued,
"See, there is a place by me where you shall stand on the rock;
[22]and while my glory passes by I will put you in a cleft of the rock,
and I will cover you with my hand until I have passed by;
[23]then I will take away my hand, and you shall see my back;
but my face shall not be seen."

PSALMODY: PSALM 99

Readings continue on p. 265

✝

SUNDAY BETWEEN
OCTOBER 23 AND 29 INCLUSIVE

OCTOBER 27, 1996   OCTOBER 24, 1999   OCTOBER 27, 2002

PROPER 25

FIRST READING: DEUTERONOMY 34:1-12

A reading from Deuteronomy:

[1]Moses went up from the plains of Moab to Mount Nebo,
to the top of Pisgah, which is opposite Jericho,
and the LORD showed him the whole land:
Gilead as far as Dan, [2]all Naphtali, the land of Ephraim and Manasseh,
all the land of Judah as far as the Western Sea,
[3]the Negeb, and the Plain—that is, the valley of Jericho,
the city of palm trees—as far as Zoar.
[4]The LORD said to Moses,
"This is the land of which I swore to Abraham, to Isaac, and to Jacob, saying,
'I will give it to your descendants';
I have let you see it with your eyes, but you shall not cross over there."

[5]Then Moses, the servant of the LORD,
died there in the land of Moab, at the LORD's command.
[6]He was buried in a valley in the land of Moab, opposite Beth-peor,
but no one knows his burial place to this day.
[7]Moses was one hundred twenty years old when he died;
his sight was unimpaired and his vigor had not abated.
[8]The Israelites wept for Moses in the plains of Moab thirty days;
then the period of mourning for Moses was ended.

[9]Joshua son of Nun was full of the spirit of wisdom,
because Moses had laid his hands on him;
and the Israelites obeyed him, doing as the LORD had commanded Moses.

[10]Never since has there arisen a prophet in Israel like Moses,
whom the LORD knew face to face.
[11]He was unequaled for all the signs and wonders
that the LORD sent him to perform in the land of Egypt,
against Pharaoh and all his servants and his entire land,
[12]and for all the mighty deeds and all the terrifying displays of power
that Moses performed in the sight of all Israel.

PSALMODY: PSALM 90:1-6, 13-17

Readings continue on p. 268

✝

FIRST READING: JOSHUA 3:7-17

A reading from Joshua:

[7]The LORD said to Joshua,
"This day I will begin to exalt you in the sight of all Israel,
so that they may know that I will be with you as I was with Moses.
[8]You are the one who shall command the priests
who bear the ark of the covenant,
'When you come to the edge of the waters of the Jordan,
you shall stand still in the Jordan.' "

[9]Joshua then said to the Israelites,
"Draw near and hear the words of the LORD your God."
[10]Joshua said,
"By this you shall know that among you is the living God
who without fail
will drive out from before you the Canaanites, Hittites, Hivites,
Perizzites, Girgashites, Amorites, and Jebusites:
[11]the ark of the covenant of the Lord of all the earth
is going to pass before you into the Jordan.
[12]So now select twelve men from the tribes of Israel,
one from each tribe.
[13]When the soles of the feet of the priests who bear the ark of the LORD,
the Lord of all the earth, rest in the waters of the Jordan,
the waters of the Jordan flowing from above shall be cut off;
they shall stand in a single heap."

[14]When the people set out from their tents to cross over the Jordan,
the priests bearing the ark of the covenant were in front of the people.
[15]Now the Jordan overflows all its banks throughout the time of harvest.
So when those who bore the ark had come to the Jordan,
and the feet of the priests bearing the ark were dipped in the edge of the water,
[16]the waters flowing from above stood still,
rising up in a single heap far off at Adam, the city that is beside Zarethan,
while those flowing toward the sea of the Arabah, the Dead Sea,
were wholly cut off.
Then the people crossed over opposite Jericho.

¹⁷While all Israel were crossing over on dry ground,
the priests who bore the ark of the covenant of the LORD
stood on dry ground in the middle of the Jordan,
until the entire nation finished crossing over the Jordan.

PSALMODY: PSALM **107:1-7, 33-37**

Readings continue on p. 271

✝

Sunday between
November 6 and 12 inclusive

NOVEMBER 10, 1996   NOVEMBER 7, 1999   NOVEMBER 10, 2002

PROPER 27

FIRST READING: Joshua 24:1-3a, 14-25

A reading from Joshua:

¹Joshua gathered all the tribes of Israel to Shechem,
and summoned the elders, the heads, the judges, and the officers of Israel;
and they presented themselves before God.
²And Joshua said to all the people,
"Thus says the LORD, the God of Israel:
Long ago your ancestors—Terah and his sons Abraham and Nahor—
lived beyond the Euphrates and served other deities.
³ªThen I took your father Abraham from beyond the River
and led him through all the land of Canaan and made his offspring many.

¹⁴"Now therefore revere the LORD,
and serve the LORD in sincerity and in faithfulness;
put away the deities that your ancestors served beyond the River and in Egypt,
and serve the LORD.
¹⁵Now if you are unwilling to serve the LORD,
choose this day whom you will serve,
whether the deities your ancestors served in the region beyond the River
or those of the Amorites in whose land you are living;
but as for me and my household, we will serve the LORD."

¹⁶Then the people answered,
"Far be it from us that we should forsake the LORD to serve other deities;
¹⁷for it is the LORD our God who brought us and our ancestors up from
        the land of Egypt,
out of the house of slavery, and who did those great signs in our sight.
The LORD protected us along all the way that we went,
and among all the peoples through whom we passed;
¹⁸and the LORD drove out before us all the peoples,
the Amorites who lived in the land.
Therefore we also will serve the LORD, for the LORD is our God."

¹⁹But Joshua said to the people,
"You cannot serve the LORD, for the LORD is a holy God,
and is a jealous God,
and will not forgive your transgressions or your sins.

²⁰If you forsake the LORD and serve foreign deities,
then the LORD will turn and do you harm, and consume you,
after having done you good."
²¹And the people said to Joshua,
"No, we will serve the LORD!"
²²Then Joshua said to the people,
"You are witnesses against yourselves
that you have chosen to serve the LORD."
And they said, "We are witnesses."
²³He said, "Then put away the foreign deities that are among you,
and incline your hearts to the LORD, the God of Israel."
²⁴The people said to Joshua,
"The LORD our God we will serve; and our God we will obey."
²⁵So Joshua made a covenant with the people that day,
and made statutes and ordinances for them at Shechem.

PSALMODY: PSALM 78:1-7

Readings continue on p. 274

✠

SUNDAY BETWEEN
NOVEMBER 13 AND 19 INCLUSIVE

NOVEMBER 17, 1996   *NOVEMBER 14, 1999*   *NOVEMBER 17, 2002*

PROPER 28

FIRST READING: JUDGES 4:1-7

A reading from Judges:

¹The Israelites again did what was evil in the sight of the LORD,
after Ehud died.
²So the LORD sold them into the hand of King Jabin of Canaan,
who reigned in Hazor;
the commander of his army was Sisera, who lived in Harosheth-ha-goiim.
³Then the Israelites cried out to the LORD for help;
for he had nine hundred chariots of iron,
and had oppressed the Israelites cruelly twenty years.

⁴At that time Deborah, a prophet, wife of Lappidoth, was judging Israel.
⁵She used to sit under the palm of Deborah
between Ramah and Bethel in the hill country of Ephraim;
and the Israelites came up to her for judgment.
⁶She sent and summoned Barak son of Abinoam from Kedesh in Naphtali,
and said to him,
"The LORD, the God of Israel, commands you,
'Go, take position at Mount Tabor,
bringing ten thousand from the tribe of Naphtali and the tribe of Zebulun.
⁷I will draw out Sisera, the general of Jabin's army,
to meet you by the Wadi Kishon with his chariots and his troops;
and I will give him into your hand.' "

PSALMODY: PSALM 123

Readings continue on p. 277

THE REIGN OF CHRIST

(Last Sunday after Pentecost)†

NOVEMBER 24, 1996   NOVEMBER 21, 1999   NOVEMBER 24, 2002

PROPER 29

FIRST READING: EZEKIEL 34:11-16, 20-24

A reading from Ezekiel:

[11]Thus says the Lord GOD:
I myself will search for my sheep, and will seek them out.
[12]As shepherds seek out their flocks
when they are among their scattered sheep,
so I will seek out my sheep.
I will rescue them from all the places to which they have been scattered
on a day of clouds and thick darkness.
[13]I will bring them out from the peoples and gather them from the countries,
and will bring them into their own land;
and I will feed them on the mountains of Israel,
by the watercourses, and in all the inhabited parts of the land.
[14]I will feed them with good pasture,
and the mountain heights of Israel shall be their pasture;
there they shall lie down in good grazing land,
and they shall feed on rich pasture on the mountains of Israel.
[15]I myself will be the shepherd of my sheep,
and I will make them lie down, says the Lord GOD.
[16]I will seek the lost, and I will bring back the strayed,
and I will bind up the injured, and I will strengthen the weak,
but the fat and the strong I will destroy.
I will feed them with justice.

[20]Therefore, thus says the Lord GOD to them:
I myself will judge between the fat sheep and the lean sheep.
[21]Because you pushed with flank and shoulder,
and butted at all the weak animals with your horns
until you scattered them far and wide,
[22]I will save my flock, and they shall no longer be ravaged;
and I will judge between sheep and sheep.

---

†*Sunday between November 20 and 26 inclusive*

²³I will set up over them one shepherd, my servant David,
and he shall feed them:
he shall feed them and be their shepherd.
²⁴And I, the LORD, will be their God,
and my servant David shall be ruler among them;
I, the LORD, have spoken.

PSALMODY: PSALM 100

The readings continue on p. 282

APPENDIX B

READINGS FROM THE APOCRYPHAL BOOKS

✞

Second Sunday after Christmas

JANUARY 3, 1999

FIRST READING: Sirach 24:1-12

A reading from Sirach:

[1]Wisdom praises herself,
and tells of her glory in the midst of her people.
[2]In the assembly of the Most High she opens her mouth,
and in the presence of God's hosts she tells of her glory:

[3]"I came forth from the mouth of the most High,
and covered the earth like a mist.
[4]I dwelt in the highest heavens,
and my throne was in a pillar of cloud.
[5]Alone I compassed the vault of heaven
and traversed the depths of the abyss.
[6]Over waves of the sea,
over all the earth,
and over every people and nation I have held sway."
[7]Among all these I sought a resting place;
in whose territory should I abide?

[8]"Then the Creator of all things gave me a command,
and chose the place for my tent.
The Creator said, 'Make your dwelling in Jacob,
and in Israel receive your inheritance.'
[9]Before the ages, in the beginning, the Most High created me,
and for all the ages I shall not cease to be.
[10]In the holy tent I ministered before God,
and so I was established in Zion.

[11]"Thus in the beloved city the Lord gave me a resting place,
and in Jerusalem was my domain.
[12]I took root in an honored people,
in the portion and heritage of the Lord."

PSALMODY: Wisdom of Solomon 10:15-21

Readings continue on p. 30

✝

Sixth Sunday after the Epiphany

FEBRUARY 11, 1996

PROPER 1

FIRST READING: Sirach 15:15-20

A reading from Sirach:

[15]If you choose,
you can keep the commandments,
and to act faithfully is a matter of your own choice.
[16]The Lord has placed before you fire and water;
stretch out your hand for whichever you choose.

[17]Before each person are life and death,
and whichever one chooses will be given.
[18]For great is the wisdom of the Lord;
the Lord is mighty in power and sees everything;
[19]the eyes of the Lord are on the God-fearing,
and the Lord knows every human action.
[20]The Lord has not commanded anyone to be wicked,
and has not given anyone permission to sin.

PSALMODY: Psalm 119:1–8

Readings continue on p. 55

✠

THE RESURRECTION OF OUR LORD
VIGIL OF EASTER

APRIL 6, 1996   *APRIL 3, 1999*   *MARCH 30, 2002*

SIXTH READING: BARUCH 3:9-15, 32—4:4

A reading from Baruch:

[9]Hear the commandments of life, O Israel;
give ear, and learn wisdom!
[10]Why is it, O Israel,
why is it that you are in the land of your enemies,
that you are growing old in a foreign country,
that you are defiled with the dead,
[11]that you are counted among those in Hades?
[12]You have forsaken the fountain of wisdom.
[13]If you had walked in the way of God,
you would be living in peace forever.
[14]Learn where there is wisdom,
where there is strength,
where there is understanding,
so that you may at the same time
discern where there is length of days, and life,
where there is light for the eyes, and peace.

[15]Who has found the place of Wisdom?
And who has entered her storehouses?

[32]But the one who knows all things knows her,
and found her through understanding.
The one who prepared the earth for all time
filled it with four-footed creatures;
[33]the one who sends forth the light, and it goes,
called it, and it hearkened, trembling;
[34]the stars shone in their watches, and were glad;
God called them, and they said, "Here we are!"
They shone with gladness for the one who made them.
[35]This is our God,
to whom no other can be compared.
[36]God found the whole way to knowledge,
and gave her to Jacob, God's servant,
and to Israel, the one whom God loved.
[37]Afterward she appeared on earth and lived with humankind.

4:1She is the book of the commandments of God,
the law that endures forever.
All who hold her fast will live,
and those who forsake her will die.
2Turn, O Jacob, and take her;
walk toward the shining of her light.
3Do not give your glory to another,
or your advantages to an alien people.
4Happy are we, O Israel,
for we know what is pleasing to God.

Readings continue on p. 145

✝

SUNDAY BETWEEN
JULY 17 AND 23 INCLUSIVE

JULY 21, 1996   *JULY 18, 1999*   *JULY 21, 2002*

PROPER 11

FIRST READING: WISDOM OF SOLOMON 12:13, 16-19

A reading from the Wisdom of Solomon:

[13]There is no deity besides you, whose care is for all people,
to whom you should prove that you have not judged unjustly.

[16]For your strength is the source of righteousness,
and your sovereignty over all causes you to spare all.
[17]For you show your strength when people doubt the completeness
    of your power,
and you rebuke any insolence among those who know it.
[18]Although you are sovereign in strength, you judge with mildness,
and with great forbearance you govern us;
for you have power to act whenever you choose.

[19]Through such works you have taught your people
that the righteous must be kind,
and you have filled your children with good hope,
because you give repentance for sins.

PSALMODY: PSALM 86:11-17

Readings continue on p. 224

$$\boxed{+}$$

SUNDAY BETWEEN
NOVEMBER 6 AND 12 INCLUSIVE

NOVEMBER 10, 1996   NOVEMBER 7, 1999   NOVEMBER 10, 2002

PROPER 27

FIRST READING: WISDOM OF SOLOMON 6:12–16

A reading from the Wisdom of Solomon:

[12]Wisdom is radiant and unfading,
and she is easily discerned by those who love her,
and is found by those who seek her.
[13]She hastens to make herself known to those who desire her.
[14]One who rises early to seek her will have no difficulty,
for she will be found sitting at the gate.
[15]To fix one's thought on her is perfect understanding,
and one who is vigilant on her account will soon be free from care,
[16]because she goes about seeking those worthy of her,
and she graciously appears to them in their paths,
and meets them in every thought.

PSALMODY: WISDOM OF SOLOMON 6:17-20

Readings continue on p. 274

INDEX

ISBN 0-8066-0434-4

9 780806 604343   90000